D1106152

SYNTAX and SEMANTICS

VOLUME 1

SYNTAX and SEMANTICS

VOLUME 1

Edited by

JOHN P. KIMBALL

University of California,
Santa Cruz

SEMINAR PRESS   1972   *New York and London*

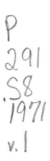

P
291
S8
1971
v. 1

SEMINAR PRESS, INC.
111 Fifth Avenue, New York, New York 10003

United Kingdom Edition published by
SEMINAR PRESS LIMITED
24/28 Oval Road, London NW1

LIBRARY OF CONGRESS CATALOG CARD NUMBER: 72-9423

PRINTED IN THE UNITED STATES OF AMERICA

99973

CONTENTS

Lahu Nominalization, Relativization, and Genitivization   237

JAMES A. MATISOFF

Navaho Object Markers and the Great Chain of Being   259

NANCY FRISHBERG

The Crossover Constraint and Ozark English   267

SUZETTE HADEN ELGIN

LIST OF CONTRIBUTORS

Numbers in parentheses indicate the pages on which the authors' contributions begin.

JUDITH AISSEN (187), *Department of Linguistics, Harvard University, Cambridge, Massachusetts*

DAVID DOWTY[1] (51), *Department of Linguistics, University of Texas at Austin, Austin, Texas*

NANCY FRISHBERG (259), *Department of Linguistics, University of California, San Diego, La Jolla, California*

TALMY GIVÓN (29), *Department of Linguistics, University of California, Los Angeles, Los Angeles, California*

JOHN GRINDER (81), *Kresge College, University of California, Santa Cruz, Santa Cruz, California*

SUZETTE HADEN ELGIN (267), *Department of Linguistics, University of California, San Diego, La Jolla, California*

JORGE HANKAMER (199), *Department of Linguistics, Massachusetts Institute of Technology, Cambridge, Massachusetts*

MICHAEL B. KAC (117, 151), *Department of Linguistics, University of Minnesota, Minneapolis, Minnesota*

LAURI KARTTUNEN[2] (1), *Department of Linguistics, University of Texas at Austin, Austin, Texas*

---

[1] Present address: Department of Linguistics, Ohio State University, Columbus, Ohio.
[2] Present address: Department of General Linguistics, University of Helsinke, Helsinke, Finland.

JOHN P. KIMBALL (21, 63), *College V, University of California, Santa Cruz, Santa Cruz, California*

GEORGE LAKOFF (113), *Department of Linguistics, University of Michigan, Ann Arbor, Michigan*

JAMES D. MC CAWLEY (139), *Department of Linguistics, University of Chicago, Chicago, Illinois*

JAMES A. MATISOFF (237), *Department of Linguistics, University of California, Berkeley, Berkeley, California*

JOHN ROBERT ROSS (157), *Department of Linguistics, Massachusetts Institute of Technology, Cambridge, Massachusetts*

ARTHUR SCHWARTZ (213), *Department of Linguistics, University of California, Santa Barbara, California*

MASAYOSHI SHIBATANI (125), *Department of Linguistics, University of California, Berkeley, Berkeley, California*

PREFACE

Volume I of *Syntax and Semantics* is the first in a planned series of volumes of papers from the Summer Linguistics Conference at Santa Cruz. The intent of these publications is to provide quick access to print for the most recent products of research in linguistic theory.

The papers in the present volume represent the results of current research on various topics in the theory of grammar. In particular, the three papers by Kac, Shibatani, and McCawley on the lexical decomposition of verbs like 'kill' provide a comprehensive discussion of the issues involved in this particular problem, as well as issues concerning the lexical decomposition in general. The papers on the transformational cycle in syntax by Kimball, Grinder, and Lakoff represent the first discussion in print of the implications of conventions for the application of transformations different from those proposed in Chomsky's *Aspects of the Theory of Syntax*.

The volume is organized by subject matter. The first group of papers concerns modality and presupposition. Following this appear papers on the syntactic cycle, lexical decomposition, and relative clauses and related matters. The final group of papers concerns miscellaneous subjects, including discussion of a dialect of English for which many putative universals seem to fail.

POSSIBLE AND MUST[1]

LAURI KARTTUNEN
University of Texas at Austin

This chapter is a limited account of the semantics of possibility and necessity in ordinary English. I will be concerned with words like *possible, may, can, perhaps,* and *conceivable* only to the extent they express epistemic or logical possibility. Whatever difference there may be between the examples in (1) remains outside the scope of the present study.

(1) a. *It is possible that it is raining in Chicago.*
     b. *It may be raining in Chicago.*
     c. *Perhaps it is raining in Chicago.*
     d. *It is conceivable that it is raining in Chicago.*

I will discuss expressions like *must, necessarily, have to,* and *is bound to* only in their epistemic sense, that is, the sense in which they appear in the following set of examples:

(2) a. *It must be raining in Chicago.*
     b. *It has to be raining in Chicago.*
     c. *Necessarily, it is raining in Chicago.*
     d. *It is bound to be raining in Chicago.*

[1] This work was supported in part by grant GS 2468 from the National Science Foundation. An earlier version of this paper was presented at the Seventh Regional Meeting of the Chicago Linguistic Society, April 1971. I am indebted to George Lakoff for suggesting a number of improvements in the manuscript.

1

I will not discuss the so-called deontic sense of *must* or the permissive use of *may* illustrated in (3):

(3)   a.   *I must finish this talk in 20 minutes.*
            b.   *May the audience ask questions?*

In discussing the notions of possibility and necessity in ordinary language, I will employ Jaakko Hintikka's notions model set and model system (Hintikka, 1962, 1969). Since these concepts may not be familiar to all linguists, I will start with a brief introduction to these concepts.

LOGICAL MODALITIES

A model set, as defined by Hintikka, is a set of formulas that can be thought of as a partial description of a possible state of affairs ("possible world"). A model set has to meet certain basic conditions, such as those in (4):

(4)   a.   Any model set W that contains some atomic formula p does
           not contain its negation; i.e., if $p \in W$, then $\sim p \notin W$.
           $(C.\sim)$
      b.   if $(p \mathbin{\&} q) \in W$, then $p \in W$ and $q \in W$. $(C.\mathbin{\&})$
      c.   If $(p \lor q) \in W$, then $p \in W$ or $q \in W$. $(C.\lor)$

In Hintikka's system, the conditions in (4) obviously play the same role as truth tables play in standard treatments of sentential logic. In a complete system, one would also need corresponding conditions for negated formulas, identities, and quantifiers, but they will not be used in this paper.

Hintikka defines a model system Q as a set of model sets related to each other by a relation of alternativeness. Intuitively, an alternative to a given model set W is a partial description of a possible state of affairs that could have been realized instead of the one described by W. The basic modal concepts of necessity L and possibility M are captured in this framework by requiring that the following three conditions be satisfied by each model system Q and its alternativeness relation:

(5)   a.   If Lp ("necessarily p") $\in W \in Q$, then $p \in W$.
      b.   If Mp ("possibly p") $\in W \in Q$, then there is in Q at
           least one alternative to W that contains p.
      c.   If $Lp \in W \in Q$ and if W^* is an alternative to W in Q,
           then $p \in W^*$.

In other words, what is possibly true in some state of affairs W is true in at least one of its alternatives. Whatever is necessarily true in W is true, not only in W itself, but in all of its alternatives as well.

There are a number of additional features that may be imposed on a model system by requiring that the alternativeness relation must also meet other constraints, such as transitivity, or symmetry. Each additional condition gives rise to a new system of modal logic. What is important to realize is that, in a sense, there is no "correct" way to construct a modal logic, no unique set of constraints on the alternativeness relation in a model set. Instead, there are a number of different systems, each of which is a legitimate object for study in its own right. Assuming that all of these systems share the same basic conditions [such as those in (4)], which define the notion of model set, they will not differ with respect to the interpretation of simple logical connectives. They are different only with respect to their modal operators, since the semantics of necessarily and possibly crucially depend on how the alternativeness relation is defined.

Assuming this framework, I shall now examine the way in which the words *possibly, may, must*, etc., are used in ordinary English. In particular, I shall investigate the sort of constraints that would have to be placed on the alternativeness relation in a model system that reflects the natural or naive modal concepts of ordinary language discourse. Not surprisingly, I will argue that the principles on which our use of *possible* and *must* in ordinary language appears to be based are different from any of the well known standard systems that have been studied by logicians. Of course, if I am right, this is an interesting fact about ordinary language, but it should not be misconstrued as evidence against other modal systems.

THE WORD *POSSIBLE*

There is an interesting constraint on the use of *possible* that we all seem to follow in our ordinary language conversation. This rule can be phrased simply as in (6).

(6)   WHATEVER IS CANNOT POSSIBLY BE OTHERWISE.

To see this principle at work, consider examples like those in (7), which are deviant utterances in ordinary English:

(7) a. *It isn't raining in Chicago, but it may be raining there.*
     b. *Mary is pretty, but perhaps she is not pretty.*
     c. *John is mistaken, but it is possible that he is right.*
     d. *It is possible that God is alive, but he is dead.*

One must be careful to note that the ill formedness of the above examples could be remedied very easily by a couple of small changes. For example, (7a) becomes perfectly acceptable if we prefix the first conjunct with *I think* or *I believe.*

(7a′)   *I think it isn't raining in Chicago, but it may be raining there.*

On the other hand, *I know* as a prefix preserves the anomaly, as shown in (7a″):

(7a″)   **I know it isn't raining in Chicago, but it may be raining there.*

I will return shortly to the difference between the *I think* and *I know* versions of (7a).

Another important feature in (7) is the mood of the verb. The ill formedness of the examples can be remedied by introducing a subjunctive conditional. Obviously, there is nothing wrong with the examples in (8):

(8)   a.   *It isn't raining in Chicago, but it could be raining there if the clouds hadn't dispersed.*
      b.   *Mary is pretty, but it is possible that she wouldn't be pretty if she didn't wear any makeup.*

Therefore, the principle in (6) must be carefully distinguished from a very similar sounding but incorrect principle (6′):

(6′)   WHATEVER IS COULD NOT POSSIBLY BE OTHERWISE.

The explicit presence of a subjunctive if clause in (8a) is not essential as long as we have *could* instead of *can.* However, it seems to me that examples such as (8a′) are to be interpreted as elliptic:

(8a′)   *It isn't raining in Chicago, but it could be.*

Some subjunctive conditional must be implicitly understood here. Example (8a′) says that it could be raining in Chicago, if something weren't the way it is. The difference between *can* and *could, is possible* and *would be possible* will be discussed again below. For the time being, let us concentrate on the first type.

The anomaly of the examples in (7) depends on the fact that the two clauses do not differ with respect to temporal and locative references. This is shown in (9):

(9) a. *God is alive, but tomorrow he may be dead.*
     b. *John is mistaken, but, under other circumstances, he might be right.*

What distinguishes the well formed examples in (8) and (9) from those in (7) is that the possibility clause makes reference to some other context than that in which the nonmodal sentence is supposed to be true.

Thus far, we have established that it is not acceptable in natural language to state in one sentence that something both is the case and possibly is not the case. The anomaly has nothing to do with syntactic well formedness in the usual sense. It is a matter of the meaning of *possible*. Consider a speaker who realizes that the rain is pouring down from the sky. He cannot honestly proclaim (10), unless he doubts his own senses:

(10)   *It is possible that it isn't raining.*

At first it may seem that, under those circumstances, (10) is not any more deviant than (11):

(11)   *It is possible that it is raining.*

However, there is a difference. One can explain the unappropriateness of (11) on the basis of a general conversational postulate formulated by Grice (1968) that requires that in general one should make one's statements as informative as one honestly can, provided that the information is relevant to the listener. In most cases, a man who is in the position to state simply *It is raining* would be extremely uncooperative if he chose to inform his listeners with (11) instead. He could certainly be accused of misleading, but not of lying. The difference shows up especially clearly in answers to the corresponding questions (12a) and (12b):

(12)   a. *Is it possible that it isn't raining?*
              b. *Is it possible that it is raining?*

A man who knows that it is raining will have to say *No* to (12a) and *Yes* (or perhaps *Well, yes*) to (12b). [Since it is likely that whoever asks (12b) is interested in whether it in fact is raining, it is somewhat uncooperative to simply say *Yes* in case one actually knows that it is raining. By answering *Well, yes*, the speaker indicates explicitly that he is not giving directly the information that the questioner is seeking. On the use of *well*, see Robin Lakoff (1971).] That is, if it really is raining, then (10) is false and (11) is true. Note also that, although the sentences in (13) could be called pointless or redundant, they are not incoherent in the same way as the examples in (7):[2]

(13) *?It isn't raining in Chicago; therefore, it is possible that it isn't raining there.*
      ?Mary is pretty, and it is possible that she is pretty.

POSSIBLE AND THE *M*-OPERATOR

Although the principle in (6) thus seems to hold for conversational English, it is not a valid principle in any of the standard modal logics.[3] Corresponding to the deviant sentences in (7), we have the formula in (14), which is not inconsistent in any standard modal system.

(14) $p \ \& \ M \sim p$ p and it is possible that not-p

There is no reason why (14) could not be a member of some model set. For example, assume that there is some model set W that contains (14). Condition (4b) requires that W must also contain the for-

---

[2] Aristotle distinguished between one-sided possibility and two-sided possibility (see Bochenski, 1961, pp. 81–83). In case of two-sided possibility, if p is possible, then not-p is also possible. On the other hand, one-sided possibility obtains whenever something in fact is known to be the case. If something is necessary, then it is also (one-sidedly) possible. One could explain the strangeness of the examples in (13) by saying that they require the one-sided sense of *possible*, which is less natural in ordinary language than the two-sided reading. However, I doubt that there is any need to postulate these two distinct senses. As far as I understand it, Aristotle's distinction is designed to account for the same facts that are also covered by Grice's conversational postulates. Assuming that the speaker is following the cooperative principle by saying that something is possible, he indicates that he is not in the position to make a stronger statement; i.e., he does not know what the facts are. Therefore, for all he knows, the contrary is also possible. The two-sided interpretation of *possible* arises from these considerations; it is not part of the meaning of *possible*.

[3] To my knowledge, the only modern logician who has proposed a system in which p and $M \sim p$ are incompatible is J. Lukasiewicz (1920). His definition of possibility makes $M \sim p$ true whenever p is either false or indeterminate. On the other hand, whenever p is true, $M \sim p$ is false. It has been argued (see Kneale, 1962, p. 573) that Lukasiewicz's three truth values (true, indeterminate, false) are not really truth values at all but certainty values. According to this interpretation, Lukasiewicz's system can be translated into ordinary two-valued logic by reading "true" as "it is certain that," "indeterminate" as "it is not certain that and it is not certain that not," and "false" as "it is certain that not." Furthermore, the Kneales suggest that "certain" can be taken as an abbreviation for "necessary in relation to what we know." This interpretation of Lukasiewicz results in a system that is very similar if not identical to the one constructed by Jaakko Hintikka in his Knowledge and Belief. The modalities in this system are epistemic modalities, defined in terms of what we know.

mulas p and $M \sim p$, as illustrated in (15). Furthermore, condition (5b) requires that there be some other model set, call it W^*, that is an alternative to W and contains the formula $\sim p$:

(15)
$$W = \{p \ \& \ M \sim p, p, M \sim p\}$$
$$W^* = \{\sim p\}$$

The two model sets, W and W^*, together form a model system that satisfies all the constraints given in (4) and (5). By constructing it, we have shown that (14) is not inconsistent.

Let us now look into the question of whether it would be feasible to add the principle.

(6)   WHATEVER IS CANNOT BE OTHERWISE.

to the set of conditions in (5), which define the notion of a model system. In this way we could perhaps obtain a new modal logic which more closely resembles natural languages than any of the standard logics. Formally, (6) would be expressed by a condition such as (16):

(16)   If $p \in W \in Q$, then $M \sim p \notin W$ [where p is any nonmodal formula].

In other words, whatever is true in some possible world is not false in any of its alternatives. An equivalent way to express the same principle is to state it as a condition on the alternativeness relation. This is given in (17):

(17)   In each model set, the subset of nonmodal formulas (= whatever is) is included in all of the alternatives of that model set as well (= cannot be otherwise).

It is obvious that if the alternativeness relation between possible worlds is constrained by a condition like (17), the formula $p \ \& \ M \sim p$ cannot be a member of any model set, since there would have to be some alternative model set containing both p and $\sim p$, which violates condition (4a). Thus, we would have a system that reflects the fact that corresponding English sentences are perceived as deviant. However, it is just as obvious that the resulting system could hardly be considered a modal logic at all. In the standard systems, the notions of necessity and possibility are interdefinable, as shown in (18):

(18)   It is possible that not-p $\equiv$ it is not necessary that p.
$$(M \sim p \equiv \sim Lp)$$

Given the standard relation between logical necessity and possibility (16) is equivalent to (19):

(19)   If $p \in W \in Q$, then $Lp \in W$ [where p is any nonmodal formula].

In other words, whatever is true is necessarily true, if it cannot possibly be otherwise. Conditions (5a) and (19) together make p logically equivalent with Lp; in effect, the notion of logical necessity simply collapses. In any standard axiomatic treatment of modal logic, the notion of possibility would consequently collapse as well. Here it does not happen except for the technical reason that model sets are defined as incomplete descriptions of possible worlds. That is, it is not required that for any formula p, a model set must contain either p or its negation. From the fact that Mp is contained in some model set, one cannot conclude from (16) that p belongs to it as well, only that its negation does not. This line of investigation leads nowhere, except that it shows explicitly that there must be a basic mistake in thinking that the words *may* and *possible* in examples like (7a) represent the same notion of possibility that is studied in modal logic. What is involved here can be seen more clearly from the distinction between (7a′) and (7a″). In saying something like *It is possible that it is raining*, the speaker states that the truth of *it is raining* is compatible with everything he knows about the world. If he knows that it is not raining, then the truth of *it is possible that it is raining* is not compatible with his knowledge. What we have here is an epistemic sense of *possible*.

EPISTEMIC LOGIC

This observation is not a new one. For example, Gottlob Frege [in his Begriffschrift in 1879] argued that modal distinctions always involve a covert reference to human knowledge; therefore, he thought that they had no place in pure logic. According to Frege, to say that something is possible is to say that the speaker knows nothing from which the negation of the proposition would follow.

More recently, Jaakko Hintikka (1962), explicitly defined epistemic possibility in terms of knowledge. In Hintikka's system, the two expressions in (20) are interchangeable:

(20) a doesn't know that $p \equiv$ for all a knows, it is possible that $\sim p$
$$(\sim K_a p \equiv P_a \sim p)$$

In order to understand what Hintikka means by the expression $\sim K_a p$, one has to keep in mind that, although Hintikka reads it as "a doesn't know that p," he is using the verb *know* in a technical sense without the usual factive presupposition. If one does not want to do that much violence to natural language, $\sim K_a p$ has to be read as suggested in (21):

(21) $\sim K_a p =$ what a knows is not that p

Hintikka shows how the semantics of epistemic statements can be stated in terms of conditions on model sets and alternativeness relations. The most important conditions are given in (22):

(22)   a.   If $K_a p \in W$, then $p \in W$.   (C.K)
       b.   If $\sim K_a p \in W$, then $P_a \sim p \in W$.   (C.$\sim$K)
       c.   If $P_a p \in W$ and if W belongs to a model system Q, then there is in Q at least one alternative W^* to W (with respect to a) such that $p \in W^*$.   (C.P*)
       d.   If $K_a q \in W$ and if W^* is an alternative to W (with respect to a) in some model system Q, then $K_a q \in W^*$. (C.KK*)

Given the interdefinability of possibility and knowledge in Hintikka's system, it follows directly that any expression of the type (7a'') is inconsistent:

(7a'')   *I know it isn't raining in Chicago, but it may be raining there.*

Example (7a'') is represented by the formula in (23a), which immediately yields the contradiction in (23b) [see (20) above]:

(23)   a. $K_a p \ \& \ P_a \sim p$
             a knows that p and, for all that a knows, it is possible that $\sim p$
       b. $K_a p \ \& \ \sim K_a p$
             a knows that p and a doesn't know that p

However, sentences of the type $p \ \& \ P_a \sim p$, such as (7a), cannot be shown to be inconsistent in Hintikka's system.

(7a)   *It isn't raining in Chicago, but it may be raining there.*

What can be shown is that (7a) has the same peculiar property as (24a) — Moore's famous example — and (24b):

(24)   a.   *The cat is on the mat, but I don't believe it.*
       b.   *The cat is on the mat, but I don't know whether the cat is on the mat.*

The latter is formally represented in Hintikka's system by (25):

(25) $p \;\&\; \sim K_a p \;\&\; \sim K_a \sim p$
           p and a doesn't know that p and a doesn't know that $\sim p$

Hintikka's explanation of the absurdity of (24b) runs as follows. When somebody makes a statement, we are normally entitled to expect that he is in the position to know that what he is saying is true. At least we would not expect the speaker to deprive himself of this possibility by the very form of the expression he is using. But the statement in (24b) is just that kind of utterance – Hintikka calls it an "epistemically indefensible" statement. It can be shown in Hintikka's system that it is impossible for the speaker himself to know that (24b) is true. If (24b) is prefixed with *I know that*, the corresponding formula in (26) turns out to be inconsistent. (Assume that a refers to the speaker himself):

(26) $K_a(p \;\&\; \sim K_a p \;\&\; \sim K_a \sim p)$

The proof of the inconsistency of (26) – not explicitly presented by Hintikka – is given in (27):

(27) 1. $K_a(p \;\&\; \sim K_a p \;\&\; \sim K_a \sim p) \in W$ I.P.
      2. $p \;\&\; \sim K_a p \;\&\; \sim K_a \sim p \in W$ 1, $(C.K)$ [see (22) above.]
      3. $\sim K_a p \in W$ 2, $(C.\&)$ [see (4)]
      4. $P_a \sim p \in W$ 3, $(C.\sim K)$
      5. $\sim p \in W^*$ 4, $(C.P^*)$
      6. $K_a(p \;\&\; \sim K_a p \;\&\; \sim K_a \sim p) \in W^*$ 5, $(C.KK^*)$
      7. $p \;\&\; \sim K_a p \;\&\; \sim K_a \sim p \in W^*$ 6, $(C.K)$
      8. $p \in W^*$ 7, $(C.\&)$

Lines 5 and 8 show that, given the initial assumption on line 1, there would have to be a model set that contained both p and $\sim p$, which is a violation of the condition $(C.\sim)$ given in (4).

As you can observe by studying the proof in (27), the third conjunct plays no role in it. Thus, the same proof also explains the absurdity of the expression in (28a), which in turn is interchangeable with (28b):

(28) a. $p \;\&\; \sim K_a p$ p but I don't know that p
      b. $p \;\&\; P_a \sim p$ p but, for all I know, it is possible that $\sim p$

Now, (28b) is just the kind of utterance that was first introduced in (7). Although Hintikka does not explicitly discuss sentences of this type, it is clear that in his system they have the same status as the examples in (24). The sentences in (7) are not inconsistent as such, but they are nevertheless epistemically indefensible—that is, self-defeating for anyone to utter, since the truth of the statement can never be known by the speaker.

The crucial condition in Hintikka's system is $(C.KK^*)$ given in (22d). It is intuitively much less obvious than the other conditions, but without it the desired result would not come about. It is interesting to note that this condition is closely related to the principle that we first presented in (6) and later unsuccessfully tried to formalize in (17). The condition $(C.KK^*)$ requires that the subset of formulas that a knows in some possible world be included in all of its epistemic alternatives as well. In simple terms, the condition can be rephrased as in (29):

(29) WHATEVER IS KNOWN TO BE CANNOT (EPISTEMICALLY) BE OTHERWISE.

Hintikka (1962) presents the following justification for the condition:

> If it is consistent of me to say that it is possible, for all that I know, that q is the case, then it must be possible for q to turn out to be the case without invalidating any of the my other claims to knowledge; that is, there must not be anything inconsistent about a state of affairs in which q is true and in which I know what I say I know [p. 17].

The interesting point is that in ordinary language, simple unqualified, nonmodal statements, such as *It isn't raining in Chicago,* carry with them an implicit claim *I know that it is so,* from which it follows that the speaker may not simultaneously admit that it might not be so without violating the rules of discourse. That is, simple declarative statements ought to be not just true, but epistemically necessary for the one who utters them. If this view is correct, it gives some insight in the problem why ordinary language words like *necessarily, must,* and *have to* most of the time seem to play a very different role in modal logic than their supposed counterpart, the necessity operator.

THE WORD *MUST*

There is a striking difference between the logical necessity operator and words like *must.* Consider the two pairs of expressions in (30) and (31):

(30) a. Lp Necessarily p
      b. p

(31)   a. *John must have left.*
                    b. *John has left.*

In any of the standard modal logics, Lp is a stronger expression than p. However, there is an inverse relation between the two sentences in (31).

Intuitively, (31a) makes a weaker claim than (31b). In general, one would use (31a) the epistemic *must* only in circumstances where it is not yet an established fact that John has left. In stating (31a), the speaker indicates that he has no first-hand evidence about John's departure, and neither has it been reported to him by trustworthy sources. Instead, (31a) seems to say that the truth of *John has left* in some way logically follows from other facts the speaker knows and some reasonable assumptions that he is willing to entertain. A man who has actually seen John leave or has read about it in the newspaper would not ordinarily assert (31a), since he is in the position to make the stronger claim in (31b).

The relation between (31a) and (31b), therefore, is of entirely different nature than the relation between the two logical formulas in (30). If we were to paraphrase (31a) without using the word *must,* the most accurate paraphrase would probably be something like the following:

(32)   *From the things I either know or regard as very probable, it logically follows that John has left (although I cannot report this as an established fact).*

This claim is supported by the following observations. Suppose you have just uttered (31a) and are now called upon to justify your statement. It seems to me that a successful defense of (31a) would have to be a list of some circumstantial evidence and some axiomatic principles of reasoning from which (31b) logically follows. For example, one might point out facts like those listed in (33):

(33)   a. *John never goes anywhere without his hat.*
        b. *John's hat was on the shelf earlier.*
        c. *John's hat is not on the shelf now.*
        d. *Nobody else but John could have removed that hat.*

The defense of (31a) is successful, provided that the premises given by the speaker are generally accepted by others and provided that the truth of (31b) in fact follows from those premises. Note also that the claim made by (31b) cannot be defended at all by logical reasoning. To defend (31b) one must be able to say something like *I saw him leave* or *I know that he did.* Anything short of that amounts to giving up (31b), it is a retreat to (31a). In trying to defend (31b) by reasoning, one essentially admits having made a stronger claim than one was entitled to make. On the basis of such observations, it seems clear that in statements like (31a) *must* is not to be interpreted as *It is logically necessary that.* . . . Just like *possible* in the earlier examples, it represents a weaker epistemic notion. The relation between the epistemic *must* and epistemic *possible* is given in (34):

(34)   *For all I know, it must be that p*
         ≡ *For all I know, it is not possible that ~p.*

A similar observation was made by Gottlob Frege (1879, translated in Geach and Black, 1966), who used it as an argument for excluding modal notions from pure logic altogether. In Frege's words:

> What distinguishes the apodeictic from the assertoric judgment is that it indicates the existence of general judgments from which the proposition may be inferred—an indication that is absent in the assertoric judgment. If I term a proposition "necessary", then I am giving a hint as to my grounds for the judgment. But this does not affect the conceptual content of the judgment; and therefore the apodeictic form of a judgment has not for our purposes any significance [Geach and Black, 1966, p. 4].

Thus, the role of *must* in (31a) is to indicate that the complement proposition is inferred but not yet known to be true independently. The intuitive feeling that (31a) is a weaker assertion than (31b) is apparently based on some general conversational principle by which indirect knowledge—that is, knowledge based on logical inferences—is valued less highly than "direct" knowledge that involves no reasoning.

It is obvious that what is true about *must* is also true of other similar words, such as *necessarily* (when it modifies a sentence), *have to,* or *is bound to.* The imperfect correspondence between these words and the logical necessity operator has been commented on by many logicians, some of whom unfortunately regard it as just another defect of ordinary language. The following syllogism is from Gerald J. Massey (1969, p. 183), who presents it as an example of how the word *necessarily* is sometimes sloppily used in places where it does not properly belong:

(35)   *If there is a sea fight tomorrow, then the Athenians will
        be victorious.
        But the Athenians will not be victorious.
        Necessarily, therefore, there will be no sea fight tomorrow.*

However, far from being an example of the misuse of *necessarily*, (35) is a perfect example of the ordinary epistemic use of this word. Following Aristotle, some logicians draw a distinction between relative and absolute necessity. Like Aristotle, they say that the conclusion of a syllogism is necessary in relation to its premises. Given a valid argument form and true premises, the conclusion cannot be false. However, at the same time, the conclusion may fail to be necessary in the absolute sense of the term. The relevant passage in Aristotle's Prior Analytics reads as follows: "One might show by an exposition of terms that the conclusion is not necessary simply, although it is necessary in relation to the premises" [i. 10(30ᵇ 32–33), quoted from Kneale and Kneale, 1962, p. 93]. It seems to me that Aristotle's distinction between relative and absolute necessity is precisely the distinction between epistemic and logical necessity. If I know that the premises of (35) are true, then it is not consistent of me to say that, for all I know, it is possible that the conclusion is false.

However, it has been argued by some logicians (e.g., Kneale and Kneale, 1962, p. 93) that, while it is important to be aware of the ambiguity of *necessarily* in order to avoid logical fallacies, ultimately the distinction can be eliminated by simply reanalyzing every case of relative necessity as a case of absolute necessity.

> In both Greek and English, the same words are used to express both absolute and relative necessity and possibility, and this is natural; for every case of relative necessity and possibility can be expressed as a case of absolute necessity and possibility. In syllogistic, for example, if a conclusion is necessary in relation to certain premises, it is absolutely necessary that if the premises are true, the conclusion should be true also. Similarly, if the truth of *p* is possible in relation to *q*, it is absolutely possible that *p* and *q* should be true. But this use, though natural, may give rise to confusion, because statements of relative necessity and possibility are often made elliptically and may for this reason be misunderstood as statements of absolute necessity and possibility [Kneale and Kneale, 1962, p. 93].

As far as I can see, this reanalysis amounts to saying that, in (35), *necessarily* is predicated, not of the conclusion, but of the syllogism as a   hole. That is, it is absolutely necessary that, if the premises are true, then the conclusion is also true.

The same advice has also been given with regard to conditional sentences. For example, Hughes and Cresswell (1968, p. 27) discuss the example in (36):

(36)   *If it rains throughout December, it is bound to rain on Christmas Day.*

Although the authors at one point correctly interpret (36) to mean that *it will rain on Christmas Day* follows from *it will rain throughout December*, they want to identify the phrase *it is bound to* with the logical necessity operator. They deplore the fact that the structure of the English sentence looks very much like (37b). For them, the logical form of (36) is the formula given in (37a):

(37)   a. $L(p \supset q)$
                       b. $p \supset Lq$

As they see it, the phrase *it is bound to* is properly used only if it expresses logical necessity. Therefore, they suspect that "most frequently what the speaker intends to assert (or at least all he is entitled to assert) is something of the form $L(p \supset q)$."

Whether the solution really works for (36) is somewhat doubtful. If we read (36) as if it had the form (37a), the sentence at first appears to be a convincing case of logical necessity. On second thought, however, one realizes that the matter depends on whether *Christmas Day* simply means "December 25" or "the birthday of Christ." In the latter case, of course, *If it rains throughout December, it will rain on Christmas Day* is not logically necessary. Its truth depends on the unstated premise that Christ was born in December, which presumably is a contingent fact. Furthermore, in most cases of this type, changing the scope of the necessity operator does not help at all. It does not convert relative necessities to absolute necessities. Consider the example in (38):

(38)   *If Bill has a diamond ring, he must have stolen it from someone.*

It is clear that *must* in (38) does not express logical necessity, no matter whether it is predicated of the conditional as a whole or of the consequent alone. It is simply a mistake to think that epistemic modalities can be made to collapse into logical modalities by rearranging the constituent structure of the sentence.

MODALS IN CONDITIONALS

Although the change in the scope of the modal in (38) does not result in a logically necessary statement, it is interesting to observe that (38) apparently is equivalent in meaning with (39):

(39)   *It must be that if Bill has a diamond ring, he has stolen it from someone.*

Consider also the following pair of examples:

(40)   a.   *This year Easter is in April. Necessarily, therefore, if
            it rains throughout April, it will rain on Easter Sunday.*
       b.   *This year Easter is in April. Therefore, if it rains
            throughout April, it will necessarily rain on Easter
            Sunday.*

It does not seem to make any difference in meaning whether the
epistemic *necessarily* has the conditional as a whole in its scope —
as in (40a) — or whether the scope of *necessarily* is limited to the consequent clause. On the other hand, note that the two formulas in (37),
which supposedly correspond to the ordinary language conditionals
in (40), are not equivalent in any of the standard modal logics. This
is what we would expect, provided that *necessarily* in (40) is analyzed
as an epistemic operator and not as a logical modality. If (40a) is true,
then the truth of *If it rains throughout April, it will rain on Easter
Sunday* follows from the truth of *This year Easter is in April.* But
this is just the same as to say that the truth of *It will rain on Easter
Sunday* follows from *This year Easter is in April* and *It will rain
throughout April.* In other words, whenever a set of premises *P*
jointly entail a conditional "If *A* then *B*," then the truth of *B* logically follows from the set *P* ∪ {*A*}, and vice versa. To make this
explanation work, one must of course assume that the ordinary language conditional in (40) is not a truth functional operator. A theory
of conditionals that seems capable of accounting for these phenomena
has recently been proposed by Stalnaker (1968). Following a suggestion by F. P. Ramsey, Stalnaker proposes that a conditional statement, such as *If it rains throughout April, it will necessarily rain on
Easter Sunday* in (40b), is to be evaluated by the following method.
You add (hypothetically) the antecedent to your stock of knowledge,
and then consider whether the consequent holds. The judgment about
the conditional as a whole should be the same as the judgment about
the consequent in the hypothetical context. Since the truth of *This
year Easter is in April* is known in (40b), the addition of the antecedent to the stock of knowledge makes it epistemically necessary
that it will rain on Easter Sunday. If I know that Easter is in April
and that it is going to rain throughout April, then it is not consistent
of me to say that it possibly won't rain on Easter Sunday.

Stalnaker's theory can also account for the fact that the indicative
conditional in (41b) is anomalous in just the same way as (41a):

(41)   a.   *It is raining in Chicago but it is possible that it isn't
            raining there.*

(41)   b.   *It is raining in Chicago, but if it isn't raining there,
       then the weather forecast was right.

In ordinary language, any indicative conditional normally commits
the speaker to the view that, for him, it is epistemically possible for
the antecedent to turn out to be true; in Stalnaker's terms, the addition of the antecedent to this stock of knowledge must not result in
inconsistency.[4] Therefore, (41b) is epistemically indefensible for
anyone to utter, just as (41a) is. As already observed, a straight nonmodal statement like It is raining in Chicago not only commits the
speaker to the belief that it is so, he ought to know that it is so. This
can be seen by comparing (41b) with the two examples in (42):

(42)   a.   I believe that it is raining in Chicago, but if it isn't
           raining there, the weather forecast was right.
       b.   *I know that it is raining in Chicago, but if it isn't
           raining there, the weather forecast was right.

Example (41b) is just as anomalous semantically as (42b) where I
know that is explicitly stated. The contrast between (42a) and (42b)
shows clearly that, if the logic of ordinary language conditionals is an
extension of modal logic, as Stalnaker proposes, the logic of indicative conditionals in particular must refer to epistemic modalities.
The antecedent of an indicative conditional ought to be epistemically possible.

Conditionals with possible bring up the same problem that we
saw in (40). Although the two formulas in (43) are not equivalent in

---

[4] By normally, I mean to exclude certain ironic uses of conditionals, such as If Harry
is a genius, then I am a monkey's uncle, which consist of an antecedent that the speaker
considers false followed by an absurd consequent. The point of such utterances obviously is to make the hearer realize that, since the consequent cannot be true, the conditional as a whole can be true only if the antecedent is false. It is an indirect way of
communicating that Harry is not a genius. This special use of conditionals is nicely
explained by truth-functional analysis, but it can be accounted for in Stalnaker's analysis as well by postulating an "absurd" world in which anything is true (Stalnaker
and Thomason, 1970). There are similar cases, which, however, seem to call for a somewhat different explanation. Namely, one may temporarily suspend one's own convic-
tions for the sake of a polite argument and pretend that some statement that one is
about to refute is possible. The refutation consists of showing that the acceptance of
the statement leads to a conclusion that even the opposition ought to recognize as in-
tolerable. For example, one might try to persuade a lexicalist of the error of his ways
by saying: "If your theory is correct, then Her hit I is a grammatical sentence." In
arguing for the truth-functional analysis of conditionals, Grice (1968) presents a couple
examples that also require the speaker to act as if he didn't know what he knows. I do
not think that they count as real counterexamples to my claim that an indicative conditional commits the speaker to the view that the antecedent is epistemically possible.

standard modal logic, similar pairs in ordinary language apparently
are synonymous:

(43)   a. $M(p \supset q)$
                              b. $p \supset Mq$

(44) a. *It is possible that, if he can get it cheap, Sam will
          smoke pot.*
      b. *If he can get it cheap, it is possible that Sam will
          smoke pot.*

The two examples in (44) have been discussed by George Lakoff
(1970). On the basis of their synonymy, Lakoff argued that the two
sentences are to be derived from the same underlying structure,
such as (45), where the *if* clause comes at the end.

(45) It is possible that Sam will smoke pot, if he can get it cheap.

In Lakoff's analysis, there would be a transformation that could
optionally move the *if* clause either to the beginning of the complement clause — yielding (44a) — or all the way to the beginning of the
main clause. Lakoff does not consider the problem of whether the
antecedent is originally inside or outside the scope of *possible*. He
seems to take the first alternative for granted, apparently for no better
reason than the fact that, were it not so, the analysis would incorrectly
predict an ambiguity in (44b). Otherwise, (44b) could have two interpretations, one corresponding to (43b), where the *if* clause has been
preposed but not raised, the other corresponding to (43a) with both
preposing and raising. On the other hand, (44a) could have only one
possible source. Since there is no such ambiguity in (44b), Lakoff must
somehow rule out as inadmissible all structures of the type (43b),
where the antecedent is outside the scope of the modal.

Once it is understood that *possible* in (44) refers to an epistemic
notion and does not correspond to the possibility operator, one may
begin to look for a more satisfactory solution. Given Stalnaker's semantics for conditionals, there apparently is no need to try to explain
the synonymy of the two examples by deriving them from the same
underlying structure. Both sentences are true just in case *Sam will
smoke pot* is possible in a situation where we know that he can get
it cheap, in addition to what else we know in the actual world.[5] Thus,

---

[5] In Stalnaker's system, "If p then q" is true in some world W if q is true in a world
$f(p,W)$ which is like W in all other respects, except possibly for the fact that p is true in
$f(p,W)$ (f is a selection function that takes a proposition and a possible world as value).
To say that "If p then q" is possible in W, therefore, is to say that q is possible in $f(pW)$.
But this is just the same condition that determines the truth of "If p, then possibly q
in W."

there is no reason to assume that the scope of the modal in the underlying structure of (44b) is different from its scope in the surface structure.

LOGICAL VERSUS EPISTEMIC MODALITIES

Thus far I have presented examples where ordinary language modals like *possible* and *must* represent epistemic modalities and should not be confused with their counterparts in modal logic. If it is true that modals in ordinary language are usually interpreted epistemically, the question arises as to how one expresses in ordinary language that something is *logically* possible or *logically* necessary. This brings us back to the distinction between (7a) and (8a'):

(7a)   *It isn't raining in Chicago, but it may be raining there.*
(8a')   *It isn't raining in Chicago, but it **could** be.*

In trying to explain why (7a) was contradictory while (8a') was not, we suggested that (8a') meant that it could be raining in Chicago if something were not the way it is. In other words, given that it is not raining in Chicago, it is not epistemically possible that it is raining there; nevertheless, it may logically be possible. It is the logical sense of possibility that is conveyed by (8a'). Consider now (46):

(46)   *It isn't raining in Chicago, and it couldn't be.*

The word *couldn't* in (46) carries the sense of logical impossibility. What (46) says is that even if things weren't the way we know they are now, it still wouldn't be raining in Chicago. Thus, something is impossible in the strong logical sense if it would not be possible even if I knew differently. The mood of the verb can be used to distinguish between epistemic and logical possibility.

However, in many cases there is a genuine ambiguity between epistemic and logical modality, just as Aristotle observed. For example, (47) can be taken in two ways:

(47)   *It isn't necessarily raining in Chicago.*

In the epistemic sense (47) means "For all I know, it doesn't follow that it is raining in Chicago." The logical sense of (47) could be paraphrased as "Even if it is raining in Chicago, it could as well be otherwise." Some similar cases are disambiguated by the presence of polarity items. For example, (48) has only the epistemic reading:

(48)   *Harry isn't necessarily all that bright.*

It will be interesting to investigate how the distinction between logical and epistemic modalities is manifested in ordinary language. At this stage, we do not yet know much about it.

REFERENCES

Bochenski, I. M. 1961. A History of Formal Logic. University of Notre Dame Press, Notre Dame, Indiana.

Geach, P. and Black, M. (eds.). 1966. Translations from the Philosophical Writings of Gottlob Frege. Blackwell, Oxford.

Grice, H. Paul. 1968. Logic and Conversation (unpublished).

Hintikka, Jaakko. 1962. Knowledge and Belief. An Introduction to the Logic of the Two Notions. Cornell University Press, Ithaca, New York.

Hintikka, Jaakko. 1969. Models for Modalities. Selected Essays. Reidel, Dordrecht, Holland.

Hughes, G. E., and Cresswell, M. J. 1968. An Introduction to Modal Logic. Methuen, London.

Kneale, W. C., and Kneale, M. 1962. The Development of Logic. Oxford University Press, Oxford.

Lakoff, George. 1970. Linguistics and Natural Logic. Synthese, 22 (1/2): 151–271.

Lakoff, Robin. 1971. Questionable Answers and Answerable Questions. In Papers in Linguistics in Honor of Henry and Renee Kahane, B. Kachru, R. B. Lees, Y. Malkiel and S. Saporta (eds.). Linguistic Research, Urbana, Illinois.

Massey, Gerald J. 1969. Understanding Symbolic Logic. Harper and Row, New York.

Stalnaker, Robert C. 1968. A Theory of Conditionals. In Studies in Logical Theory, Nicholas Rescher (ed.). Oxford University Press, Oxford.

Stalnaker, Robert C. and Thomason, Richmond H. 1970. A Semantic Analysis of Conditional Logic. In Theoria, 36:23–42.

THE MODALITY OF CONDITIONALS—A DISCUSSION OF "POSSIBLE AND MUST"

JOHN P. KIMBALL
University of California, Santa Cruz

Professor Karttunen's excellent paper sheds light on a problem that has long been brushed aside by logicians. I shall not comment on the main argument of his thesis, but should like to discuss a matter touched on by him in section six of his chapter, concerning sentences like (1)—parallel to Karttunen's (40) and (44).

(1)   a. *It* $\begin{Bmatrix} may \\ must \end{Bmatrix}$ *be the case that if Stone space is compact, then truth is hyperarithmetic.*

      b. *If Stone space is compact, then it* $\begin{Bmatrix} may \\ must \end{Bmatrix}$ *be the case that truth is hyperarithmetic.*

      c. *If Stone space is compact, then truth* $\begin{Bmatrix} may \\ must \end{Bmatrix}$ *be hyperarithmetic.*

In (1) I have chosen an example with the modals *may* and *must*, while *possible* and *necessarily* appear in Karttunen's examples. However, everything I have to say about sentences containing the modals applies with equal force to the adjectival and adverbial carriers of modality.

I will first recapitulate the arguments adduced in Kimball (1970),

21

Chapter 4, independently of Lakoff (1970), for the existence of a transformational relation between (1a) and (1b). I shall argue that (1a) is in fact the only source for (1b), thus meeting the problem discussed by Karttunen that (1b) is not ambiguous, although an analysis that derives (1b) from (1a) seems to predict an ambiguity if (1b) is generated separately by the base. Finally, I shall argue that the fact that (1b) can be derived only from (1a) illustrates a deep fact about the construction of conditional sentences, as well as inducing a classification in which modality falls together with negation and certain kinds of belief sentences.

As discussed by Lindholm (1969) and Kimball (1970) a sentence like (2) has two readings.

(2)   *I believe that the world is not round.*

In one sense, (2) is the expression of a belief on the part of the speaker, and in this sense it is synonymous with (3), where *neg transportation* has applied.

(3)   *I don't believe that the world is round.*

In the other sense, (2) is an assertion that the speaker is in a certain state of belief; in this reading, (2) is not synonymous with (3), for to assert that a proposition, not-S, is among the beliefs of someone, is quite different from asserting that proposition S is not among that person's beliefs. Hence, it is only on one reading of (2) that *neg transportation* can apply. Lindholm treats this fact by positing disparate lexical decompositions for verbs like *believe,* claiming, in effect, that such verbs are ambiguous. My treatment of this matter is to locate the difference in meaning at the sentence level, which has the happy consequence that *believe* remains one verb in deep structure. This matter is worth scrutiny, for the operation that maps (1a) into (1b)— which I shall term *protasis lifting*—also operates to map (4a) into (4b), but again subject to the restriction on *negative transportation* observed in (2).

(4) a. *I believe that if Stone space is compact, then truth is*
         an ultrafilter.
     b. *If Stone space is compact, then I believe that truth is*
         an ultrafilter.

Thus it is that the properties of sentences like (2) are relevant to the existence of an operation relating (1a) and (1b). I will now take up the properties of such sentences in some detail, after which it will be possible to return to sentences like (1) and (4).

Let us term the different readings of sentences like (2) the expressive and the reportive; it is in the expressive sense of (2) that *negative transportation* can apply to yield (3). There seem to be other classes of sentences that manifest the difference between expressive and reportive use, noticed first by Wittgenstein (1953, article 244 ff.). He writes:

> How do words *refer* to sensations? — There doesn't seem to be any problem here; don't we talk about sensations every day, and give them names? But how is the connexion between the name and the thing named set up? This question is the same as: how does a human being learn the meaning of the names of sensations? — of the word "pain" for example. Here is one possibility: words are connected with the primitive, the natural, expressions of the sensation and used in their place. A child has hurt himself and he cries; and then adults talk to him and teach him exclamations and, later, sentences. They teach the child new pain-behavior.
> "So you are saying that the word 'pain' really means crying?" — On the contrary: the verbal expression of pain replaces crying and does not describe it.

Thus, a sentence like *It hurts* can either replace pain-behavior, and constitute an expression of pain; or it can be an assertion, a report that the speaker is in a certain state. In the expressive use, sentences do not carry truth value, any more than a groan has truth value; thus, they can neither be answers to yes–no questions nor can they be negated. If one responds to a question such as *Does it hurt?* with a groan, the response is not a direct answer, but something from which an answer can be deduced. In the same way, an expressive *It hurts* is not a possible answer to a question. Likewise, just as a groan has no negation, so also expressive sentences are incapable of carrying negation.

I shall not discuss the question of whether the difference between expressive and reportive uses of a sentence lies in a difference of underlying performative, although I suspect that no performative analysis can shed much light on the problem. It is evident, at any rate, that the difference between the two readings of *It hurts* does not reside in an ambiguity in the word *hurt*, nor in the word *it* for that matter, but rather the difference in senses is a property of the sentence as a whole. I would like to claim that the same is true of belief sentences like (2), in spite of Wittgenstein's (1953) remark in article 317:

> Misleading parallel: the expression of pain is a cry — the expression of thought, a proposition.

Notice, now, if expressive sentences can have no negation, then the expressive sense of a sentence like (3) must find its origin with (2);

so here we have proof of the existence of *neg transportation* on purely semantic grounds. I shall attempt now to show that a sentence like (4b) must come from (4a) by *protasis lifting*. Conditionals will be represented in deep structure with protasis in initial position, with no justification greater than Greenberg's universal 14: "In conditional statements, the conditional clause precedes the conclusion as the normal order in all languages" (Greenberg, 1963, p. 66).

Protasis lifting maps a structure like (5a) into (5b).

(5)

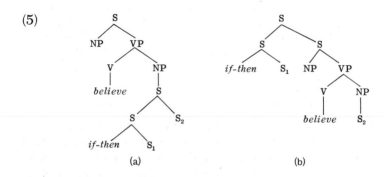

(a)   (b)

In (5), S_1 is the protasis, and S_2 the apodosis. A later rule distributes the *if–then* morphology of the conditional sentence.

It is easy to see that the *I believe* of (4b) is not a parenthetical. Parentheticals do not contain internal negation, as attested by sentences like (6).

(6)   George is, $\begin{cases} you \ (*don't) \ know \\ we \ (*don't) \ say \\ they \ (*don't) \ believe \end{cases}$, not a resident of any country.

However, if (4a) is replaced by a sentence with a negative in the second clause of the conditional, this negative can raise by *neg transportation*, and thus we would get a derivation like that from (7a) to (7c).

(7)   a.   *I believe that if Mike smokes, then Betsy doesn't smoke.*
      b.   *If Mike smokes, then I believe that Betsy doesn't smoke.*
      c.   *If Mike smokes, then I don't believe that Betsy smokes.*

In (7c) we find a negated belief expression, showing that the *believe* of this sentence and of (7b) and (4b) is not a parenthetical.

It is evident, furthermore, that only in the expressive sense of belief sentences like (4a) can protasis lifting apply. If the belief sentence is reportive, so that the believe clause carries a truth value, then (4b) is read such that the belief of the speaker is contingent on the protasis. Given that protasis lifting operates in expressive belief sentences, let us turn now to an examination of other classes of sentences to which it may apply.

One form of negation of a conditional in the surface structure of English is illustrated by (8a), where the negative appears before the entire sentence. However, (8a) also has a surface realization given in (8b), in which the negation occurs in the apodosis; though (8b) is also the surface manifestation of a sentence in which the apodosis carries negation in deep structure.

(8) a. *It is not the case that if you pick the violets, you will be arrested.*
    b. *If you pick the violets, you won't be arrested.*

The reading of (8b) that is not synonymous with (8a) is that in which your not being arrested is contingent on your picking the violets.

In mapping (8a) to (8b), *protasis lifting* operates just as in (5), as illustrated in (9).

(9)

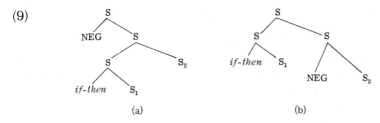

(a)   (b)

Finally, *protasis lifting* applies to (1a′) yielding (1b′), while (1c′) comes from (1b′) by an auxiliary lowering rule;

(1′)

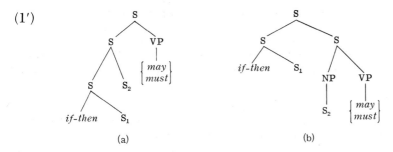

(a)   (b)

It is possible now to establish that (1b) could come only from (1a) by *protasis lifting*. It could not be generated independently in the base, thus explaining why (1b) is not ambiguous. Syntactic evidence for this claim exists in the form of ungrammatical sentences like (10).

(10) *It $\begin{Bmatrix} may \\ must \end{Bmatrix}$ be the case that if you pick the violets, you

$\begin{Bmatrix} may \\ must \end{Bmatrix}$ get arrested.

In (10) we see that modals cannot simultaneously appear over the whole conditional and over the apodosis. It is as though formulas of the form (11) were ungrammatical in natural language.

(11)   a. $L(p \supset Lp)$
                                         b. $M(p \supset Lp)$
                                         c. $L(p \supset Mp)$
                                         d. $M(p \supset Mp)$

The ungrammaticality of (10) establishes the syntactic fact that conditionals with modals in the apodosis like (1b) can be derived only from conditionals that appear in the scope of the modal in question, e.g., (1a). If we allow modals to be generated freely both over conditionals and apodoses independently, we are faced with a combinatorial problem of considerable complexity—that of insuring that in no conditional is there a modal over both the whole and the apodosis. Further, as I shall show below, conditionals with modals in the apodosis have readings as though the modal were over the whole conditional. It is thus clear that the latter is the unique position of the modal in deep structure.

Consider sentences such as (12) from the point of view of what would falsify each:

(12) a. *It may be that if you pick the violets, you will be arrested.*
      b. *If you pick the violets, you may be arrested.*

Sentence (12a) will be false if it is necessarily the case that you can pick the violets and not be arrested. Likewise, (12b) will be false if you can pick the violets with impunity and never be arrested, that is, if it is necessarily the case that you can pick the violets and not be arrested.

Finally, concerning the class of those items to which *protasis lifting* applies, it has been shown that this operation applies to expressive belief sentences, and to conditionals in the scope of modals and negation. Perhaps all these items share some semantic feature. *Believe* can be treated on the model of a two-place predicate, relating a subject and a proposition; furthermore, if Karttunen's analysis is correct, then the epistemic modals serve the same function. Pursuing the analogy, it may be correct to treat negation likewise as a relational term holding between subjects and propositions. If this is the case, we should have achieved a partial semantic characterization of the class of structures to which *protasis lifting* may apply.

REFERENCES

Greenberg, J. 1963. Some Universals in Grammar. in Universals of Language (J. Greenberg, ed.). Cambridge, Massachusetts, MIT Press.

Kimball, J. 1970. Categories of Meaning. Ph.D. thesis, MIT, Cambridge, Massachusetts.

Lakoff, G. 1970. Linguistics and Natural Logic. Synthese 22:151–271.

Lindholm, J. M. 1969. Negative Raising and Sentence Pronominalization, in Papers from the Fifth Chicago Linguistics Society Meeting.

Wittgenstein, L. 1953. *Philosophical Investigations.* New York, Macmillan.

FORWARD IMPLICATIONS, BACKWARD PRESUPPOSITIONS, AND THE TIME AXIS OF VERBS

TALMY GIVÓN
University of California, Los Angeles

INTRODUCTION

In this discussion of the semantics of verbs requiring sentential complements, I will assume familiarity with previous works by Kiparsky (1968) and Morgan (1969), but will take off more or less where Karttunen (1970a, b) has left off, although in a different direction. Two classes of verbs whose memberships show a considerable overlap will be discussed. Their initial subclassification is given in (1), (2) below, roughly following Kartunnen (1970a).

Perception/Knowledge Verbs (P/K)

Ordinarily these verbs take a that-S complement and do not require, when used in this sense, identity of the subject of the main verb with that of the complement verb. The term "factive" is used below to mean presuppositional [disregarding Kiparsky's "fact" classification (1968)].

I have put in parentheses those verbs that Karttunen (1970b) found, under test environments that involve modals such as *necessary* and *possible*, to be semifactive. For example: *He'll learn that she was*

29

(1)   INITIAL SUBCLASSIFICATION OF P/K VERBS

Factive	Neg-factive	Nonfactive
know, remember, forget, see, hear[a]*, guess, understand, regret, suspect, be aware, (learn), (realize), (discover), (find out)*	*pretend, dream, imagine*	*decide, agree, hope, be afraid, think, believe, doubt, feel, assume, suppose, be sure, judge,*

[a] The presuppositional status of *hear* is somewhat baffling. Under normal intonation, it seems that only the negative, not the affirmative, of this verbs implies the truth of the complement: *John didn't hear that Mary left* ⊃ *Mary left; John heard that Mary left*° ⊃ *Mary left.* A *stress change*, as well as question environment, seem to convert *hear* into factivity: *John hear'd that left?* ⊃ *Mary left.* Both alternants clearly change the presuppositional environment of the utterance.

there ⊃ *She was there;* but: *It's possible that he'll learn that she was there* * ⊃ *She was there.* So far as I can see, this new extension of the classification does not impinge upon the phenomena with which this paper is mostly concerned.

Aspectual/Modal Verbs (A/M)

These verbs ordinarily take an infinitival or gerundive complement in English, and require, when used in this sense, an identity of the subject of the main verb with that of the complement verb.

(2)   INITIAL SUBCLASSIFICATION OF A/M VERBS

Implicative	Neg-implicative	Nonimplicative
begin/start continue, repeat[a]*, succeed, manage, remember, condescend*	*finish/end/stop*[b] *avoid, neglect, fail, (refuse)*[c]*, (decline)*[c]*, forget, pretend*[d]	*want, plan, try, decide, prefer, agree, be afraid, hope, intend, hate, dread*

[a] The verb *repeat* in English takes only nominalized complements, as in: *He repeated his request.* However, it belongs in this group semantically. For the purpose of this paper, I will simply assume that the verb may be correctly paraphrased with the adverb *again*, so that *He repeated his request* will be taken to mean the same as *He requested again.*

[b] Verbs of termination have been erroneously classified in the past as positive implicative. I will show that it is their presuppositions, rather than implications, that carry a sense of factivity.

[c] *Refuse* and *decline* are neg-implicative in many uses but nonimplicative when one forces the issue, so that one may say that they invite the inference of neg-implicature.

[d] *Pretend* again stands out of pattern, as is briefly shown below. For some more peculiarities of this verb, see Neubauer (1971).

A cursory glance at (1) and (2) will show a considerable overlap in their membership; or, in terms used here, many verbs exist that have both a P/K and A/M sense. The possibility that this polysemy is systematic will also be discussed.

PRESUPPOSITION AND IMPLICATION

Because of the potentially systematic nature of the polysemy mentioned above, one would like to know whether a verb that is factive in its P/K sense will turn out to be implicative in its A/M sense. While a definitive answer cannot be given at the moment — due among other facts to the extremely small size of the sample (*remember, forget, pretend, learn*) — the question is nevertheless of considerable interest. To take *pretend* first, it turns out that it remains not only implicative but also factive in its A/M sense:[1]

(3) a. *John pretended that he was sick ⊃ John wasn't sick*
     b. *John didn't pretend that he was sick ⊃ John wasn't sick*
     c. *John pretended to be sick ⊃ John wasn't sick*
     d. *John didn't pretent to be sick ⊃ John wasn't sick*

Further, it seems that (a)/(c) and (b)/(d) above are identical in meaning. In other words, the change in complement form, from *that-S* to infinitive, carries no change in meaning. As I will attempt to show later on, the change in complement form normally involves a considerable reanalysis of the verb's meaning.

The verb *learn* is only spuriously considered implicative, as in:

(4)   *He learned to speak French ⊃ He speaks French*

On closer examination, one finds that the *to* complementation for this verb is semantically identical with the *how to* complementation, so that (5) below is an adequate paraphrase of (4):

(5)   *He learned how to speak French ⊃ He speaks French*

Further, the implication in both (4) and (5) is not with respect to any act/action, but rather with respect to ability, so that the implied

---

[1] For the purpose of factivity tests, only the internal negation of the affirmative utterances will be considered. The external negation has, as one of its readings, a negation of the presuppositions of the utterance.

sentence

(6)   *He speaks French*

in both (4) and (5) could not mean (7), but only (8):

(7)   *He always speaks French*

(8)   *He has aquired the ability to speak French*

That *to* and *how to* complements do not always mean the same
thing can be seen from the contrast between (9) and (10) below:

(9)   *Mary remembered to put her pants on* ⊃
                              Mary put her pants on

(10)   *Mary remembered how to put her pants on* *⊃
                              Mary put her pants on

With respect to *remember* and *forget*, both are factive in their P/K
sense, though as A/M verbs they are negatively paired with respect to
their implication, as discussed in Givón (1970). However, I will show
that this seeming discrepancy is due to a time axis alignment of (backward-looking) presuppositions and (forward-looking) implications,
and that the negative pairing of these two verbs already exists with respect to their implications in their P/K sense. To sum up, one does expect to find some crossover from the presuppositions and implications
of a P/K sense of a verb to its A/M sense, but a more detailed analysis
is required before valid predictions can be made.

BACKWARD PRESUPPOSITIONS
AND THE TIME AXIS OF VERBS

In this section I will begin discussion of a small group of A/M verbs,
all of them implicative, either positive or negative, in the sense of
Karttunen (1970a). I will show that in addition to the implications observed by Karttunen, these verbs also exhibit definite presuppositions,
and that, while their implications refer to the time following the time
axis of the act, their presuppositions refer to the time prior to the same
time axis. The verbs in this subgroup denote concepts such as inception, termination, continuation, or repetition. A smaller subgroup,
including *succeed, manage,* and *fail,* involve additional semantic material and will be discussed under a separate heading. Later, I will
also show that the time-axis separation between presuppositions and

implicatures is not unique to this group of verbs, but may be extended, not only to other A/M verbs but also to many P/K verbs.

(11)   Implications
    At 2 pm John began to work ⊃
                *Sometime **after** 2 pm John was working*
    At 2 pm John didn't begin to work· ⊃
                Sometime after 2 pm John wasn't working
    At 2 pm John continued to sleep ⊃
                Sometime after 2 pm John was asleep
    At 2 pm John didn't continue to sleep ⊃
                Sometime after 2 pm John wasn't asleep
    At 2 pm John again entered the room ⊃
                Sometime after 2 pm John was in the room
    At 2 pm John didn't again enter the room ⊃
                Sometime after 2 pm John wasn't in the room
    At 2 pm John finished writing ⊃
                Sometime after 2 pm John wasn't writing
    At 2 pm John didn't finish writing ⊃
                Sometime after 2 pm John was writing

With respect to their forward-looking implications, then, *begin, continue* and *repeat* are positive-implicative, while *end* is neg-implicative.

(12)   Presuppositions[2]
    At 2 pm John began to work ⎫
    At 2 pm John didn't begin to work ⎬ ⊃
                *Sometime **before** 2 pm John wasn't working*
    At 2 pm John continued to sleep ⎫
    At 2 pm John didn't continue to sleep ⎬ ⊃
                Sometime before 2 pm John was asleep
    At 2 pm John again entered the room ⎫
    At 2 pm John didn't again enter the room ⎬ ⊃
    Sometime before 2 pm John had been in(and then out of)
                              the room
    At 2 pm John finished writing ⎫
    At 2 pm John didn't finish writing ⎬ ⊃
                Sometime before 2 pm John was writing

With respect to their backward-looking presuppositions, *end, continue,* and *repeat* (the latter with the added presupposition of interruption), are positive-factive, while *begin* is neg-factive.

---

[2] See footnote 1.

The presuppositions shown in (12) above remain truly factive (rather than semifactive) under Karttunen's more strigent test (1970b):

(13)   *It is possible that John started working at 2 pm* ⎱ ⊃
       It is possible that John didn't start working at 2 pm ⎰
           *At some time **before** 2 pm John wasn't working*

THE SEMANTICS OF SUCCESS AND FAILURE

Succeed and *fail* are time axis verbs of the type discussed in the preceding section, though they carry, in addition, some extra semantic baggage. To begin with, I claim that both verbs show a systematic ambiguity; while one of their senses involves true predication of the subject of the sentence, the other is a mere affirmation (*succeed, manage*) or negation (*fail*) of the sentence. Thus, observe the following:

(14)   a.   *(We were waiting, but) he failed to arrive =*
                            He didn't arrive   [mere neg]
       b.   *He has failed to solve the problem =*
                            He tried but failed

(15)   a.   *He succeeded in alienating everybody =*
                            He alienated everybody   [ironic]
       b.   *He succeeded in solving the problem =*
                            He tried and succeeded

(16)   a.   *He managed to get killed in action =*
                            He got killed in action   [ironic]
       b.   *He managed to swim ashore =*
                            He tried hard and succeeded

The (a) and (b) senses of these verbs share their implications. But it is only the senses under (b), those that presuppose trying, which show the characteristic backward presuppositions with respect to the time axis of the action:

(17)   *John failed to solve the problem **by 2 pm*** ⎱ ⊃
       John didn't fail to solve the problem by 2 pm ⎰
         *Sometime **before** 2 pm John was trying to solve the problem*
         *John succeeded in solving the problem **by 2 pm*** ⎱ ⊃
         John didn't succeed in solving the problem by 2 pm ⎰
       *Sometime **before** 2 pm John was trying to solve the problem*

The feature [actively trying] thus characterizes the presuppositions of these verbs, taken in their subject–predicative sense. With respect to the time axis, they share the backward presuppositions of the others: the action takes place prior to the time-axis. *Succeed* also shares the time axis implication of *end:* no further action after time-axis. (*Fail* doesn't seem to carry this implication). Finally, they are negatively paired (see below) with respect to the implication of accomplishment: *succeed* positive, *fail* negative.

A summary of the presuppositions and implications associated with our time axis verbs is given in tabulation (18).

(18) PRESUPPOSITIONS AND IMPLICATIONS ASSOCIATED WITH TIME AXIS VERBS

Verb	Presuppositions with respect to prior time	Implications with respect to subsequent time
end/stop/finish	+action	−action
start/begin	−action	+action
succeed/manage	+action,(+try)	−action,(+goal)
fail	+action,(+try)	(−goal)
continue	+action	+action
repeat	+action,(then −action)	+action

It is perhaps not an accident that all the presuppositions involved concern time prior to the time axis of the verb, while all the implications concern time subsequent to that same time axis. I will show below that the time axis phenomenon per se is not at all limited to this small group of verbs and that in other instances it is also the case that presuppositions and implicatures divide in the same manner on both sides of the time axis. Thus, for example, the intensional A/M verbs *want, plan, decide, agree, hope, try* all share a negative backward presupposition with respect to time prior to the time axis of the verb, as in:

(19)   *At 2 pm John* $\begin{Bmatrix} wanted \\ decided \\ agreed \end{Bmatrix}$ *to work* ⊃

   Directly before 2 pm John wasn't working

  At 2 pm John didn't $\begin{Bmatrix} want \\ decide \\ agree \end{Bmatrix}$ *to work* ⊃

   Directly before 2 pm John wasn't working

What differentiates these verbs from our time axis group, however, is that they do not carry any implications with respect to performing the action after the time axis. They only imply intent. With the exception of *succeed* and *fail*, both of which involves added presuppositions and implications, time axis verbs primarily delimit the action time before and after the time axis. As we shall see, some interesting selectional and systactic phenomena seem to correlate with this semantic function.

TIME AXIS AND ANTONYMY

In view of the observations above, one must reasses the concept of antonymy, or as I have alluded to it elsewhere (Givón, 1970), negative pairing. The concept of negative pairing is clearly not rich enough to describe the facts. Thus, notice that the pair *begin/end* are negatively paired with respect to their (backward) presuppositions and (forward) implications. *Continue/end*, on the other hand, share their backward presuppositions, but are negatively paired with respect to their implications. The same is also true of the P/K sense of *remember/forget;* they share their backward presuppositions of knowledge before time axis, but are negatively paired with respect to their implication of knowledge after the time axis. Likewise, the pair *agree/refuse* share their negative presuppositions with respect to action prior to the time axis, but are negatively paired with respect to the implication of intended action after the time axis. Antonymic pairs such as *enter/exit* and *to/from* are negatively paired with both their implications and their presuppositions, while *go/come* are negatively paired only with respect to their backward presuppositions, as shown in tabulation (20).

(20)

Item	Backward presupposition	Forward implication
enter	−in place	+in place
exit	+in place	−in place
to	−at place	+toward place
from	+at place	−toward place
go	−toward speaker	motion
come	+toward speaker	motion

Although neg-pairing is most often used in connection with the neg-pairing of implications, the concept must clearly be refined to accommodate the various combinations of implications and presuppositions.

ANIMACY OF SUBJECT

Of the entire A/M group of verbs, only the time axis verbs can take inanimate or nonagentive subjects. This conforms to what was observed above, namely that most of the other verbs in the group are intentional/volitional, a property ordinarily predicative only of agentive nouns. One thus finds:

(21)   *The stone started to roll downhill.*
         The house continued to burn.
         The rocks stopped falling on the highway.
         The clothesline snapped again.

but never:

(22)   **The stone forgot to roll downhill.*
         **The house planned to burn.*
         **The rocks decided to roll downhill.*
         **The clothesline tried to snap.*

The status of *succeed/fail* is again of some interest. Although they are time axis verbs in their "try and succeed/fail" sense, they cannot predicate nonagentive subjects:

(23)   **The stone succeeded in rolling downhill.*
         **The house failed to burn.*

In their sentential, nonintensional sense, however, these verbs (or at least *fail*) may predicate nonagentives:

(24)   *Bruce threw the Molotov cocktail at the house,*
         { *but it (the house) failed to burn. = It didn't burn.* }
         { *but it (the cocktail) failed to explode. = It didn't explode.* }

It is thus clear that the restriction in (23) has to do with the presence of the presupposed *try* in the semantic structure of these two verbs; thus it is linked to the selectional restrictions of *intend*, as in:

(25)   *The plague killed many people.*
         **The plague murdered many people.*
         **The plague killed many people intentionally.*

PREDICATES OF NOMINALIZATIONS

In the preceding sections, I have shown that a small group of A/M verbs, named time axis verbs, are distinct from other, intensional A/M verbs in both their presuppositional and selectional properties. In this section I will discuss an interesting syntactic correlate of this difference.

In their normal usage, A/M verbs are two-place predicates, taking a nominal subject and a sentential complement–object. Of all the A/M verbs, it is only time axis verbs that are capable of developing the following subsense, whereby they become predicates of nominalized sentential objects. In the examples below, the implication sign is not intended to suggest a full meaning equivalence, nor, for that matter, a transformational derivation, but only a meaning relationship and perhaps a weak implication:

(26)   *They started to celebrate. ⊃ The celebration started.*
       They finished dancing. ⊃ The dancing ended.
       They continued to debate. ⊃ The(ir) debate continued.
       They stopped quarreling. ⊃ The(ir) quarrel ended.

In contrast, with intensional A/M verbs:

(27)   *They forgot to celebrate. ⊃ *The celebration forgot.*
       *They wanted to dance. ⊃ *The dancing wanted.*
       *They intended to debate. ⊃ *The(ir) debate intended.*
       *They tried to quarrel. ⊃ *The(ir) quarrel tried.*

One may of course argue that the restriction in (27) is merely due to the selectional properties of intensional verbs, that is, the fact that they may not take nonagentive subjects. While the fact itself is true, its validity in this argument seems at best derived. Rather, we are dealing here not with the same sense showing up in two different syntactic patterns, but with a distinct meaning transformation, by which a verb that originally predicated the act of a nominal subject is reinterpreted to become the time axis predicate of the act itself—the nominalized event sentence. Further, time axis verbs are capable of this transformation because their primary function is to convey the time axis dimensions of the event, rather than to describe the internal mental state of the actor–agent.

In this connection, it would be of interest to consider the behavior of *succeed/fail*, which are time axis verbs but also presuppose trying and thus presuppose intent. Notice that in (28), although the sentences on the right are grammatical, they are not correctly infered from those on the left:

(28) *They succeeded in celebrating. * ⊃ The celebration succeeded.*
     *They failed to debate each other. * ⊃ Their debate failed.*

This failure of implication may be due to the fact that the trying involved in the sentences on the left in (28) refers at best to the initiation of the action (at worst these sentences involve the mere negation or mere affirmation senses of these verbs); while in the sentences on the right, trying must have involved the successful conclusion of the action. Thus, sentence (29a) below does not imply (29b) but only (29c):

(29)   a.   *He failed to kill the dragon.*

     * ⊃ b.   *?The killing of the dragon failed.*
     ⊃ c.   *His attempt to kill the dragon failed.*

Similarly:

(30)   a.   *He succeeded in taming the shrew.*

     * ⊃ b.   *The taming of the shrew succeeded.*
     ⊃ c.   *His attempt to tame the shrew succeeded.*

The oddity or inappropriateness of (29b) and (30b) may also be due to
the factive nature of result nominalizations. In (29a) and (30a), the
verbs *succeed/fail* presuppose trying to achieve the goal, while the
nominalizations in (29b) and (30b) presuppose that the goal has already been achieved. Therefore, the use of *succeed/fail* with their
success/failure implications, is odd if only for its redundancy. In (29)
it is also odd due to the clash between the factivity of *the killing* and
the neg-implicature of *fail*. It seems, then, that the added implications and presuppositions of *succed/fail* over and above the time axis
presuppositions and implications [see (18)] removes them from the
normal pattern of time axis verbs (26), though they by no means conform entirely to the pattern of the intensional A/M verbs (27).

SOME DIACHRONIC NOTES ON THE RISE OF SENTENTIAL MODALITY SENSES OF M/A VERBS

I have shown above (p. 34) that *succeed/fail* have developed an
added, nonintensional sense, not really predicating the agent–subject
of the utterance, but rather, serving as a negation or affirmation marker
for the entire sentence. I have also shown (p. 38) that other time
axis verbs may become predicates of (nominalized) sentences. Elsewhere (Givón 1969, 1971) I have suggested that M/A verbs in diverse
linguistic groups are extremely productive, historically, giving rise to
tense–aspect–modality markers. That is, they give rise to semantic
categories that predicate the entire sentence. The participation of
time axis verbs in diachronic developments of this type is of course
expected, since they involve primarily the delimitation of time boundaries of the action. In Bantu languages, for example, one finds in some
cases three successive condensations of the verb *finish* into sentential

tense–aspect markers. The oldest one occurred in Proto-Bantu and involved the current modified-base suffix *-ile,* reconstructed as a perfective/terminative past aspect. Then, in Swahili the verb **-mala* 'finish' has more recently given rise to the imperfect past aspect marker *-me-,* as in:

(31)   *ni-me-lala*
                                  'I **have** gone to sleep.'

More recently, the verb *-isha* 'finish' has given rise in Swahili to a recent past perfective marker '*sha*', as in:

(32)   *ni-me-sha-pika*
                                  'I have **just finished** cooking.'

It is of course not an accident that a verb with the implications and presuppositions of *end* would give rise to a past marker [see (18)]. It is hardly an accident that *begin,* on the other hand, should give rise to future senses, as in Siluyana:

(33)   *ni-mba-kela*
                                  'I **will** work.'   (*-tamba* 'begin')

   One wonders whether it is accidental that in many languages volition/intent verbs such as 'want,' 'plan,' 'intend' have given rise to future sentential sense. One finds this in Swahili (where the verb *-taka* 'want' has given rise to the future marker *-ta-*), as in:

(34)   *ni-ta-kuja*
                                  'I **will** come.'

or in Palestinian Arabic, with the ambiguity:

(35)   **biddi ashrib**
                                  'I **want** to drink.' 'I **will** drink.'

As noted in (19), intensional verbs have a negative presupposition with respect to action at the time prior to the time axis. One would therefore not expect them to give rise to past tense markers. By implication, the intended action is intended for some time after the time axis — i.e., in the *future.* This may be demonstrated by the infelicities in (36) and (37):

(36)   Max $\begin{Bmatrix} wants \\ plans \end{Bmatrix}$ to deflower his cousin,

                              $\begin{Bmatrix} and\ he'll\ do\ it\ tomorrow \\ {}^*but\ he\ did\ it\ yesterday \end{Bmatrix}$.

(37) *Max has deflowered his cousin, and he $\begin{Bmatrix} wants \\ plans \end{Bmatrix}$ to do it.

An interesting case involves the verbs *go/come.* In many languages they have joined the A/M group with the meaning 'in order to' or 'intending to':

(38)   *I've come (here) to talk business.*
            I went (there) to get back my sousaphone.

Since both imply intent, one would expect future sense to arise from both. But in fact one finds that the verb *go* has given rise to future tense markers in English, French, Spanish, Hebrew, and probably many other languages. The verb *come*, on the other hand, seems to have given rise only to past tense aspects, as in French:

(39)   *Il vient de partir*
                  'He **has just** left'

or in the negative past marker in Swahili (from *-ja* 'come'):

(40)   *ha-wa-ja-enda*
                  'They **have not** gone'

Since in their A/M usage both verbs imply intent and thus futurity, I suggest that the source of their difference should be found in their presuppositions. As motion-in-space verbs, *go* presupposes 'from the speaker's place' and *come* 'toward the speaker's place,' or:

(41)   come   SPEAKER   go
                  ----------→   ----------→
                              PLACE

Diagram (41) is spatial. Suppose it were transformed into a temporal space diagram, to yield:

(42)   past (come)   SPEAKER   future (go)
                  ----------→   ----------→
                              TIME

Now the movement toward speaker's time is past, whereas the movement away from it (in the time medium) is *future*. While this explanation is highly speculative, its plausibility is enhanced by the fact that both *go* and *come* retain their presuppositions involving the speaker's position in their A/M senses.

Finally, the neg-sentential sense developed by *fail* has already been noted. It is not altogether an accident that neg-implicative verbs such as *fail, avoid, lack,* or *refuse* often give rise to sentential neg-markers.

To sum this up, one may view the diachronic process of sense development discussed above as a transformational change, involving some variant of subject identity and *equi-NP deletion,* as well as the deletion of much of the semantic material of the erstwhile A/M verb. This leaves only the appropriate implication or presupposition, which remains associated with the new sentential predicate:

(43)

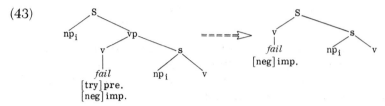

Furthermore, this presumed diachronic transformation is in essence quite similar to the synchronic one discussed earlier, through which time axis verbs become predicates of nominalized sentences:

(44)

ON THE POLYSEMY OF A/M AND P/K VERBS

As mentioned earlier, memberships of P/K and A/M groups of verbs show a considerable overlap. It is possible that this overlap or polysemy exhibited by some of these verbs is anchored in some deep semantic regularity. The subject is as frustrating as it is fascinating. At this juncture it is impossible to give more than an initial exposition of some of its intricacies.

If, given the list of A/M verbs, one first attempts to predict which ones may also show a P/K sense, one winds up with initial classification (45).

(45)

Only A/M sense	Also P/K sense
begin, end, repeat, continue, succeed, fail, *try, avoid, condescend, refuse, decline,* *neglect, manage, want, plan, prefer, hate,*	*remember, forget, hope, agree,* *learn, pretend, decide,* *intend(?), be afraid, regret*

This classification seems to show no correlation with implication, either positive or negative. There seems to be a weak correlation with stativity, in that in their P/K senses the verbs on the right are mostly stative. This correlation is illusory, however. To begin with, stative verbs such as *want, plan,* and *prefer* do not develop P/K senses. Further, *pretend* and *hope* in their A/M sense are not stative, at least by the progressive test:

(46)   *I am pretending to be sick.*
         I am hoping to finish this paper by tomorrow.

Finally, since perception/knowledge verbs are overwhelmingly stative in English, it is not altogether an accident that P/K senses turn out to be mostly stative. The strongest prediction it is possible to make is that time axis verbs do not have P/K senses. Whether this is significant or not I do not know at the moment.

Conversely, one may try to predict, given the list of P/K verbs, which ones also show an A/M sense. This task seems to be a little more rewarding, though as will be seen below, the tentative suggestions arising from this investigation are at best just suggestions. An initial classification of the P/K verb list with respect to A/M senses is given in (47).

(47)

Only P/K sense	Also A/M sense
know, realize, suspect, suppose, find out, hear, see, feel, guess, dream, discover, think, believe, doubt, fear, assume, be sure, judge	*remember, forget, decide, agree, pretend, be afraid, hope, regret, learn*

Before going into any analysis, note that the list on the right in (47) may be extended to almost all the verbs on the left by allowing the *how to* sense to be counted. As pointed out earlier, however, in most verbs that can show this sense, the sense does not correspond to the normal infinitival complementation sense (see p. 31). For this reason, it may seem strange to include *learn* in the list on the right. However, notice that there are potentially two senses of *learn to:*

(48)   *He learned to speak French.* =
                   He learned how to speak French.
         He learned to keep his mouth shut. =

                   $\begin{cases} \textit{He learned \textbf{how} to do it} \\ \textit{He learned \textbf{that} he \textbf{should} do it} \end{cases}$

The obligation sense of *learn to* is quite legitimate, and in fact closely parallels a similar A/M sense of *remember* and *forget*.

Going back to the lists in (47), they seem to correlate neither with factivity nor with stativity. They seem, however, to correlate with an interesting syntactic behavior. This involves a personal passive construction. Most of the purely P/K verbs in (47) seem to allow this pattern. This does not necessarily mean that items (c) below are transformationally derived from (b) or (a), but only that there exists some kind of semantic relatedness between patterns (a), (b), and (c):

(49) a. . . . *knew that John loved roses.*
      b. *It was known (to . . .) that John loved roses.*
      c. *John was known to love roses.*

      a. . . . *thought that Mary was beautiful.*
      b. *It was thought (by . . .) that Mary was beautiful.*
      c. *Mary was thought to be beautiful.*

      a. . . . *discovered that Bill was a fool.*
      b. *It was discovered (by . . .) that Bill was a fool.*
      c. *Bill was discovered to be a fool.*

With a number of interesting exceptions, to be discussed later, other verbs in this subgroup also allow the (c) pattern of personal passive:

(50) *Bill was suspected (by . . .) of being a coward.*
      Bill was assumed (by . . . ?) to have stolen the diamonds.
      Bill was understood (by . . . ?) to have left the country.
      Bill was believed (by . . . ?) to have been mistaken.
      Bill was supposed (by . . . ?) to have left long before.
      Bill was found to have been missing from his house.
      The airplane is feared lost over the Atlantic.
      Bill was judged to have made a fool of himself.
      Bill is sure to come home sooner or later.

The last sentence in (50) requires a brief comment. Syntactically, it is out of the passive pattern. Semantically, however, it seems to fall squarely in the paradigm of (49):

(51)   a. . . . **is sure** *that Bill will come home.*
          b. *It is sure/certain that Bill will come home.*
          c. *Bill is sure/is certain to come home.*

As I will argue below, for several verbs, nonpassive forms seem to have suppleted the passive ones in the (c) pattern.

Although several verbs that have no A/M sense, do not show the (c) pattern above, lexical suppletion may be involved. Let us first take *see*. While it is true that *be seen* may not appear in the pattern, semantically suppletive passive–stative forms such as *seem, look like,* and *appear* do crop up in the (c) and (b) patterns:

(52) a. . . . *saw that Bill loved spinach.*
  b. *?It was seen (by . . .) that Bill loved spinach.*
   It seemed (to . . .) that Bill loved spinach.
   It appeared (to . . .) that Bill loved spinach.
   It looked (to . . .) like/that Bill loved spinach.
  c. **Bill was seen to love spinach.*
   Bill seemed to love spinach.
   Bill appeared to love spinach.
   Bill looked like he loved spinach.

A similar argument may be advanced regarding *hear*, whose passive *be heard* is not admited in patterns (b) and (c) above. However, the semantically suppletive passive–stative *sound like* does appear in the pattern:

(53) a. . . . *heard that Mary was pretty.*
  b. *?It was heard (by . . .) that Mary was pretty.*
   It sounded (to . . .) like Mary was pretty.
  c. **Mary was heard to be pretty.*
   ?Mary sounded pretty.
   Mary sounded (to . . .) like she was pretty.

Let us turn next to the verb *feel*. As a P/K verb, it is not really a perception/sensation verb, but rather a diluted *think*:

(54) *I feel that you're right. ≠ I have perceived through one of my senses that you are right.*
      = I have a vague conviction that you're right.

It may be that the absence of personal passive (c) pattern for *feel* may be again due to a suppletive interaction with either *think* or *believe*, both of which do show the pattern. One may also argue that perhaps *feel* does show the (c) pattern, but not in its passivized form. Thus, note:

(54') a. *I feel that Mary is a bit weird today.*
  b. *It feels like Mary is a little weird today.*
  c. *Mary feels a little weird today.*

In short, it may well be that *be felt* is suppleted by *feel* the same way

as *be seen* is supplanted by *seem, look (like), appear,* and *be heard* by
sound(like).

One may perhaps argue a case of suppletion for *realize.* Like *feel,* it
does not exhibit the pattern:

(55)   **John was felt to have been lost.*
              *John was realized to have been lost.

However, *be realized* may have well been suppleted by *be found* or
be discovered in their senses shown in (50).

This leaves *guess, doubt,* and *dream* for the absence of the (c) pattern of which there is no ready explanation, except to suggest that I
don't see any principled grounds explaining why the sentences in (56)
are unacceptable:

(56)   ?*The answer was guessed to have been*
              cleverly hidden between the lines.
              ?*Angela was doubted to have been guilty.*
              ?*Mary was dreamed to have left Bill.*

Now, to complete the generalization, notice that all the verbs in (47)
that show an A/M sense in addition to their P/K sense seem never to
exhibit the personal passive pattern:

(57)   **Bill was remembered to have loved spinach.*
              *Bill was forgotten to have been a fool.
              *Mary was hoped to have swallowed her pill.
              *Bill was pretended to have been the champion.
              *Mary was decided to have been pretty.
              *Bill was afraid to have been wrong.
              *Bill was regretted to have been a fool.
              *Bill was agreed to have passed his orals.
              *Bill was learned to have been wrong.

It may well be that the sense of *learn* ruled out in the last sentence is
so ruled out because of possible suppletion by *find(out), discover,* or
realize.

A case of some interest in that of *fear/be afraid.* Off hand, they seem
rather alike. Why, then does *fear* exhibit the personal passive pattern
while *be afraid* does not? Perhaps this may have to do with the restriction on passivization of adjectives or stative verbs. However, *be sure*
has managed to circumvent the restriction simply by not passivizing,
as in:

(58)   *John **is sure** to turn up eventually.*

An alternative explanation would hold that *fear* in

(59)   *The plane is feared lost.*

has nothing whatever to do with 'being afraid,' but rather involves the nonpassive verb *suspect* or *believe*. Similarly, in

(60)   *I am afraid that John has already left.*
          I am afraid that Mary must leave immediately.

be afraid is used in the sense of *believe* or *think*, with an added mitigation and perhaps an implied regret, but no implication of fear. It is with this sense of *fear/be afraid* that *be feared* patterns in (59).

Initially, I would have liked to explain the syntactic test described above as differentiating between pure perception/knowledge verbs, which may exhibit the personal passive pattern, and emotive/intentional verbs, which may not. Exceptions such as *guess, doubt,* and *dream*, on one hand, and semantic exceptions such as *forget/remember*, on the other, make this explanation somewhat tainted. Instead of pursuing it further (and, undoubtedly, to its ultimate demise), I should like next to discuss the possibility of predicting what type of A/M intensional sense may arise from P/K verbs.

INTENSIONAL A/M SENSES OF P/K VERBS

As mentioned above, many P/K verbs may develop a *how to* sense. The list may be divided as in (61):

(61)

Capable of *how to* sense	Incapable
know, realize, suspect, find out, hear, see, guess, dream, discover, be sure, remember, forget, decide, learn, agree, (judge?)	*feel, think, believe, doubt, hope, regret, fear, be afraid*

If anything, the division seems to be between verbs of knowledge or acquisition of knowledge (left), as against verbs of belief/conviction/feeling. Whether the *how to* sense can be described as a true A/M sense is an open question, mostly because *how to* seems to stand for an abstract nominal object 'the manner in which,' so that it is possible to argue that this sense does not involve a sentential complement, but rather a sentential/relative clause modification on the object–noun *manner*.

Next, a suggestion made by Karttunen (private communication) has cast considerable doubt on the universal validity of the distinction drawn in the preceding section. Karttunen has observed that in Finnish almost all P/K verbs may develop A/M senses (quite apart from *how to*). While the list is not at the moment available to me, one can consider the case of *forget/remember* in English. With respect to their semantic structure as P/K verbs, one may characterize them the following way:

(62)

	Presupposed (before time axis)	Implied (after time axis)
remember	+knowledge	+know
forget	+knowledge	−know

As A/M verbs, an interesting shift occurs in both presuppositions and implications:

(63)

	Presupposed (before axis)	Implied (after axis)
remember	+knowledge of obligation	+performance
forget	+knowledge of obligation	−performance

A familiar change is shown with *learn* [in its obligation sense, see (48)]. As a P/K verb it involves:

(64)

	Presupposed (before axis)	Implied (after axis)
learn	+truth, −knowledge of it	+knowledge of truth

The same is probably true for *discover, realize, find out, see,* and *hear.* In its obligation sense as an A/M verb; however, *learn* shows:

(65)

	Presupposed (before axis)	Implied (after axis)
learn	+obligation, −compliance	+compliance with obligation

In English, cases of this kind are for some reason quite limited. In Hebrew they are more numerous. Both *remember/forget* and *learn* show a pattern identical to the one described above for English. That is, as A/M verbs they develop the presuppositon of obligation. The verb *know* also develops this sense, as in:

(66)   *hu yada laasot et ze bazman*
         'He **knew** well enough to perform it on time'

An added possibility in Hebrew is the development of *volition/ intention* senses from P/K verbs that do not ordinarily possess them. This is the case with both *think* and *dream*, the first extending to *plan*, the second to *hope*:

(67)   *Hu ḥašav lavo haerev.*
         'He **planned** to come this evening.'

which paraphrases *plan*, as in:

(68)   *Hu tixnen lavo haerve.*
         'He **planned** to come this evening.'

And with *dream*:

(69)   *Hu ḥalam linsoa le-London.*
         'He **hoped/yearned** to travel to London.'

which paraphrases *hope*:

(70)   *Hu kiva linsoa le-London*
         'He **hoped** to travel to London.'

Since the development of A/M senses from P/K senses is not unrestricted in Hebrew, not enough data exists to generalize on this phenomenon. It seems, from the small sample discussed above, that two major classes of A/M senses may arise from quite bona fide P/K verbs: volition/intent and obligation. Whether one could ultimately predict which P/K verb would give rise to what A/M sense remains to be seen.

SOME CONCLUDING REMARKS ON THE
TIME AXIS PHENOMENON

As shown above, the time axis division between the presuppositions (prior to axis) and implications (after axis) is much more widespread than originally envisioned. It has been shown in inception/termination verbs (*begin, end, continue, repeat, succeed, fail*); in volitional/ intensional verbs (*want, plan, try, intend, decide*); in perception/

knowledge verbs (*remember, forget, learn, discover, find out, realize*), and in motion verbs (*come, go, exit, enter, to, from*). One can easily demonstrate that causative verbs (such as *give, kill,* or *break*) show the same division, and we may tentatively conclude that the time axis phenomenon in the semantic structure of verbs is perhaps another candidate for eventual admission into the hall of fame of linguistic universals.

ACKNOWLEDGMENTS

I am indebted to Lauri Karttunnen, Andy Rogers, Larry Horn, and Sandra A. Thompson for valuable comments and criticism of an earlier version of this paper. The opinions expressed remain strictly my own. A much expanded and revised version of this paper will appear in *Language*.

REFERENCES

Givón, T. 1969. Studies in ChiBemba and Bantu Grammar. Unpublished dissertation, University of California, Los Angeles.

Givón, T. 1970. Notes on the semantic structure of English adjectives. *Language* 46.4.

Givón, T. 1971. Historical syntax and synchronic morphology: An archaeologist's field trip. IN Papers from the 7th Regional Meeting, Chicago Linguistics Society.

Karttunen, L. 1970a. On the semantics of complement sentences. IN Papers from the 6th Regional Meeting, Chicago Linguistics Society.

Karttunen, L. 1970b. Some observations on factivity. Linguistics Society of America. winter.

Kiparsky, P. and Kiparsky, C. 1968. Fact, IN (Bierwiesch and Heidolph, eds.) Recent advances in Linguistics Mouton, The Hague.

Morgan, J. 1969. On the treatment of presupposition in transformational grammar. IN *Papers from the 5th Regional meeting, Chicago Linguistic Society.*

Neubauer, P. 1971. The 2^3 Surface Verbs *pretend*, University of Michigan (mimeographed).

TEMPORALLY RESTRICTIVE ADJECTIVES

DAVID DOWTY
University of Texas at Austin

In this paper I will propose an analysis of sentence-final modifiers like those in sentences (1) and (2):

(1)   *The girl married* $\begin{cases} young. \\ on\ the\ streetcorner. \\ wearing\ a\ white\ dress. \end{cases}$

(2)   *I saw John* $\begin{cases} asleep. \\ studying\ in\ the\ library. \end{cases}$

I will refer to these modifiers as temporally restrictive adjectives (TRAs). First, I will show several ways in which TRAs behave like time adverbs and like relative clauses introduced by *when*. Then I will propose an underlying structure for TRAs that explains these facts.

Sentences like (2), in which the adjective modifies the object rather than the subject, are discussed in Georgia Green's article "How Abstract is Surface Structure?" (Green, 1970). In this paper she contrasts temporal adjectives (3a) with those expressing result (3b), and those expressing a psychological judgment (3c):

(3)   a. Temporal   *John saw Harry alive.*
        b. Result   *John shot Harry dead.*
        c. Psychological   *John considers Harry obnoxious.*

51

Since I use examples with the verb *find* below, I should point out that it can appear as a psychological construction as well as in a temporal one. These two senses can, if necessary, be distinguished by the test of entailment. With TRAs, the speaker assumes the truth of the proposition expressed by the adjective; with the psychological constructions, he does not. Thus (3'a) is psychological while (3'b) is temporal:

(3')   a.   *John found Harry stupid, but I didn't think he was*
             stupid at all.
       b.   **John found Harry asleep, but I didn't think he was*
             asleep at all.

This paper will apply only to temporal adjectives. Green claims that the above adjectives cannot be the same as the postnominal modifiers which follow indefinites, as in (4).

(4)   *John wrote about someone dead.*

She gives four arguments for this claim, which I will merely summarize here:

   1.   Only postnominal modifiers can answer the question *What kind of.*
   2.   Postnominal modifiers can occur only following indefinite pronouns such as *someone, everyone,* or *something.*
   3.   Postnominal modifiers are paraphrases of relative clauses, the others are not.
   4.   Only the NPs with postnominals can undergo *passive;* thus, (5) is the passive of (4), but (6) as the passive of (3c) is impossible.

(5)   *Someone dead was written about by John.*

(6)   **Harry alive was seen by John.*

Green does not directly discuss sentences like (1), in which the adjective modifies the object rather than the subject, but her first three arguments apply to (1) as well. Hence in neither case can TRAs arise from the reduction of relative clauses (the obvious source of the postnominals).

Sentences with TRAs, first of all, can always be paraphrased by sentences with *when*-clauses.[1] However, they are never synonymous with sentences having relative clauses:

---

[1] Some speakers object that the sentences in (1) and (2) are more accurately paraphrased by (i) and (ii) than by (7a) and (8a) as I claim:

(*Continued on next page*)

(7)   a. *The girl married when she was young.*   (= 1)
       b. *The girl who was young married.*   (≠ 1)

(8)   a. *I saw John when he was asleep.*   (= 2)
           b. *I saw John, who was asleep.*   (≠ 2)

A time adverb that occurs in the main clause can be moved to the adjective phrase with no change in meaning; (9a) and (9b) are synonymous:

(9) a. *Thursday night I* $\begin{Bmatrix} found \\ observed \\ discovered \end{Bmatrix}$ *John studying in the library.*

     b. *I found John studying in the library Thursday night.*

The same applies to *when*-clauses; (10a) and (10b) are synonymous:

(10) a. *Thursday night I found John when he was studying in the library.*

      b. *I found John when he was studying in the library Thursday night.*

With different time adverbs, however, both kinds of sentences become meaningless:

(11)   **Friday morning I found John studying in the library Thursday night.*

(12)   **Friday morning I found John when he was studying in the library Thursday night.*

Notice for comparison that this restriction does not apply to relative clauses:

(13)   *Friday morning I found John, who was studying in the library Thursday night.*

(i)   *When the girl married she was young.*
(ii)   *When I saw John he was asleep.*

These paraphrases do seem intuitively more satisfying, but it is difficult to describe what difference there is, if any, between (7a) and (i) or between (8a) and (ii). These sentences amount to an assertion of co-temporality, and since the relation *is co-temporal with* is logically reflexive, one form entails the other and vice-versa. Since all the arguments I give in the paper would support a source for TRAs resembling (i) and (ii) as well as the one I argue for, I wish to leave the question open. My guess is that the difference is simply one of focus; that is, (i) (and perhaps (1)) assert something like "speaking of the girl's marriage, it occurred when she was young," whereas (7a) is more like "speaking of the girl's youth, she got married then."

Nor does it apply to outwardly similar constructions involving complementizers:

(14)   *Friday morning I* $\begin{Bmatrix} found \\ observed \\ discovered \end{Bmatrix}$ *that John was studying in*
       the library Thursday night.

Mary Gallagher (1970) noticed an interesting class of predicates which are semantically anomalous with time adverbs:

(15)   a.   *John said that the Washington Monument was heavy*
            (*in 1934*).
       b.   *The man who sold the house knew more languages*
            (*at noon*) *than anyone else.*
       c.   *Whoever stole the piano had strong arms* (*a week*
            ago Thursday).

Whatever the source of this anomaly, these predicates are just as bad when they appear as either TRAs or *when*-clauses:

(16)   a.   *John saw the Washington Monument heavy.*
            John saw the Washington Monument when it was
            heavy.
       b.   *The man sold the house knowing more languages*
            than anyone else.
            The man sold the house when he knew more languages
            than anyone else.
       c.   *Someone stole the piano having strong arms.*
            Someone stole the piano when he had strong arms.

Gallagher used the facts of (15) to argue that *Tense* is not an obligatory category in underlying structure, and she assumes that the class of predicates which cannot take time adverbs consists simply of all statives. But this cannot be true, since there are statives which do take time adverbs:

(17)   *John was* $\begin{Bmatrix} asleep \\ alone \\ drunk \end{Bmatrix}$ *yesterday at noon.*

(18)   *Did you see John* $\begin{Bmatrix} asleep? \\ alone? \\ drunk? \end{Bmatrix}$

Even worse, there are adjectives that are tensable when predicated of some nouns, but nontensable when predicated of others:

(19)   *The traffic light*⎱
         *The avocado   ⎰ *was green a moment ago.*

(20)   *The beach ball*⎱
         *John's head ⎰ *was round yesterday afternoon.*

Especially interesting are the sentences of (21):

(21)   *Did you see the nude dancing girls?*
         Did you see the dancing girls nude?
         Did you see the nude statue?
         *Did you see the statue nude?

         The dancing girls were nude at midnight.
         *The statue in the garden was nude at midnight.

A little reflection on the meanings of these sentences reveals what is going on here. The asterisked sentences in (21) seem to imply that the statue is nude at some times and not nude at others, a state of affairs that would be counter to our knowledge of statues in the real world. Examination of Gallagher's examples suggests, in fact, that a property predicated of an individual cannot appear with a time adverb in cases where the property cannot be lost or acquired by that individual as time passes. For instance, the Washington Monument is either heavy once and for all or it is not; it cannot lose or gain weight. This distinction is referred to by traditional grammarians as "essence" versus "accident" (see Bolinger, 1971).

This observation strongly suggests that the "ungrammaticality" of (16)–(21) is to be explained in terms of the speaker's beliefs about the real world, rather than by the form of the grammar of English (unlike the categories stative and nonstative). These beliefs may vary from speaker to speaker. For example, (22) would probably not be accepted by most speakers of English, but for residents of Austin, Texas it is perfectly normal.

(22)   *Did you see the tower orange?*

In Austin it is generally known that the University of Texas has a conspicuous tower, normally lighted with white lights at night, but lighted with orange lights after major athletic victories. This serves as a signal to the nation's number one football fans to jump into their cars and drive around town honking their horns and drinking beer.

A strange fact is that technology advances, the number of predicates which cannot be tensed decreases. Only in recent years has it become possible to ask someone whether he has seen the secretary blond, or to assert that Mary had blue eyes yesterday.

A language like Finnish gives further evidence of the relation between TRAs and time adverbs. Lauri Karttunen has pointed out to
me that sentences in Finnish that correspond to TRAs have an adjective in the essive case, which is a case used to mark time adverbials.

(23)   *Tyttö meni naimisiin nuorena.*
         'The girl married young.' (Essive of *nuori*, 'young')

(24)   *Tyttö meni naimisiin tiistaina.*
         'The girl married on Tuesday.' (Essive of *tiistai*, 'Tuesday'.)

In fact, Finnish grammarians have traditionally analyzed the adjective in (23) as a time adverbial.

When sentences like (1) and (2) are negated, many of them acquire
an invited inference to the effect that the action described by the main
clause did take place, but at a different time or under different conditions from that referred to by the adjective. Thus *The girl didn't marry
young* leads us to suppose that she married later in life; *I didn't find
John asleep* suggests that I found him at some other activity. Hence
the continuations in (25) are natural:

(25)   *The girl didn't marry young.* (She married at 40.)

(26)   *I didn't find John asleep.* (I found him swinging from the
         chandelier.)

My purpose here is not to argue what kind of inference this is
(whether conversational implicature in the sense of Grice (1968) or
presupposition that can be canceled), but simply to point out that
when-clauses have the same property.

(27)   *The girl didn't marry when she was young.* (She married
         at 40.)
         I didn't find John when he was asleep. (I found him
         when he was swinging from the chandelier.)

This kind of continuation is not possible with relative clauses:

(28)   ??*The girl who was young didn't marry.* She married at 40.
         ??*I didn't find John, who was asleep.* He was swinging
         from the chandelier.

A fact I cannot explain is that the TRAs differ from the *when*-clauses
in terms of their own respective presuppositions. That is, a sentence
with a TRA only entails the truth of the TRA, whereas a sentence

with a *when*-clause presupposes the truth of the *when*-clause. This is illustrated by (29) and (30):

(29) a. *John found Harry alone.* $\Vdash$ (Harry was alone)

    b. *John didn't find Harry alone.*
      Did John find Harry alone? $\left.\rule{0pt}{60pt}\right\}$ $\Vdash\mkern-8mu/$ (Harry was alone)
      It is possible that John found
      Harry alone.

(30) a. *John found Harry when he was* $\Vdash$ (Harry was alone)
      alone.

    b. *John didn't find Harry when he*
      was alone.
      Did John find Harry when he $\left.\rule{0pt}{60pt}\right\}$ $\Vdash$ (Harry was alone)
      was alone?
      It is possible that John found
      Harry when he was alone.

Schematically,

$$S_1\text{-}TRA_1 \ \Vdash\ TRA_1 \qquad \text{but} \qquad S_1\text{-when-}S_2 \gg S_2$$

It has been argued in recent literature—e.g., Gallagher (1970), Ross (1967), and McCawley (1971)—that *Tense* is a higher predicate. It has also been claimed by Kiparsky (1968), McCawley (1971), and Gallagher (1970) that surface structure tense morphemes are the surface reflexes of underlying time adverbs. If these proposals are correct, as I assume they are, then *Tense* must be a two-place predicate (as McCawley observed), taking as its arguments a proposition and a time expression. This time expression must have a structure something like that of a noun phrase, for it can be relativized, as (31)–(32) shows.

(31)   *The guests arrived at a time that was inconvenient for everyone.*

(32)   *John was here Monday, which was the worst possible day.*

If this possibility for *relativation* is allowed, then there is a natural source for relative clauses introduced by *when;* these are relative clauses having as head noun a time expression that does not appear in surface structure. In fact, Michael Geis (1970) has argued that such sentences are to be derived by a rule which deletes *the time at which.* I propose that the underlying structure of both *when*-clauses and TRAs is something like (33).

(33)

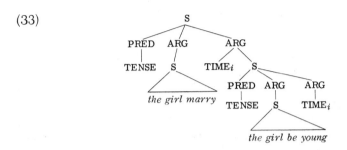

This structure will explain the cooccurrence restriction on time adverbs observed above. Notice that the structure I have proposed would automatically be subject to the well-formedness condition that applies to all relative clauses, namely, that there be an identical occurrence of the head noun within the embedded clause. Thus, in this analysis, the ungrammatical sentence (11) would have a time index as head noun that is not identical to the one in its relative clause.

My arguments here do not support any difference in underlying structure between subject-modifying TRAs and object-modifying TRAs (other than the obvious difference that the NPs with which their subjects are coreferential are in subject position and object position, respectively), though they may turn out to be quite dissimilar. Green (1970) showed in her article that in surface structure, object-modifying adjectives are within the VP, whereas subject-modifying adjectives are not. How this difference arises in the course of the derivation remains to be explained in any case.

The analysis of TRAs as higher predicates suggests that one would find parallels between their properties and those of quantifiers, which have also been analyzed as higher predicates. Such a case is the behavior of TRAs under negation observed above. In Carden (1970), it is claimed that the quantifier *many* in (34a) is derived from a higher predicate, while *many* in (34b) originates within the NP, that is, from a relative clause.

(34) a. *John doesn't think many girls left.*   (negates *many*)
      b. *John doesn't think the many girls left.*   (negates *left*)

In (34a), the negation is understood to apply to *many* in the most common reading; John thinks few girls left. But in (34b), John thinks the many girls stayed; the negation applies to the verb. With adjectives, the same variation is observed according to whether the adjective is temporal and thus a higher predicate as in (35a), or originates within the NP as in (35b).

(35)   a. *John doesn't think the girl married young.*
         (negates *young*)
         b. *John doesn't think the young girl married.*
         (negates *married*)

Finally, my analysis predicts that if TRAs are really higher predicates, there should be cases where a difference in meaning can arise when the *precedence/command constraint* on quantifiers is violated. This constraint, which is discussed in Lakoff (1969), requires that "if an underlying asymmetric command relationship (between quantifiers) breaks down in SS, a precedence relation takes over." This can be shown with subject-modifying TRAs, since—as Green (1970) observed—these adjective phrases can ordinarily be moved to the beginning of the sentence with no change in meaning. Each of the pairs of sentences in (36)–(39) is synonymous:

(36)   a. *The sailor returned home tired and disillusioned.*
       b. *Tired and disillusioned, the sailor returned home.*
          (= 36a)

(37)   a. *John left his office exhausted.*
       b. *Exhausted, John left his office.*   (= 37a)

(38)   a. *John watched TV alone in his apartment.*
       b. *Alone in his apartment, John watched TV.*
          (= 38a)

(39)   a. *John listened to Traffic stoned.*
       b. *Stoned, John listened to Traffic.*   (= 39a)

If, however, the sentence is negated, as in (40), or a temporal quantifier such as *frequently, often, twice,* or *seldom* is introduced, as in (41)–(44), then the sentences are no longer synonymous. There is considerable dialect variation here, as is usually the case with the quantifier constraint, but for many speakers at least, the quantifier changes its scope in these sentences:

(40)   a. *The sailor didn't return home tired and disillusioned.*
       b. *Tired and disillusioned, the sailor didn't return home.*
          (≠ 40a)

(41)   a. *John frequently left his office exhausted.*
       b. *Exhausted, John frequently left his office.*   (≠ 41a)

(42)   a. *John often watched television alone in his apartment.*
       b. *Alone in his apartment, John often watched television.*
          (≠ 42a)

(43) a. *John listened to Traffic three times stoned.*
      b. *Stoned, John listened to Traffic three times.* (≠ 43a)

In (40a), the TRA falls within the scope of the negation; that is, this sentence is the negation of (36a). It is actually ambiguous as to whether the sailor was ever tired and disillusioned or not (though as we saw above, there is an invited inference to the effect that he did return but in a different condition). On the other hand, (40b) asserts unambiguously that the sailor was in fact tired and disillusioned, but that he did not return home. In (41a), *exhausted* is within the scope of *frequently;* that is, it suggests that John was exhausted on many different occasions. In (41b), however, *frequently* is within the scope of *exhausted;* it asserts that John was exhausted for some period of time and that during that time it was frequently the case that he left the office. He was exhausted once in this sentence, and not frequently. The distinctions between the remaining pairs of sentences can be accounted for in the same way. Some speakers find a similar scope distinction with a time adverb such as *on Tuesday.* Thus, (44a) could refer to either a single Tuesday or three different Tuesdays; (44b) refers only to a single Tuesday:

(44)   a. *John was arrested three times on Tuesday.*
            b. *On Tuesday, John was arrested three times.*

Lakoff's (1969) constraint on quantifiers accounts for these different readings as follows. Notice that in the a sentences of (41)–(43) quantifiers such as *frequently, often* precede the TRA, and that the quantifier and the TRA command each other. In the b sentences it is the TRA that precedes the other quantifiers, but the same symmetric command relationship holds. What the quantifier constraint specifies is that if one quantifier precedes another in surface structure, and their command relationship is symmetric, then the leftmost quantifier must be the higher in the underlying structure. Thus, the constraint requires that the TRAs are in the scope of the other quantifiers in the a sentences, but that this relation is reversed in the b sentences.

One more qualification must be made about these readings. For some speakers of dialects that have the rule of *Y movement*, there is a second reading of the b sentence that is synonymous with the respective a sentence. If this reading is indeed produced by the *Y movement* rule, then it is evidence for rather than against my hypothesis, since it has already been shown on other grounds that the quantifier constraint does not affect *Y movement* (see Lakoff, 1969).

As Green (1970) observed (in her footnote 2), the readings associated with Y *movement* have a characteristic rise–fall pitch contour (and no pause for the "comma"), whereas the normal readings do not. Thus, most speakers can distinguish Y *movement* readings from other readings on this basis, and it is in fact only the Y *movement* readings that violate the quantifier constraint.

I will conclude with one more observation about the preposed TRAs. For some speakers, a preposed adjective phrase can only precede a verb in the past tense, as (45b) shows, though the same phrase in sentence-final position allows any tense, as in (45a):

(45) a. *John* $\begin{Bmatrix} left \\ leaves \\ will\ leave \\ may\ leave \end{Bmatrix}$ *his office exhausted.*

  b. *Exhausted, John* $\begin{Bmatrix} left \\ {}^*will\ leave \\ {}^*leaves \\ {}^*may\ leave \end{Bmatrix}$ *his office.*

The exception to this is when sentence (45b) is understood to be in the historical present—then present and present perfect are also grammatical. I do not understand why this is so, but I suspect that it may have to do with the quantifier constraint again. In (45b), the TRA precedes the tense morpheme on the main verb, and they command each other. Since this tense morpheme presumably also comes from a higher predicate, the quantifier constraint may apply to it as well. If so, this would seem to require that the tense of the TRA is higher in the tree than the past tense on the main verb. Even if this wild speculation turns out to be true, it still remains to be explained just what the configuration of underlying tenses in (45b) looks like, and why only the past tense should be acceptable here.

ACKNOWLEDGMENT

I wish to thank Stanley Peters, Lauri Karttunen, and Robert Wall for many helpful comments on an earlier version of this paper, without, of course, implying that they necessarily agree with my conclusions.

REFERENCES

Bolinger, D. 1971. The Nominal in the Progressive. Linguistic Inquiry 2(2); pp. 246–250.

Carden, G. 1970. On Post-Determiner Quantifiers. Linguistic Inquiry, 1(4), pp. 415–428.

Gallagher, M. 1970. Adverbs of Time and Tense. Papers from the Sixth Regional Meeting, Chicago Linguistic Society, pp. 220–225 (R. I. Binnick et al., eds.). University of Chicago, Chicago.

Geis, M. L. 1970. Adverbial Subordinate Clauses in English. Ph.D. thesis, MIT, Cambridge, Massachusetts.

Green, G. M. 1970. How Abstract is Surface Structure? Papers from the Sixth Regional Meeting, Chicago Linguistic Society, pp. 270–281 (R. I. Binnick et al., eds.). University of Chicago, Chicago.

Grice, H. P. 1968. The Logic of Conversation. Unpublished manuscript presented in The William James Lectures, Harvard University.

Kiparsky, R. P. V. 1968. Tense and Mood in Indo-European Syntax. Foundations of Language 4.30–57.

Lakoff, G. 1969. On Generative Semantics. Semantics: An Interdisciplinary Reader in Philosophy, Psychology, Linguistics and Anthropology (L. Jacobovits and D. Steinberg, eds.). University of Illinois Press, Urbana, Illinois.

McCawley, J. D. 1971. Tense and Time Reference in English. Studies in Semantics, pp. 97–114. (Charles Fillmore and Terrence Langendoen, eds.) Holt, New York.

Ross, J. R. 1967. Auxiliaries as Main Verbs. (mimeograph) MIT, Cambridge, Massachusetts.

CYCLIC AND LINEAR GRAMMARS

JOHN P. KIMBALL
University of California, Santa Cruz

INTRODUCTION

Although current work in generative grammar derives its origins from Chomsky's "Aspects" (Chomsky, 1965), recent research has led increasingly to divergence on a number of fundamental points. One basic point on which such divergence has been manifested concerns the conventions under which transformations are applied in derivation of surface structure from deep structure.

Conventions for the application of rules are not part of the grammar of any language. Thus, the statement of such conventions, although empirical in content, is universal in application. We should expect that investigations into the nature of the conventions will be of greatest interest and importance and will interact with particular syntactic analysis in many ways; they will also be among the most difficult to pursue. The reason for the former is clear, for in sketching universal properties of grammars we are thereby characterizing properties innate in the mind's organization of perceptual experience. The reason for the latter is that the consequences of positing different conventions that interact with data of the particular language only by lengthy chains of inference, in which one frequently is forced to make assumptions concerning as yet unestablished points. Furthermore, since the conventions for applying transformations are linguistic universals, the child already has knowledge of them (in the sense that the child may be said to have any linguistic knowledge) when he begins the task of language learning. In other words, the child never has to make a decision concerning alternate formulations of conventions as if he had to decide whether such-and-such a transformation is in the language, and also concerning other facts particular to his language. Thus, whereas there must be evidence in the speech the child hears regarding particular facts about his language, there never need be evidence in any language concerning conventions for applying transformations, since every child brings complete knowledge about the subject with him from birth.

There are certain requirements that must be met a priori by any set of conventions for applying transformations. As conceived in "Aspects," the base of the grammar generates structures that are arbitrarily large in size. If the set of transformations is to be finite (as it must be if the speaker's knowledge of a potentially infinite set of sentences is to be finitely represented), and if each simplex sentence within any deep structure must have at least one transformation applied to it (where a simplex sentence is the structure dominated by an S within which no other S occurs), then a provision must be made for iterative (recursive) application of transformations. Such a provision for iterative application of transformations is incorporated in the framework of "Aspects" in at least two ways: first, a transformation applies to all subdomains of its domain of application, which meets its structural description (SD); and second, the sequence of linearly ordered transformations applies cyclically (in a sense to be specified below) in a derivation.

It is the motivation for the second of the above provisions that may be brought into question and for which an alternative has been proposed, principally by John Ross. Under cyclic conventions, a sequence of transformations applies in order first to the most deeply embedded sentence of a deep structure, and then successively to each higher sentence. Alternatively, under linear conventions, each transformation would apply, in its turn, to the whole deep structure processing S-dominated substrings from the bottom up. After a transformation had applied, it would not be available for further deep structure processing. Grammars in which the transformations apply as described in "Aspects" are called cyclic grammars, and those in which the above transformations apply may be called linear grammars.

I will not give a formal definition of either kind of grammar, but for purposes of exposition, transformational derivations of a given deep structure in a particular grammar will be carried out according to cyclic and linear conventions. The rules for the grammar are as follows:

Phrase structure:

$$S \longrightarrow abc \; S$$
$$S \longrightarrow abc \; s$$

Transformations:

$$T_1: X \; a \; b \; Y \longrightarrow X \; b + a \; \emptyset \; Y$$
$$T_2: X \; a \; c \; Y \longrightarrow X \; \emptyset \; c + a \; Y$$

The symbol $+$ represents sister-adjunction.

A cyclic derivation in this grammar would go as follows:

$[a \; b \; c \; [a \; b \; c \; [a \; b \; c \; s]_s]_s]_s$	Base string
$[a \; b \; c \; [a \; b \; c \; [b \; a \; c \; s]_s]_s]_s$	T_1 first cycle
$[a \; b \; c \; [a \; b \; c \; [b \; c \; a \; s]_s]_s]_s$	T_2 first cycle
$[a \; b \; c \; [b \; a \; c \; [b \; c \; a \; s]_s]_s]_s$	T_1 second cycle
$[a \; b \; c \; [b \; c \; a \; [b \; c \; a \; s]_s]_s]_s$	T_2 second cycle
$[b \; a \; c \; [b \; c \; b \; a \; [c \; a \; s]_s]_s]_s$	T_1 third cycle
$[b \; c \; a \; [b \; c \; b \; [c \; a \; a \; s]_s]_s]_s$	T_2 third cycle

The linear derivation of the same base string is:

$[a \; b \; c \; [a \; b \; c \; [a \; b \; c \; s]_s]_s]_s$	Base string
$[a \; b \; c \; [a \; b \; c \; [b \; a \; c \; s]_s]_s]_s$	T_1 within lowest S
$[a \; b \; c \; [b \; a \; c \; [b \; a \; c \; s]_s]_s]_s$	T_1 within second lowest S
$[b \; a \; c \; [b \; a \; c \; [b \; a \; c \; s]_s]_s]_s$	T_1 within highest S
$[b \; a \; c \; [b \; a \; c \; [b \; c \; a \; s]_s]_s]_s$	T_2 within lowest S
$[b \; a \; c \; [b \; c \; a \; [b \; c \; a \; s]_s]_s]_s$	T_2 within second S
$[b \; c \; a \; [b \; c \; a \; [b \; c \; a \; s]_s]_s]_s$	T_2 within highest S

Thus, in general, in a grammar G with transformations $T_1 \cdots T_k$, a cyclic derivation of a deep-structure string will have a transformational history that is some word in the regular language $(T_1 \cup T_2 \cup \cdots \cup T_k)^*$, whereas a linear derivation will have a transformational history which is some word in the regular language $(T_1)^* \cdots (T_k)^*$. The reader will notice that the language generated by this grammar under cyclic conventions is different from that generated under linear conventions. We may then consider the problem of whether the class of languages weakly generated by cyclic grammars is the same as that weakly generated by linear languages. This question has been answered in the affirmative, for it has been shown that any recursively enumerable language can be generated by cyclic and linear grammars (see Kimball, 1967).

In proposing a new way of doing derivations in syntax, one must show not only that it can adequately account for facts covered by the old method, but also that it captures certain generalizations about syntax that the old way could not. Thus, for example, for linear conventions to be considered seriously, it is necessary to show that derivations computed in the cyclic grammar can also be done in the grammar under linear conventions. As noted above, there is no reason to expect a transformational grammar to give the same language under different conventions, and so, it is rather surprising to find that, with some adjustments, certain major subportions of English grammar will yield the same language under either convention. (Of course, if the grammar as a whole yielded the same language under either way of doing transformational derivations, the differences between the conventions would be immaterial to syntax.)

Using the analysis of complement constructions in English recently proposed by Kiparsky and Kiparsky (1971), I shall demonstrate the manner in which different conventions yield the same language for a grammar of English which contains only transformations of subject *raising*, *passive*, and *extrap*.

The rule of *extrap*, which is a last-cyclic rule, is stated as follows: $X[(NP) S]_{NP} Y \Rightarrow X[(NP)]_{NP} Y S$. This transformation relates sentences like *That the President should be so scurrilous surprised the Congress* and *It surprised the Congress that the President should be so scurrilous*. The rule of subject raising brings the subject of a sentence embedded in either subject or object position of certain verbs (nonfactive, by Kiparsky's analysis) and sister-adjoins it to the NP that dominates the embedded sentence. Thus, from the deep structure $[[[Charles\ lost\ his\ head]_S]_{NP} [seems]_{VP}]_S$ we get by subject raising $[[Charles]_{NP}[[[lost\ his\ head]_{VP}]_S]_{NP} [seems]_{VP}]_S$, and then the application of *extrap* yields *Charles seems to have lost his head*. In Kiparsky's analysis, VPs exhaustively dominated by Ss become infinitives. *Passive* relates sentences like *John loved Merry* and *Merry was loved by John*. Both *passive* and *subject raising* apply within the domain of each S in a deep structure.

The interaction of *passive* and *subject raising* yields the possibility of moving a NP, which is both the most deeply embedded and the right-most major category of a deep structure, to a position which is left-most and the least embedded major category constituent. Thus, from a deep structure like *Mary believes Bill to expect the cat to eat the mouse*, we can get *The mouse was believed by Mary to be expected by Bill to have been eaten by the cat*. What is interesting is that such a derivation can be carried out by either convention with the same results using the above transformations if *passive* is ordered before *subject raising*. There is some debate concerning this ordering, and it will be discussed in detail below. We will carry out the derivation first by the cyclic and then by the linear convention.

The base structure is as follows:

(1)

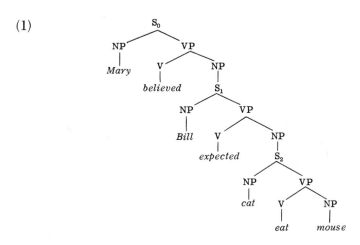

On the first cycle (S_2) of the cyclic derivation, *passive* applies yielding a derived S_2 structure (2).

(2)

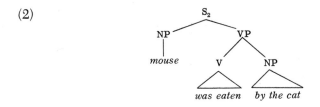

Subject raising fails to apply on the S_2 cycle. On S_1, *passive* again applies yielding a derived S_1 structure:

(3)

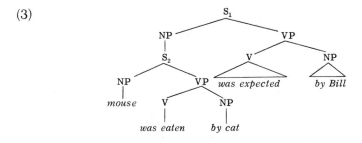

Subject raising next applies on S_1 yielding:

(4)

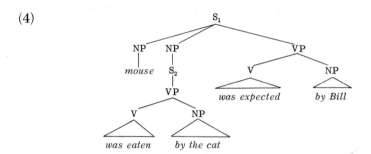

Passive applies on S_0 yielding:

(5)

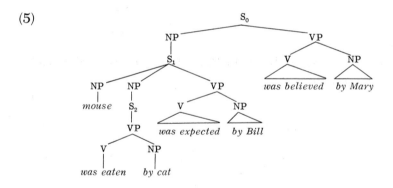

Subject raising then applies to S_0 yielding:

(6)

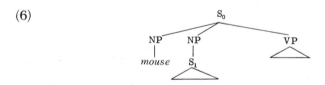

Finally, *extrap* applies last-cyclically, moving S_2 to the end of S_1 and S_1 to the end of S_0 simultaneously. The final derived structure is:

(7)

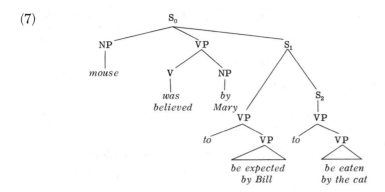

A linear derivation of (7) from (1) proceeds as follows: *Passive* applies to (1) on the lowest cycle (S_2) yielding (2). Then *passive* applies on S_1 yielding (3). Finally, *passive* applies on S_0 yielding:

(8)

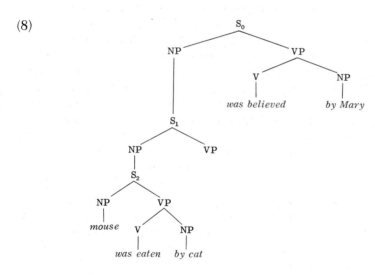

Subject raising fails to apply then on S_2, but moves the subject NP of S_2 up sister-adjoining it to the subject NP of S_1 in application to S_1. The derived S_1 structure is that:

(9)

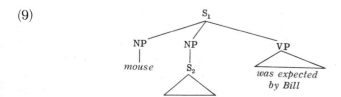

Subject raising applies on S_0 yielding structure (6). Then extrap applies to (6) as in the cyclic case, yielding the final derived structure (7).

SOME FORMAL PROPERTIES OF CYCLIC AND LINEAR GRAMMARS

I shall now discuss a formal characterization of the following two classes of transformational grammars:

Class I: Grammars that generate the same language under cyclic and linear conventions. (we write: $L(G)_c = L(G)_l$).

Class II: Grammars that are cyclic (linear) such that their transformations may be reordered and applied linearly (cyclically) to yield the same language.

For a grammar to be in classes I or II, we demand more than a simple set theoretic identity of $L(G)_c$ and $L(G)_l$. What is demanded is what we will call derivational identity, which may be expressed as follows: Let us conceive of a transformational grammar as specifying a set of ordered pairs $\langle D_{ij}, \delta_i \rangle$, where δ_i is a structure generated by the base of the grammar, and D_{ij} is a derivation of δ_i into a surface structure σ_{ij}, D_{ij} consisting of a sequence of names (or indices) of transformational rules (see Kimball, 1967, for further discussion). For a grammar to be class I (or II), we require that for each cyclic derivation D_{ij}^c of a base string δ_i, there be a corresponding linear derivation D_{ij}^l, which uses the same transformations as D_{ij}^c. That is, we require that there be a one-to-one function $f; D_{ij}^c \rightarrow D_{ij}^l$, such that for each transformation T_k, we have $f(T_k) = T_k$. In fact, we want to impose the further condition that if a certain T_k in D_{ij}^c applied within the domain of a certain S node S_t, then $f(T_k)$ applied within the same domain in D_{ij}^l. From now on we will take the expression $L(G)_c = {}_D L(G)_l$ to imply derivational as well as set theoretic identity.

We should perhaps remark on the motivation for and effect of imposing this stronger kind of identity on the cyclic and noncyclic languages generated by a grammar as a condition for it to be class I or class II. A requirement of derivational identity is usually implied by linguists when it is said that a certain sentence can be derived either cyclically or linearly, or that a grammar yields the same language by either convention for applying transformations. Generative grammarians say they have explained a sentence when they have found a deep structure from which it may be derived by a sequence of well motivated transformations. What has remained relatively stable over years of research are the transformations, whereas the phase structure rules have undergone and continue to undergo rather far-reaching changes. Thus, what is perhaps most central to an explanation of a sentence is that in its history certain transformations applied in certain domains. Frequently one argues back to a specific deep structure for a sentence (and thus, indirectly, to a certain set of base rules) by arguing that certain transformations must have been applied to it. Further, these transformational arguments are used to determine the set of nonterminals that must exist in a language under the dictum that such-and-such is a nonterminal only if at least one transformation must mention it in its structural description. In positing a certain deep structure for a sentence, we are stating what it has in common with all other sentences of the language, and the particular sequence of transformations that apply to it determine the idiosyncracies of its surface form. If a deep sturcture is mapped into various different surface forms, there must be a unique transformational history particular to each one. And if a certain surface structure were generated from a set of different deep structures (resulting in an ambiguity), then each of its deep structures must be uniquely recoverable by virtue of a different transformational history.

The effect of this requirement of derivational identity of languages is that of imposing greater structure on the problem of characterizing classes I and II, and thus enabling a correspondingly stronger conclusion. For example, if we require only set theoretic identity, it would be easy to find a grammar that met this condition whose language contained an infinite subset of surface forms, such that for each form, the deep structure from which it was derived cyclically would be different from that from which it was derived linearly.

A simple example of such a grammar is as follows:

$$S \implies ab \ (S) \qquad T_1: \ [ab \ [b \ X]_s]_s \overset{t}{\implies} [bab \ [X \ ]_s]_s$$

$$S \implies (t)ba \qquad T_2: \ [ab]_s \implies [ba]_s$$

$$T_3: \ XtaY \implies XaY$$

In this grammar, deep structures whose right-most S node dominates ab are mapped cyclically into strings of the form $b(ab)^*a$, and are mapped linearly into strings of the form $(ab)^*ba$. Base strings whose right-most S node dominates ba are mapped both cyclically and linearly into strings of the form $b(ab)^*a$. And base strings whose right-most S node dominates tba get mapped cyclically and linearly into strings of the form $(ab)^*ba$. Thus $L(g)_c = L(G)_t = b(ab)^*a = (ab)^*ba$, but a string of the form $b(ba)^*$ comes cyclically from the first type of base structure mentioned above and linearly from the second type of base structure.

Formal Properties of Transformations

The first problem to be dealt with in characterizing classes I and II above is to find the conditions under which a grammar may fail to be class I. For example, our discussion previous to this section indicated that an English grammar with just the rules of *passive, subject raising,* and *extrap* would be a class I grammar. However, the example given does not prove this, and it is possible that some deep structure (of some great complexity) could exist from which the cyclic and noncyclic derivations give different results. So far, no such deep structure has been found, but of course, only a finite number of deep structures have been or could ever be examined. Thus, we must find reason based on formal considerations for supposing that the grammar of English with the three rules mentioned above is a class I grammar.

Let us assume that all recursion in the base of the transformational grammar must pass through the initial symbol S (see Chomsky, 1965, p. 142), so that there is a fixed bound on the maximum distance between any two S nodes in a base structure, one of which dominates the other with no intervening S nodes. Let us further assume that the S nodes in each base string are indexed according to their level of embedding in the structure, with the top S node receiving the index 0. With this indexing of levels of embedding in a tree, we may make the following definitions:

DEFINITION 1   In a tree structure τ, we have $S_i <_k S_j$ if $i > j$ and $i - j = k$.

DEFINITION 2   A transformation T_i in a TG, G is k-limited if in no derivation in G is the structural description (SD) of T_i met by a factorization $\psi_1 \cdots \psi_k$ of the derived structure where there are two factors, ψ_i, ψ_j, each of whose lowest exhaustively dominating S nodes, S_{ti}, S_{tj}, are such that $S_{ti} <_m S_{tj}$ where $k < m$.

Intuitively speaking, a transformation is k-limited if it never relates material in two sentences, one of which is embedded more than k sentences deeper than the other.

Note that if a transformation is k-limited for some k, then it is k'-limited for all $k' > k$.

DEFINITION 3   A grammar is k-limited if all its transformations are k-limited.

DEFINITION 4   Let Δ^n be the set of deep structures generated by the base of a transformational grammar, the longest chain of sequential embeddings in each of which is no greater than n. (That is, a deep structure δ is in Δ^n iff its bottom layer of most deeply embedded sentences is indexed by an integer no greater than n.)[1]

Let G be a k-limited grammar for which it is true that the transformational derivations on all structures in Δ^{k+1} give the same result by the cyclic and linear conventions. Suppose that G is not a class I grammar. There is, then, some deep structure δ for which the outcome of applying the transformations cyclically to δ is not derivationally equivalent to the result of applying the transformations linearly—we will write $T_c(\delta) \neq T_l(\delta)$. Let δ_0 be a deep structure with the least number of embeddings for which the derivational equivalence fails to hold. For ease of proof, we will set $k = 1$; it will be evident that everything we say about such a grammar generalizes immediately to grammars with arbitrary values of k. δ_0 has a depth of embedding of n for some $n > k$ (by the induction assumption). Let $S_1^n \cdots S_t^n$ and $S_1^{n-1} \cdots S_s^{n-1}$ be the bottom-most and next bottom-most sequences of embedded sentences in δ_0, where a certain subsequence of the former (possibly null) is embedded in each S_i^{n-1} ($i = 1, \ldots, S$) of the latter, respectively. Now let δ_0' be formed from δ_0 by applying all the transformations on the lowest domain (the S^n domains) and the next-lowest (the S^{n-1} domains) by the cyclic conventions. Let $\bar{\delta}_0$ be formed from δ_0 by dropping from δ_0 all the S_i^n domains. By construction of δ_0, we know that $\bar{\delta}_0$ will give the same result when the transformations are applied by either the cyclic or noncyclic conventions. The most deeply embedded structures in $\bar{\delta}_0$ are the S_i^{n-1} domains, which differ from the $S_i'^{n-1}$ domains only by virtue of the fact that the latter were derived by application of the transformations to Δ^1 structures. We conclude that for at least one i, the derived structure $S_i'^{n-1}$ differs from the deep structure S_i^{n-1} in a way that plays a crucial role in the fact that $T_c(\delta_0) \neq T_l(\delta_0)$. That is, if the base of the grammar generated $S_i'^{n-1}$ directly (minus any remains of embedded sentences, since the grammar is 1-limited), then we would have $T_c(\delta_0) \neq T_l(\delta_0)$. In this way $_S{'}_i^{n-1}$ differs crucially from

---

[1] There are clearly transformations that are not k-limited for any k. In general, these are the transformations that make an essential use of a variable. Examples of such transformations, which we will call unlimited transformations, are *wh-front* and *relative clause formation*. Examples of k-limited transformations are *subject raising* (1-limited) and *passive* (0-limited). Note that if a transformation is k-limited for some k, then it is k-limited for all $k' > k$.

any simplex deep structure generated by the base of the grammar. By simplex deep structure, we mean a structure with no embedded sentences.

It is possible to conclude from these considerations that if the formal properties or strings generated by the base are preserved across the application of each transformation in the transformational component; and if it is the case that $T_c(\delta) = T_l(\delta)$ for all $\delta \in \Delta^{k+1}$; then $L(G)_c = L(G)_l$. This is an intuitive way of seeing that the above-mentioned grammar of English with three transformations is a class I grammar, for strings generated by the base are of the form NP $[V(NP)(NP)]_{VP}$. The output of both of *passive* and *subject raising* are likewise of this form, and although the application of *extrap* does not preserve strings of this form, this rule is last cyclic so that its application could not result in some base string being derived differently either cyclically or linearly.

This leads us to a digression, in which we will discuss the difference between two important classes of transformations. Under either the cyclic or linear conventions, it is necessary to distinguish those transformations that apply in the domain of each successive S node moving upward in the tree in a derivation versus those applying only on the top-most S node.[2] This latter class of transformations has been called the class of last-cyclic transformations. Those transformations that are not last-cyclic we will call all-cyclic, as they apply to all cycles of the derivation. Examples of last-cyclic transformations are: *appositive clause formation, extrap, topicalization, extrap from NP,* and *relative clause reduction.* Examples of all-cyclic transformations are: *equi-NP deletion, subject raising,* to *dative,* and there *insertion.*

Previous grammars incorporating the notion of last-cyclic transformations have treated the difference between these and all-cyclic transformations simply by making two lists, i.e., marking each transformation idiosyncratically. However, one can discern a formal difference between transformations which are last-cyclic and all-cyclic. In brief, it seems that those transformations that preserve properties of base strings across their application (the output of such transformations is essentially of the same form as the input) are all-cyclic; the transformations that radically derange the structure to which they are applied, producing as output a structure not generable by the base, are last-cyclic.

[2] A transformation that applies on the last cycle only may still apply to material that is not within the simplex sentence immediately dominated by the top most S node. The reason is that, by definition, a transformation applies to all subsequences of the bracketed string under consideration that meet its structural description.

We may also note that transformations that we have called all-cyclic do not introduce structural ambiguities. In other words, if T_i is an all-cyclic transformation, then it is not the case that after T_i has applied to a structure K, the result $T_i(K)$ could also have been produced from a different deep structure by a different sequence of operations.

Ross and Lakoff, in their work on the problem of variables in SDs of transformations and use of exception features, have hypothesized that transformations that make essential use of variables may not to be excepted. Their class of transformations that do not use variables and that have exceptions turns out to be exactly our class of all-cyclic transformations. This work on formal classes of transforms is summarized in Table I.

TABLE I *Formal Classes of Transforms*

All-cyclic	Last-cyclic
1. Preserve base-like structures across application	1. Produce structures not generated by the base
2. Make no essential use of variables	2. Make essential use of variables
3. May be excepted	3. May have no exceptions
4. Do not introduce structural ambiguities	4. May introduce structural ambiguities
5. Several may apply within one S	5. Only one may apply within one S
6. May apply working upward in a tree	6. May apply only on the topmost S
7. Are essentially ordered with respect to one another[a]	7. No reason to be ordered with respect to one another

[a] Note that property 7 seems to follow from 5.

Finally, it can be proved that the problem of determining whether a given arbitrary transformational grammar is in class I is not recursively solvable. This follows immediately from the following theorem.

THEOREM 1 For any two context-free grammars G_1 and G_2, there is a recursive procedure for finding a transformational grammar G such that $L(G)_l = 0$ always, and such that $L(G)_c = \emptyset$ iff $L(G_1) \cap L(G_2) = 0$.

PROOF: Given the CF grammars G_1 and G_2 with terminal vocabularies V_{T_1}, V_{T_2} and initial symbols S_1 and S_2, let the base of G contain the following rules:

$$S \longrightarrow S \begin{Bmatrix} r \\ x \end{Bmatrix} \qquad \text{for all } x \in (V_{T_1} \cap V_{T_2})$$
$$S \longrightarrow S_1 S_2 t$$

where t and r are new terminal symbols different from any in V_T ($i = 1, 2$). G has the following transformations, the second of which is a filter transformation (in the sense of Chomsky, 1965, p. 139).

$$T_1: \quad [[[Xx]_{S_1}[Yy]S_2 z]_S w]_S$$

where x, y, z, and w are single terminal symbols, and $x = y = z$.

Operation: delete x and y.

$$T_2: \quad [[Xx]_{S_1}[Yy]_{S_2} WZz]_S$$

where x, y, z, and w are single terminal symbols, and $x = y = z$.

Operation: delete x and y.

$$T_3: \quad XyT$$

Operation: delete t.

$$T_4: \quad [[x]_{S_1}[y]_{S_2} Zzr]_S$$

where x, y, z are single terminal symbols, and $x = y = z$.

Operation: delete x, y, and r.

T_4 is a post cyclic filter (see Kimball, 1967).

In this grammar, neither of the filters T_1 nor T_2 will apply in any linear derivation, and so all strings will be excluded from the language. In the cyclic derivation, T_3 will apply on the first cycle erasing t, allowing T_1 and T_2 to apply on the second cycle. T_2 continues to apply on successive cycles, and T_4 applies on the last cycle ensuring that neither of the strings dominated by either S_1 or S_2 in the derivation is longer than the string to the right of the latter. Thus the output of the set of cyclic derivations is exactly $L(G_1) \cap L(G_2)$.

From Theorem 1 it follows that there is no recursive procedure for determining if an arbitrary transformational grammar is in class I. Suppose there were such a procedure; then, given any CF grammars G_1 and G_2, one could effectively construct the transformational grammar G mentioned in the theorem; and G would be in class I iff $L(G_1) \cap L(G_2) = 0$. Thus, we would have a recursive procedure for determining, given any CF G_1 and G_2, whether $L(G_1) \cap L(G_2) = \emptyset$. But it is known that this is impossible. (Theorem 6.1:a, p. 160 of Bar-Hillel et al., 1961). One can use theorem 1 to prove directly that both cyclic and linear grammars with filter and post-cyclic transformations can generate any recursively enumerable language without going via a lemma of Haines as has been done before. One can show by similar methods that the problem of determining whether an arbitrary transformational grammar is in class II is likewise recursively unsolvable.

When one restricts the class of CF grammars that may be in the base of a transformation grammar to those that are like those of natural languages in permitting recursion through only the initial symbol, one arrives at a class of transformational grammars for which it is easy to see that the problem of determining membership in class I is recursively solvable. Because for such a transformational grammar, it is clear that the smallest deep structure that will give different results cyclically and linearly will have a depth of embedding that is some arithmetic function of the number of transformations in the grammar and the variety and length of the longest simplex structures generated by the base. It is not necessary to go further into this matter, since it is as of little linguistic interest as the results remarked upon immediately above. Our investigations, however, will be limited to grammars with CF bases of the sort discussed by Chomsky (1965, p. 141).

Class II Grammars

There is an asymmetry between cyclic and linear grammars, which expresses itself in the study of class II grammars. Suppose we have a grammar G such that $L(G)_c \neq L(G)_l$, but by some reordering of the transformations of G, giving G', we know that $L(G)_c = L(G')_l$. Thus, it seems to be generally the case that we will have $L(G')_l = L(G')_c$. More work needs to be done on this problem to specify exactly the class of exceptions, but it appears at first glance that a grammar that is an exception exhibits complex interactions between transformations not realized in natural languages.

The asymmetry comes out when it is seen that the analog of this fact for the case of reordering noncyclic grammars does not seem to hold. The meaning of these facts for the theory of grammar is as follows: If we have a grammar of a natural language that gives the right results cyclically and the wrong results linearly, but it is possible to reorder the transformations to give the right output linearly, then the reordered grammar will be a class I grammar. In this manner one can see that the kind of arguments relevant for determining the correct set of conventions reduce to arguments concerning the ordering of transformations. The structure of such arguments will be detailed later in this section.

Class I Grammars

We initiate the study of class I grammars by considering a subclass of their limiting cases. We will then generalize the features of the grammars in this subclass relevant to their being in class I in constructing a rather simple but linguistically relevant characterization of all class I grammars.

The limiting case to be considered is that of a grammar that contains only 0-limited transformations. It is clear that such a grammar is class I, for the derivation of each simplex sentence will be exactly the same, regardless of whether the first transformation was applied to all sentences in the deep structure at one, or whether each sentence was derived separately, working from the most deeply embedded up.

The feature of 0-limited grammars crucial to their being class I is that in no derivation is it the case that the application of any transformation in the domain of any sentence is relevant to the application of any other transformation on any other cycle. By "relevant to" here is meant the full range of possibilities, namely, that the application of T_i on S_n is relevant to the application of T_j on S_m if any one of the following holds: (1) if T_i did not apply on S_n then the output of T_j on S_m would be different than if T_i did apply; (2) the environment for T_j to apply on S_m is created by the application of T_i on S_n; (3) the environment for T_j to apply on S_m is destroyed by the application of T_i on S_n.

Condition (1) above relates to set-theoretic identity of languages, and conditions (2) and (3) relate to derivational identity. We may introduce the following definition:

DEFINITION 5   In a transformational grammar G, T_i is *isolated* from T_j if in no derivation in G is any application of T_j relevant to any application of T_i on another cycle.

It is clear that a transformational grammar, all of whose transformations are pairwise isolated, is a class I grammar, and in fact, in such a grammar there would be no motivation for the convention that the most deeply embedded sentences are processed first in a derivation. Note also that the relation of isolation as defined above is in general asymmetrical, so that T_i being isolated from T_j does not necessarily imply that T_j is isolated from T_i.

In terms of these notions, we can state sufficient conditions for a grammar to be class I. As noted, in the case of a 0-limited grammar, no transformation is relevant to the application of any other transformation on another cycle. Thus, the cases in which a grammar fails to be class I must essentially involve transformations which are 1-limited. Thus, we arrive at the following statement of sufficient conditions for membership in class I:

PROPOSITION I   A grammar is class I if each 1-limited transformation in the grammar is pairwise isolated from every transformation following it in the ordering of transformations. (T_i is pairwise isolated from T_j if T_i is isolated from T_j and T_j is isolated from T_i.)

One can see intuitively that these pairwise isolation conditions are sufficient to guarantee membership in class I by the following considerations: CASE i: A cyclic derivation will fail to be equivalent to the corresponding linear derivation if either some 1-limited transformation T_i apply on S_{k-1} depends on the output of some later transformation having applied on S_k, or if some transformation applying on S_k depends on some earlier 1-limited transformation not applying on S_{k-1}.   CASE ii: A noncyclic derivation will fail to be equivalent to the corresponding cyclic derivation if some 1-limited T_i applying on S_{k-1} depends on some later T_j not having applied on S_k, or if some transformation applying on S_k depends on some earlier 1-limited transformation having applied on S_{k-1}.

The characterization given in proposition I may be interpreted linguistically as follows: The problem of determining the correct conventions for applying transformations can be seen as that of determining the correct definition of the notion "domain of syntactic process." The cyclic theory the domain of syntactic process is each S-dominated subtree of the whole tree structure; in the noncyclic case, the domain is that of the entire deep structure generated by the base.

In terms of this difference it is apparent that there are certain ranges of facts incorporable by a cyclic grammar that are essentially out of the range of any noncyclic grammar, and vice versa. For example, in a cyclic grammar, one can order the rules $(\cdots T_i \cdots T_j \cdots)$, while it is the case that in certain constructions it is necessary that T_j will apply before T_i. If such a case were found to hold in natural language, one would have shown the cyclic conventions to be correct.

Likewise, by using the linear conventions one can make the application of a transformation in a certain domain S_k dependent on the previous application of an earlier transformation in a domain in which S_k is embedded. It is essentially impossible to obtain such a derivational structure in a cyclic grammar.

We will conclude with the following observations concerning the difference between cyclic and linear grammar. In a linear grammar, the order in which transformations are stated will be that in which they are to be applied in any given S-dominated domain. On the other hand, it is not difficult to show the existence of a cyclic grammar in which transformations are ordered $(T_1 \cdot \cdot \cdot T_k)$ $(k > 1)$, but for an infinite number of deep structures generated by the base, there will be a subdomain in which the transformations are, in fact, applied in reverse order in the derivation. In this sense, the linear theory of grammar offers the stronger hypothesis concerning language, for the set of possible derivational histories of surface structures in linear grammars is a proper subset of those in cyclic grammars.

REFERENCES

Bar-Hillel, Y., Perles, M., and Shamir, E. 1961. On Formal Properties of Simple Phrase Structure Grammars. Zeitschrift fur Phonetik, Sprachwissenschaft, und Kommunikations forchung 14(2).
Chomsky, N. 1965. Aspects of the Theory of Syntax. MIT Press, Cambridge, Massachusetts.
Kimball, J. 1967. Predicates definable over transformational derivations by intersection with regular language. Information and Control, Volume 11.
Kiparsky, P. and Kiparsky, C. 1971. Fact. Progress in Linguistics (Bierwisch and Heidolph, eds.). Mouton, The Hague.

ON THE CYCLE IN SYNTAX

JOHN GRINDER
University of California, Santa Cruz

In generative grammar, as in every discipline, there exist a number of background assumptions made by researchers that are rarely stated, but without which many of the results reported would lose much of their coherence. In the last ten to fifteen years, the analysis of natural language systems within the framework of transformational grammar has yielded a number of rules. Within this collection of rules. This distinction is perhaps most easily grasped by a schema; consider (1):

(1)

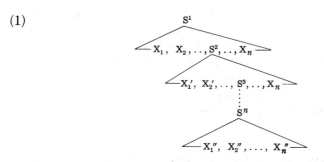

The present system of transformational grammar assumes the cyclic principle of rule application (Chomsky, 1965); with the exception of

Kimball's paper (this volume), this principle is explicitly or implicitly assumed in every discussion of ordering of transformations in the transformational literature. The set of cyclic rules are grouped in a block, ordered with respect to each other, and applied to the most deeply embedded clause; in terms of (1), the set of cyclic rules apply first to the elements in the domain defined by S^n. When all of the cyclic rules have applied to the elements of S^n, the first cycle is said to be completed. This set is then applied to the elements in the domain defined by S^{n-1}, the clause which immediately dominates S^n. The process is recursive; the set of cyclic rules work their way up the tree structure, applying to the elements of each succeeding more inclusive S node, until the entire tree has been subjected to the cyclic rules. The last cycle occurs when the set of cyclic rules is applied to S^1. At this point in the derivation, the set of noncyclic rules may apply.

A casual examination of articles appearing in transformational literature that deal with syntactic phenomena will reveal that constant reference is being made to the cyclic principle of rule application.[1] The purpose of this paper is quite modest: I intend to show that the classic arguments that have been taken to provide motivation for the cyclic application of transformations do not warrant that conclusion. There is little contained in the ensuing discussion which is new. I hope that by raising this issue generative grammarians will be challenged to find phenomena that unequivocally establish the cyclic or noncyclic principle. This will, I hope, balance the fact that the findings in this paper are primarily negative. Settling the question of a cyclic or noncyclic principle for the application of transformations is particularly desirable, as the cyclic principle at present occupies such a priviledged position in the area of syntax.

We may begin by distinguishing cases of what will be referred to as primary motivation for the cyclic principle of rule application from cases of secondary motivation. Primary motivation for the cyclic principle of rule application is provided by cases where the derivation of surface structures enumerated *requires* that some rule of grammar r_i apply both before and after some distinct rule of grammar r_j. Schematically, in terms of a derivation, the case of primary motivation can be depicted as in (2):

---

[1] I do not mean to imply that the semantic and syntactic portions of derivations can be separated in some principled way.

(2)   Underlying structure

        Intermediate structure$_1$ by rule 1

        Intermediate structure$_2$ by rule 2

.   .

.   .

.   .

        Intermediate structure$_i$ by rule i

.   .

.   .

.   .

        Intermediate structure$_{i+k}$ by rule j

.   .

.   .

.   .

        Intermediate structure$_{i+k+j}$ by rule i

.   .

.   .

.   .

        Surface structure   by rule n

This statement is equivalent to the following:

The derivation of a surface structure will be said to provide primary motivation for the cyclic principle if and only if the derivation includes two applications (minimal) of some rule r_i and one application (minimal) of some distinct rule r_j such that:

a.   the output string enumerated by r_j is properly analyzable with respect to the structural index of r_i

b.   the input string to r_j is not properly analyzable with respect to the structural index of r_i

c.   the output string enumerated by (the first application of) r_i is properly analyzable with respect to the structural index of r_j

d.   the input string to (the first application of) r_i is not properly analyzable with respect to the structural index of r_j.

More intuitively, the derivation involves two applications of r_i and a single application of r_j. No intermediate string in the derivation is properly analyzable with respect to r_j except the string created by (the first application) of r_i. The application of r_i produces a structural change that prevents it from applying to its own output. Subsequent to the first application of r_i, no intermediate string is properly analyzable with respect to r_i except the output string of r_j. Thus, the two (minimal) applications of r_i are possible only in case r_j applies between them to create the proper structural configuration.[2]

Primary motivation for the cyclic principle differs from secondary motivation in that the former requires the cyclic principle simply to achieve descriptive adequacy—i.e., simply to enumerate the surface structure involved with an intuitively satisfying tree representation—while the latter is consistent with the cyclic principle. In other words, phenomena that are cases of secondary motivation for the cyclic principle may be formulated adequately in either a cyclic or noncyclic grammar. I will argue that only the latter cases exist; what have been taken to be cases of primary motivation for the cycle can be reduced to cases of secondary motivation. More interesting in the present context, such a reduction is possible without doing violence to the standard claims regarding the nature of the transformational processes in question.

CLASSIC MOTIVATION FOR THE CYCLIC
PRINCIPLE IN SYNTAX

Case I — Pronominalization

Surely one of the most striking arguments developed within the framework of transformational grammar is that presented by J. R. Ross (1969a). It is easy to show, however, that this argument is one of the category II—one of secondary motivation, a syntactic phenomenon that is consistent with the cyclic principle but does not require it. The crucial structures for the argument are those of (3):

(3)   a.   *Discovering that he$_i$ was sick disturbed Harry$_i$.*
        b.   *Discovering that Harry$_i$ was sick disturbed him$_i$.*

The intuition regarding the chain of coreference in (3a) is that the terms *he, Harry,* and the missing subject term of the predicate *dis-*

---

[2] Gilles Fauconnier (1971) has pointed out that the characterization given in the text allows the case where r_i applies both before and after r_j within the same domain of application of the rules. Within the usual terminology, one would be uncertain as to whether to call this a case of cyclic application of rules, as "different cycles" usually refers to different domains of application. Fauconnier's case, however, is cyclic in the sense in which I am interested. Since there are no instances of this phenomenon, I will let the characterization stand as it is. If such a case is discovered, the decision as to whether it ought to be referred to as cyclic can be easily decided as it is a matter of definition.

cover refer to the same individual. This contrasts with the situation in (3b), where the same chain of coreference cannot be established between those three elements. This is somewhat perplexing in that by the Ross–Langacker constraints (Ross, 1967; Langacker, 1966) on pronominalization, since the subject term of the predicate *sick* precedes the object/dative term of the predicate *disturb*, it should be possible for the former to serve as antecedent for the latter. For example, in (4), a parallel structural configuration is found, and both possibilities are grammatical:

(4)   a.   *That he$_i$ was sick disturbed Harry$_i$.*
               b.   *That Harry$_i$ was sick disturbed him$_i$.*

I begin by reviewing Ross's argument. The following assumptions are being made: (i) Pronominalization is a transformational rule subject to the Ross–Langacker constraints. (ii) Pronominalization and *equi-NP deletion* are distinct transformational rules. While (ii) has yet to be challenged[3] the first assumption has been explicitly denied by both Bach (1968) and Lakoff (1968), as well as numerous writers working under a distinct conceptual framework (e.g., Jackendoff, 1969; Dougherty, 1969; and Chomsky, 1969).

The derivation of the sequences of (2) proceeds from an underlying structure of the form (5):

(5)

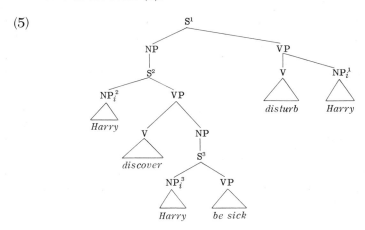

---

[3] In his doctoral dissertation, Gilles Fauconnier (1971) argued that certain rules involving a condition of coreference (*equi-NP deletion, pronominalization, . . .*) are complex operations consisting of a number of more elementary operations. Further, when considered from this point of view, it is possible to abstract from these operations certain of the elementaries which are identical. By doing so, one achieves interesting generalizations concerning the parallelism in such processes.

There are three pairs of coreferential NP nodes in the tree structure: $\langle NP_i^1, NP_i^2 \rangle$, $\langle NP_i^2, NP_i^3 \rangle$, and $\langle NP_i^1, NP_i^3 \rangle$. Ross's task is to provide a natural explanation for the fact that while both pronominalization possibilities are well formed in (4), only the configuration (3a) is possible from the tree structure (5).

Assume the cyclic application of rules. On the cycle on S^3, nothing of interest occurs; on the S^2 cycle, the pair $\langle NP_i^2, NP_i^3 \rangle$ is available. Notice that NP_i^2 both precedes and commands NP_i^3. Thus by the Ross–Langacker constraints, only NP_i^3 may be marked for reduction to a pro form; never NP_i^2, as the ill formedness of (6b) shows:

(6)   a. *Harry$_i$ discovered that he$_i$ was sick.*
            b. **He$_i$ discovered that Harry$_i$ was sick.*

On the S^1 cycle, the rule of *equi-NP deletion* applies, marking NP_i^2 for reduction to the null anaphor. Although the proper structural configuration for the application of pronominalization obtains for the pair $\langle NP_i^1, NP_i^3 \rangle$, the rule will not apply, since on the preceding cycle, NP_i^3 was marked for reduction to a pro form under coreference with NP_i^2. Ross' argument predicts that just in case NP_i^2 is not coreferential with NP_i^3, it will be possible for NP_i^3 to pronominalize NP_i^1 on the S^1 cycle. This prediction is correct as the grammaticality of both of the strings of (7) shows:

(7)   a. *Maria's discovering that he$_i$ was sick disturbed Harry$_i$.*
            b. *Maria's discovering that Harry$_i$ was sick disturbed him$_i$.*

We then need only point out the repercussions of giving up the cyclic principle of rules application. In particular, note that for some derivation proceeding from the underlying tree structure (5), the following rule applications are possible and fully consistent with the Ross–Langacker constraints on pronominalization: (i) For the pair of NP, $\langle NP_i^1, NP_i^2 \rangle$, mark NP_i^2 for reduction to the null anaphor by *equi-NP deletion*. (ii) For the pair of NP, $\langle NP_i^1, NP_i^3 \rangle$, mark NP_i^3 for reduction to a pro form. Given these rule applications, the ungrammatical surface structure (3b) results. Hence, the ill formed surface structure results even though for each pair of coreferential NP at each point in the derivation the Ross–Langacker constraints are respected; Ross concludes from this that English *pronominalization* is a cyclic phenomenon.

On a closer examination of the argument, we see that *pronominalization* provides not primary motivation for the cyclic principle, but only secondary motivation. Recall the paradigm for the case of primary motivation for the cycle. It minimally involves two rules, r_i and

r_j, where r_i applies twice in the derivation, and the application of r_j *necessarily* intervenes between the two applications of r_i. What the argument actually shows is that the sequence of rule applications of the same rule (*pronominalization*) is not free with respect to the order in which the pairs of coreferential NP undergo the rule. In particular, the string (3b) will be automatically excluded by any grammar, cyclic or noncyclic, where the rule of pronominalization is constrained to apply with an upward orientation on the tree structure (5). By "upward orientation" on a tree structure, I mean simply that the convention for rule application is such that the rule applies first to the most deeply embedded clause, then to the clause dominating the clause to which the rule(s) have just applied, and so forth until the rule(s) have been applied to the entire tree structure. In terms of the example used in reconstructing Ross's argument, the ungrammatical string (3b) will be excluded, but the grammatical string (3a) generated, just in case in the derivation that proceeds from (5), the rule of pronominalization, applies first to the pair, $\langle NP_i^2, NP_i^3 \rangle$. This will occur naturally if the rule of pronominalization applies with an upward orientation on the tree; that is, first to the subtree dominated by S^3 (no application), then to the subtree dominated by S^2, and finally to the entire tree, which is dominated by S^1. Since NP_i^1 is not available for the rule of pronominalization until the cycle after which the NP pair $\langle NP_i^2, NP_i^3 \rangle$ has undergone the rule, which must by the Ross–Langacker constraints mark NP^3 for reduction, it will never be the case that the pair $\langle NP_i^1, NP_i^3 \rangle$ will be considered for application of that rule.

The notion of orientation of rule application on a tree structure is independent of the question of the cyclic–noncyclic principle. The argument by Ross, then, does not constitute primary motivation for the cyclic principle. The derivation of the strings under consideration involve the application of but a single rule,[4] that of *pronominalization;* thus failing to meet the specifications for a case of primary motivation for the cycle as outlined above.

---

[4] It should be clear from the discussion in the text that the rule of *equi-NP deletion,* mentioned initially in the discussion of the pair (3a,b), is not crucially involved in the ordering of the two applications of the rule of *pronominalization.* Further, in dialects where *equi-NP deletion* is optional for structures of the form (3), the sentences (8a) and (8b) contrast in grammaticality, showing that the phenomenon is independent of the interaction of *equi-NP deletion* and *pronominalization.*

(8)   a. *Harry'$_i$s discovering that he$_i$ was sick disturbed him$_i$.*
             b. °*His$_i$ discovering that Harry$_i$ was sick disturbed him$_i$.*

Case II — The Passive–Raising Interaction

A remarkable characteristic of natural languages is the ability for certain rules, or sets of rules, to interact in such a way as to introduce gross distortions in what has been argued to be the underlying constituent structure and word order. In English, a NP that appears in the object position of the most deeply embedded clause in underlying structure may come to occupy the surface subject position of the matrix clause in surface structure. One way this is possible involves a derivation in which there is an interaction of the rules of *passive* and *raising*.

In his lucid discussion of the *passive–raising* interaction, Postal (1968b) uses the strings (9) as an example of a pair of strings related by the transformation *raising:*

(9)   a. *Lucy believes that Harry is a Greek.*
            b. *Lucy believes Harry to be a Greek.*

In a later paper, Postal (1971) presents extensive motivation for this rule of Raising. For the purposes of the exposition here, we will accept the informal account of the rule as:

A.   Raising is a transformation that moves an embedded subject NP from its clause into the clause that immediately dominates it.

Schematically, the rule applies to tree structures of the form (10) converting them into structures of the form (11) (cf. McCawley, 1970, regarding the verb initial formulation for English assumed here).

(10)
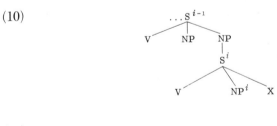

(11)
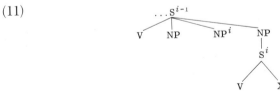

Further, I assume for the purposes of discussion that the following informal description of the rule of *passive* is essentially correct:[5]

   B.   Passive is a transformation that moves the subject NP right to the end of its clause and that introduces a marking on the verb that is eventually spelled out in its passive form.

Schematically, the rule of *passive* maps trees of the form (12) onto those of the form (13):

(12)

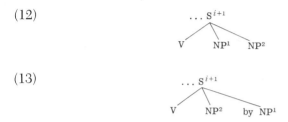

(13)

Using the structure underlying (9) as an example, we notice that there are two possible passive forms (14).

(14)   a.   *That Harry is a Greek is believed by Lucy.*
           b.   *Harry is believed by Lucy to be a Greek.*

The derivation of both sentences in (14) involves in addition to the *passive* an application of the rule of subject formation. *Subject formation* moves the NP contiguous to the verb to a preverbal position. Notice that in the surface structures (9), the *passive* has not applied, and the rule of *subject formation* moves the underlying subject NP to the preverbal position. In the surface structures (14), the *passive* has applied, moving the underlying subject NP to the end of the clause, thus effectively disqualifying that NP from undergoing *subject formation*. The interesting question regarding the interaction of *passive* and *raising* now arises. In the derivation of (14a), there has been no application of the rule of *raising*; therefore, when the rule of *subject formation* applies, the NP contiguous with the verb is the NP that dominates the entire clause *Harry is a Greek*. In the derivation of the surface structure (14b), on the other hand, the rule of *raising* has been applied

---

[5] The final surface order of constituents within a clause appears to be an extremely late phenomenon. This late re-arrangement rule is discussed by both Ross (1967) and Postal (1968a). It is often referred to as heavy NP drift.

to create a derived object NP that is contiguous with the verb. Consequently, when the rule of *subject formation* applies, the NP contiguous with the verb is the former subject of the embedded clause, the NP *Harry*.

Consider the structure underlying (15) and the set of grammatical surface structures involving the application of the rule of *passive:*

(15) a. *Lucy believed that Harry kissed Maxine.*
      b. *That Harry kissed Maxine is believed by Lucy.*
      c. *Harry is believed by Lucy to have kissed Maxine.*
      d. *Lucy believed that Maxine was kissed by Harry.*
      e. *That Maxine was kissed by Harry is believed by Lucy.*
      f. *Maxine is believed by Lucy to have been kissed by*
          Harry.

The crucial string is (15f). It is clear that the object of the embedded clause, the NP *Maxine*, has, through a series of transformations, been promoted to the surface subject position of the matrix clause. From the preceding discussion, we know that the rule that creates new clause mates must have applied to move the NP *Maxine* out of the embedded clause into the matrix clause for the rule of *subject formation* subsequently to have moved the NP *Maxine* into surface subject position. Thus, the derivation of (15f) involves application of the rule of *raising*. Further, both matrix and embedded verb forms show morphological evidence that the rule of *passive* has applied to them. We can establish immediately that the rule of *passive* must have applied in the embedded clause prior to application of the rule of *raising*. This is so, since the rule of *raising* lifts NP that are in subject position in the embedded clause. Since the NP *Maxine* is the derived subject, and since it is in fact derived subject by the application of the rule of *passive*, it follows that the rule of *passive* must have applied in the embedded clause before the rule of *raising*. The final step in establishing this phenomenon as a case of primary motivation for the cyclic principle is to show that the second application of the rule of *passive* necessarily follows the application of the rule of *raising*. In fact, this has been the conclusion most often found in the literature. This conclusion is, however, completely unwarranted. If the account B of the *passive* is accepted, the data do not constitute a case of primary motivation for the cyclic principle. Under this system (accepting both B and the rule of *subject formation*), the noncyclic derivation of the surface structure of (15f) would proceed as follows:

a.   Given the underlying form:

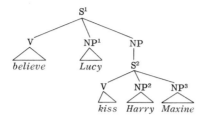

b.   Apply the *passive* to S² yielding:

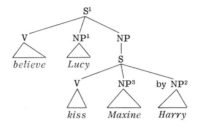

c.   Apply the *passive* to S¹ yielding:

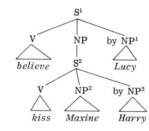

d.   Apply *raising* yielding:

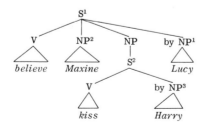

e.   Apply *subject formation:*

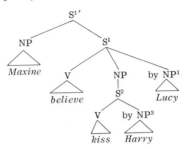

f.   The spelling of the passive markings on the verb forms
     S[1] and S[2] yields the surface structure (15f):   *Maxine is
     is believed by Lucy to have been kissed by Harry.*

Notice that the derivation of the surface structure (15f) does indeed
involve two applications of the *passive* rule and a single application
of the rule of *raising;* the two applications of *passive* (steps b and c
above), however, are contiguous in the derivation.

The above derivation involves no rules other than those commonly
accepted as independently motivated rules of English syntax. At most,
the data indicate that the rule of *subject formation* must be ordered
after the rule of raising (optional). What has been shown is that under
the present conception of form and function of the rules of *passive,
raising,* and *subject formation,* the *passive–raising* interaction constitutes a phenomenon that is consistent with the cyclic principle as
well as the noncyclic principle; that is, a case of secondary motivation.

Under the conception of grammar current when Postal (1968b)
presented this data as a case of primary motivation for the cycle in
syntax, (B) was not considered accurate; rather something like the
following was generally accepted:

C.   Passive is a transformation that moves the subject NP
     right to the end of the clause that introduces a mark-
     ing on the verb that is eventually spelled out in its
     passive form, and that moves the object NP into sur-
     face subject position.

The underlined portion of the older formulation of passive corre-
sponds in present terms to the separate transformation which I have
been referring to as subject formation.

In J. Kimball's paper (this volume), it is shown that it is possible
under the older conception of the rule of *passive* (i.e., formulation
(C)) to reduce the *passive–raising* interaction to a case of secondary

motivation. Kimball's account involves one additional rule, VP *extraposition*.[6]

The linear derivation of (15f) by Kimball's account would begin from an underlying structure suggested by (16):

(16)

```
                    S¹
              ╱           ╲
           NP¹             VP
                      ╱         ╲
         Lucy       V            NP
                                 │
                  believe        S²
                            ╱         ╲
                         NP²            VP
                         △          ╱      ╲
                       Harry       V        NP³
                                   △        △
                                 kiss      Maxine
```

Application of the rule of *passive* to both the embedded clause S² and the matrix clause S¹ yields the structure (17):

(17)

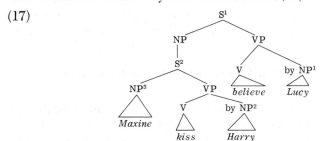

Finally, the application of *raising* and VP *extraposition* produce the structure (18):

(18)

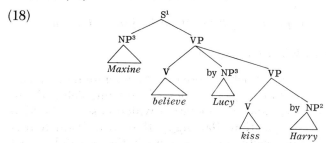

---

[6] Kimball refers to this transformation as *extraposition*. It differs, however, from the ordinary rule of *extraposition* in that in this case the constituent moved is a VP (what will surface as a VP). The usual rule of *extraposition* moves the constituent S. As far as I am able to determine, this rule is an artifact of the non-verb-initial formulation for English.

Spelling rules for the verbal forms of the *passive* apply to (18) to produce the surface structure (15f). Hence, we see that even under the older notion of the rule of *passive*, the *passive–raising* interaction constitutes data only consistent with cyclic principle of rule application.

CYCLIC AND NONCYCLIC TREATMENTS OF PASSIVE–RAISING INTERACTION

There appear to be at least two differential empirical predictions between cyclic and noncylic treatments of the *passive–raising* interaction.

In his monograph "Cross-Over Phenomena," P. M. Postal (1968a) points out that for a certain class of transformations (constant movement rules) crossover violations occur only if the two nominals involved are clause mates at the point in the derivation where the particular transformation applies. Assume this formulation is accurate. The cyclic grammar claims that in a string such as (19) the derived surface subject was a clause mate of the underlying subject of the predicate *except* at the point of application of *passive*. The noncyclic grammar claims, on the contrary, that the derived subject never occupied the derived object position of the predicate *expect*.

(19)   *Mary was expected by John to be fair with the war criminals.*

If there is a systematic difference in the relative grammaticality of (20a) and (20b), where the a version is judged to be less deviant than the b version, the noncyclic analysis provides an explanation. Conversely, if no such systematic difference is detectable, the noncyclic approach is at variance with Postal's final formulation of crossover.

(20)   a. *John$_i$ was expected by himself$_i$ to be fair to the war criminals.*
        b. *John$_i$ was killed by himself$_i$.*

Assume that there is a distinction between the operation that raises embedded subject NP into subject position of the immediately dominating clause, Raising$_{subj}$, and the operation which raises embedded subject NP into object position, Raising$_{obj}$. If such a distinction is granted, then in the noncyclic analysis there is the possibility that for some particular predicate, P$_i$, *raising*$_{subj}$ is allowed but *raising*$_{obj}$ is excluded (and vice versa). No such distinction for a single predicate is available within a cyclic grammar. There are predicates in

English that appear to meet the specifications of P_i. Consider the contrast in the pair (21).

(21)   a.   *Martha was* $\begin{bmatrix} said \\ rumored \\ \cdot \\ \cdot \\ \cdot \end{bmatrix}$ *by many people to be a friend*

of John's.

   b.   **Many people* $\begin{bmatrix} said \\ rumored \\ \cdot \\ \cdot \\ \cdot \end{bmatrix}$ *Martha to be a friend of*

John's.

I do not explore these differences further here, as the purpose of this paper is to argue that there are no cases of primary motivation for the cyclic principle, not to attempt to motivate the noncyclic principle.

Case III — The Raising–Reflexivization Interaction

The third and final of the phenomena usually understood to constitute primary motivation for the cycle also crucially involves the rule of *raising;* specifically, the interaction of this rule with the rule of *reflexivization.* We will continue to assume the formulation of the *raising* rule (A) given in the previous section. The rule of *reflexivization* has been assumed since it was first proposed by Klima and Lees (1963) to be the paradigm case of a rule applying to clause mates, that is, the domain of the rule is the clause. Informally, then, we will assume the following version of the rule of *reflexivization:*

   D.   Reflexivization is a feature-introducing rule that marks
        the rightmost of two coreferential NP for reduction to
        a reflexive form if the two coreferential NP are clause
        mates.

As seen in the last section, raising has the effect of creating new clause mates by lifting an embedded subject term into the immediately dominating clause. Thus, raising creates additional cases of the configuration necessary for the application of *reflexivization.* Consider, now, the underlying tree (22):

(22)

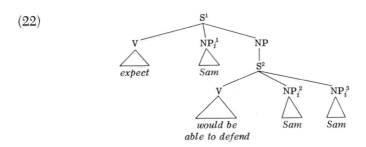

From an inspection of the tree structure, we see that the pair of NP, $\langle NP_i^2, NP_i^3 \rangle$, meet the required structural configuration for the application of *reflexivization*. This observation is accurate as the grammaticality of the sentence (23) shows:

(23) *Sam$_i$ expected that he$_i$ would be able to defend himself$_i$.*

We next observe that the verb *expect* takes *raising:*

(24)   **Sam$_i$ expected him$_i$ to be able to defend himself.*

The ungrammaticality of (24) follows naturally from the fact that the structural index of the obligatory transformation *reflexivization* with respect to the pair (NP^1, NP^2) was met, but the transformation failed to apply. The grammatical surface structure resulting from a derivation precedes from the underlying structure (22) and that includes an application of the rule of *raising* is (25):

(25)   *Sam$_i$ expected himself$_i$ to be able to defend himself$_i$.*

There is in (25) unequivocal morphological evidence that the rule of *reflexivization* has applied twice. We need only show that the two applications of this rule are necessarily separated by the application of the rule of *raising* in order to establish this as a case of primary motivation for the cycle.

Assume that the two applications of *reflexivization* are contiguous in the derivation of (25). If so, then *raising* either precedes or succeeds the application of reflexivization. If *raising* precedes *reflexivization*, then at the point where *reflexivization* applies, the pair (NP$_i^2$, NP$_i^3$) will be in the proper structural configuration for the transformation, but the pair (NP$_i^1$, NP$_i^2$) will not, as the embedded subject term NP$_i^2$ has not yet been raised into the clause S^1, and thus is not a clause mate of NP$_i$. The subsequent application of *raising* will allow the ungrammatical string (24) to be generated. On the other hand, in the derivation where the *raising* rule applies prior to the two applications of *reflexivization*, the pair (NP^1_i, NP^2_i) will be in the proper structural configuration for the reflexive rule, but the pair (NP^2_i, NP^3_i) will not, NP^2_i having been lifted out of the clause S^2, and thus no longer qualifying as a clause mate of NP^3_i. This sequence of rule applications results in the ungrammatical string (26):

(26) *Sam$_i$ expected himself$_i$ to be able to defend him$_i$.

It is clear that given the formulation of the rules of *raising* and *reflexivization*, (A) and (D), respectively, this phenomenon constitutes a case of primary motivation for the cycle. The derivation of the well formed surface structure (25) must proceed as follows:

a. Apply *reflexivization* to the pair (NP^2_i, NP^3_i), marking NP^3_i for reduction to a reflexive form.
b. Apply *raising* to NP^2_i, moving that term from the embedded subject position of S^2 into the object position of S^1.
c. Apply *reflexivization* to the pair (NP^1_i, NP^2_i), marking NP^2_i for reduction to a reflexive form.

The structural index of *reflexivization* will not be met for its application to the pair (NP^1_i, NP^2_i) unless the rule of *raising* applies. Thus, the second application of *reflexivization* is literally defined on the output of the rule of *raising*. This is the paradigm case of primary motivation for the cycle as outlined above.

Subversion of Case III

The *raising–reflexivization* interaction case is rather easily subverted. In order to handle the same set of surface structures, it is necessary simply to accept an alternative formulation for the rule of *raising*:[7]

E. Raising is a copying transformation which copies the embedded subject NP from its clause into the clause which immediately dominates it.

---

[7] Since I first considered this possibility, I have discovered two places in the literature where authors have independently suggested that Raising is a copying rule: Postal (1968a:163) and Ross (1969b:283). In a sense, the way I have stated the problem is misleading. All permutation rules are composed of two parts: a copying and the subsequent deletion of the original. The real distinction between copying and chopping rules to use Ross's terminology (1967) is whether there is some distinct rule which applies after the copy is made but before the original is deleted.

The derivation of the critical string (25) would then proceed as follows:

a. Apply *raising* (version E) to NP_i^2, copying that term from the embedded subject position of S^2 into S^1.
b. Apply *reflexivization* to the pair (NP_i^2, NP_i^3), marking NP_i^3 for reduction to a reflexive form.
c. Apply *reflexivization* to the pair (NP_i^1, NP_i^2), marking $NP_i^{2'}$ for reduction to a reflexive form where $NP_i^{2'}$ is the copied version of NP_i^2.

This sequence of rule applications would yield an intermediate structure of the form (27):

(27)

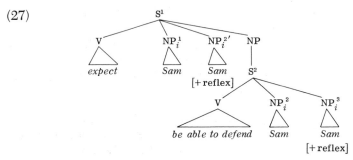

The final step in the derivation of interest to us is the application of the generalized rule of *equi-NP deletion*. Notice that the structural index of that rule will find between the original embedded subject term NP_i^2 and its copy $NP_i^{2'}$. The former will be deleted with the copy serving as controller. As a general result, then, if the rule of *raising* is reformulated as a copying rule, the subsequent application of the rule of *equi-NP* will always delete the original without any special statement being necessary. The application of *equi-NP* removes the original NP_i^2, the derivation yielding the grammatical string (25). The derivation of the critical string (25) as presented above includes two applications of the rule of *reflexivization*, but these are, in fact, contiguous; thus the derivation is noncyclic.

SOME ADDITIONAL DATA

Three additional cases have been proposed as candidates for cases of primary motivation for the cyclic principle of rule application: *there insertion* by John Kimball, and Greek case agreement and *tag questions* by George Lakoff (both personal communications). I should now like to show that these cases as well as the three discussed above reduce to cases of secondary motivation.

There Insertion and Raising

The sentences cited by John Kimball (credited by him to Haj Ross) were:

(28)   a.   *There were believed to be lions in the forest.*
         b.   *There were lions believed to be in the forest.*

The derivation of the a version of the above pair is quite straight-forward. From an underlying structure of the form (29a) by a combination of *there insertion, raising,* and *passive,* we obtain the tree structures (29b–d), respectively.

(29)

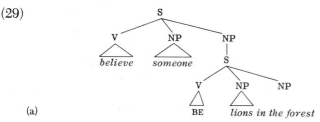

(a)

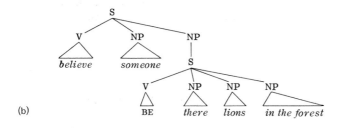

(b)

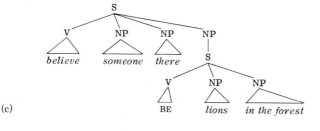

(c)

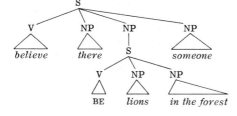

(d)

The NP that dominates the lexical item *someone* in the above tree fails to have a lexical realization in the surface structure (by *unspecified agent deletion*), and the spelling out of the appropriate morphological markings on the matrix verb *believe* yields the surface structure (28a). Notice that in the derivation of that string the order was *there insertion > raising.*

Notice that the pair of sentences cited by Kimball do not meet the definition for a case of primary motivation for the cyclic principle presented earlier. Rather, for the *there insertion–raising* interaction to constitute a case of primary motivation, it would be necessary to find a derivation in which the application of either *raising* or *there insertion* was necessary for the structural index of the other rule to be met. It would then be necessary simply to show that the second rule had also applied prior in the derivation. The derivation of (28a) indicates that the transformation of *there insertion* must apply before *raising* in order for the latter to be able to lift the inserted element into the upper clause. However, I have been unsuccessful in constructing a case where the raising of the inserted element *there* into a higher clause causes the sequence of elements in that higher clause to meet the structural index for a second application of *there insertion*. The example would have a form something like (30):

(30) **There* $\left\{ \begin{array}{c} is \\ is\ expected \end{array} \right\}$ *there to be a sign saying* "ASA NISI MASA."

If the lack of success in constructing such an example is the result of the relative independence of the two rules,[8] rather than lack of imagination, then it is clear that the converse case will also be impossible to construct, since it involves a situation in which the application of the rule of *there insertion* must *necessarily* follow the first application of *raising*. If these results are general, as they seem to be, then it follows that the *there insertion–raising* interaction cannot, in principle, provide a case of primary motivation.

Let us turn now to a consideration of the sentence (28b). I assume that the example is designed to show that the derivation from which it proceeds involves the order of rule application: *raising > there insertion*. That is, the assumption is that the derivation of (28b) be-

---

[8] By the term relative independence of two rules, I mean to suggest that two rules will be independent just in case the application of one neither creates nor destroys a proper environment for application of the other and vice versa. That is, the set of phrase markers properly analyzable with respect to one rule is constant across the set of derivations whether the second rule has applied in those derivations or not, and vice versa.

gins from the same underlying structure as does the derivation of
(28a), and that the tree structures (21)–(33) represent the intermediate
stages of the derivation of (29b) as specified by the transformations
of *raising, passive,* and *there insertion* respectively:

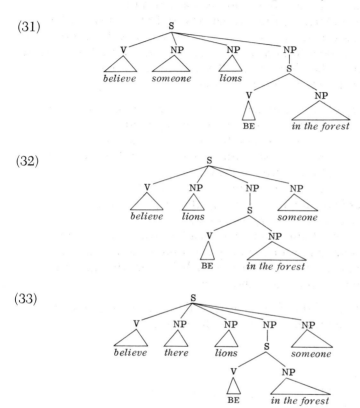

(31)

(32)

(33)

The subsequent application of *unspecified agent deletion* and the
spelling of the appropriate morphological markings for the passive
verb forms yield the string (28b). Obviously, if the above derivation
is correct, then the order of application of the two rules must have
been   *raising > there insertion.*
Assuming for the moment that the derivations described above are
correct, we have the following situation:

Given some underlying structure US_i, there exist two derivations,
D_i and D_j, each of which includes the application of two rules r_i and
r_j, such that (a) in D_i, the order of application is $r_i > r_j$, and (b) in D_j,
the order of application is $r_j > r_i$.

The question which now arises is whether this situation is to be considered a case of primary motivation for the cyclic principle. It seems that in each such case it is trivial to construct a noncyclic alternative; that is, the situation described is one of secondary motivation. Note first of all that under the assumptions made regarding the identity of the structure underlying the two strings of (28), it must be the case that there exists at least one phrase marker P_i that is properly analyzable with respect to both r_i or r_j prior to the application of either r_i or r_j. Consider the alternatives; that is, consider the possibility that no such P_i exists. There are three cases:

I. The set of phrase markers in all derivations proceeding from US_i prior to the application of either r_i or r_j contain at least one tree that is properly analyzable with respect to the structural index of r_i but not with respect to the structural index of r_j.

II. The inverse of condition I; that is, where there exists at least one tree structure that is properly analyzable with respect to r_j and not r_i.

III. The set of phrase markers in all derivations proceeding from US_i prior to the application of either r_i or r_j contain no tree structure which is properly analyzable with respect to either r_i or r_j.

An examination of the three cases will reveal that necessarily the only well formed result of case I is the order:

$$r_i > r_j = D_i$$

and of case II:

$$r_j > r_i = D_j$$

and of case III:

no application of either r_i or r_j.

Hence, we may conclude that the situation described necessarily involves the existence in the derivation prior to the application of either r_i or r_j of some phrase marker, P_i, which is properly analyzable with respect to both r_i and r_j. If this line of reasoning is correct, then we have, in effect, the classic case for unordered rule application. Hence, for every pair of rules, $\langle r_i, r_j \rangle$ for which the description holds, there is an alternative noncyclic analysis that simply maintains that the r_i and r_j are unordered with respect to each other. Further, given the existence of the phrase marker P_i, the two derivations in question are guaranteed; D_i, just in case r_i applies to P_i prior to r_j, and D_j, just in case r_j applies to P_i prior to r_i. Hence, the situation could never in principle offer a case of primary motivation for the cycle.[9]

However, I wish to challenge the claim that the two sentences of (28) are surface realizations of the same underlying form. Notice first of all, that if the derivation described for (28b) were correct, it would involve the application of the transformation *there insertion* on the cycle on the predicate *believe*. In general, however, *there insertion* is not possible with this predicate, as (34) shows:

(34)   a.   *There believed John that Mary was sick.*
       b.   *There was believed by John that Mary was sick.*
       c.   *There was John believed that Mary was sick.*

.

.

.

If the derivation were claimed to be as indicated in the preceding discussion, then a principled way of deciding under what structural conditions the predicate *believe* could take *there insertion* would have to be found.

I suggest that the derivation of (28b) involves the structure (35) as a more remote structure.

(35)   *There were lions which were believed to be in the forest.*

The suggestion entails a number of predictions that distinguish nicely between the syntactic possibilities of (28). It makes the claim, for example, that the constituent represented by the surface lexical items *in the forest* is inside a relative clause in the structure (28b), but not in (28a). If this is correct, then the constituent represented by the phrase *in the forest* will be extractable by any of a series of movement rules in the case of (28a) but not (29b), since in the latter case the constituent is within a syntactic island defined by a relative clause (cf. Ross, 1967, the Complex NP Constraint). This prediction is quite accurate as the pairs (36) and (37) indicate.

---

[9] There are, however, interesting variations on this theme. Consider the effect of relaxing the stipulation in (33) that the two derivations D_i and D_j proceed from the same underlying structure. The same result will obtain. Notice that in either case that the existence of some third rule, which can be shown to be ordered between r_i and r_j, will remove the possibility of claiming that r_i and r_j are unordered with respect to each other, and apparently will convert such cases of those described in (33) into cases of primary motivation. Thus, the characterization of what constitutes a case of primary motivation for the cyclic principle is both accurate and exhaustive for two rule interactions, but not exhaustive for cases of n rule interactions where n is greater than 2.

(36)   a. *Where are there believed to be lions?*
              b. **Where are there lions believed to be?*

       a. *I never seen the forest in which there are believed to be
           lions.*
       b. **I never seen the forest in which there are lions believed
           to be.*

I conclude not only that the *there insertion–raising* interaction does
not constitute a case of primary motivation for the cycle, but that the
sentences in (28) are derived from distinct underlying structures.

Greek Case Agreement

George Lakoff (1970) has noted the existence of a grammatical
phenomenon that requires reference to the node in the derivation
designated in a cyclic grammar as cyclic subject. The definition of
cyclic subject is quite easily obtained in a cyclic grammar. Cyclic
subject is the node that is in the structural position shown in (37) (the
choice between the a and b version of the definition is contingent
upon the decision as to whether the rule of *subject formation* is cyclic
(configuration a) or noncyclic (configuration b).

(37)

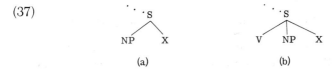

                (a)   (b)

Lakoff's characterization of the Greek Case Agreement phenomenon
seems to be correct; that is, the agreement in case marking between
some NP and a predicate nominal, adjective, or past participle is
determined by the surface structure position occupied by that NP.
However, determining which NP the various categories must agree
with must be decided cyclically. This is accurate, as there are rules
that will change the syntactic position of the NP in question, thus
changing the surface case marking. Notice that the same set of rules
that change the syntactic position of the NP have the effect of moving
that NP a (potentially) infinite distance away from the predicate nominal, adjective, . . . which must agree with that NP.[10] Hence, the case
marking that the predicate nominal, adjective, . . . will bear is de-

[10] In a paper delivered at the same conference, Postal argued for the necessity of referring to the notion of cyclical subject for a principled account of a rule he refers to
as *Q float.*

termined by the structural position that its NP controller comes to occupy in surface structure – that position is determined only post-cyclically. The NP that will serve as the controlling NP for purposes of case agreement is the NP in the structural position shown in (37) at the end of the first cycle on the predicate nominal, adjective, . . . ; that NP is determined only cyclically.

The reconstruction of the notion of cyclic subject in a noncyclic grammar is quite easily accomplished. Consider the set of rules that create derived subjects; in other words, the set of rules that move NP into the structural configuration displayed in (40). There are two such rules in both the cyclic and noncyclic grammars – *passive* and *raising*.[11] I argued above for the order *passive* > *raising*. Further, I argued for the formulation of *raising* as a copying transformation. Given these arguments, cyclic subject in a cyclic grammar can be identified with the NP in the structural configuration shown in (37). At this point in the derivation, all applications of the two rules that move elements into the appropriate structural configuration have applied, and none of the rules (*equi-NP deletion, Wh-Q movement,* . . .) that destroy that configuration have applied. The reconstruction of the notion of cyclic subject can therefore be accomplished by simply referring to the NP in the structural position (37) at the point in the derivation defined by a particular rule – the rule of *raising*.

Tag Questions

As pointed out by George Lakoff, another case of what appears to be primary motivation for the cyclic principle may be found in an article by Robin Lakoff (1969). The argument involves the two rules of *negative transportation* and *tag question formation*.

I must confess some hesitation in attempting to discuss the inter-action of these two rules; *negative transportation* is relatively well defined, the rule of *tag question formation*, however, as well as the shape of the underlying structure for tag questions, is less than trans-parent. I agree with R. Lakoff's suggestion regarding an underlying

---

[11] The sentences involving case agreement in Greek involve only the transformations of *raising* and *passive*. There is in English, however, a third rule that has been claimed to create derived subjects – the rule of *tough movement* (see Postal, 1968a). Since the notion of cyclical subject must be Postal's arguments be reconstructed for English, it follows that a noncyclic grammar of English will order *tough movement* before the rules that destroy the configuration that defines cyclical subject in a noncyclic grammar; specifically, prior to the rules of *equi-NP deletion, Wh-Q movement,* etc. This is a con-sistent ordering as far as I have been able to determine.

performative *suppose.* The argument for the cycle presented by her
is misleading as the subsequent discussion in the text will show.

The following relatively neutral statements concerning the process
are accurate first approximations to a final formulation:

 i.   The shape of the tag (disregarding the question of its
       negative–positive value) is determined by the shape of
       the highest nonperformative clause in the left conjunct.
 ii. The positive–negative value of the tag is determined by
       value of the highest nonperformative clause in the left
       conjunct. If the value of the highest nonperformative
       in the left conjunct is designated by α, then the tag is
       necessarily $-\alpha$.

Thus the following strings meet both the requirements and consequently are well-formed:

(38)   a. *Peter laughs a lot, doesn't he?*
       b. *Peter doesn't laugh a lot, does he?*
       c. *Pam thinks that Peter doesn't laugh a lot, doesn't she?*
       d. *Pam doesn't think that Peter laughs a lot, does she?*

Clearly, the above strings can be easily generated in a non-cyclic
grammar by the ordering *negative transportation > tag question
formation.*

In particular, if, as argued by Robin Lakoff, the pair (38)c and (38d)
are to be derived from the same underlying structure, one need only
allow the optional rule of *negative transportation* to apply. After the
last application of *negative transportation,* apply *tag question formation* (represented by i and ii). The derivations produce the correct
outputs noncyclically; in the derivation of (38c), the optional rule of
negative transportation has failed to apply, leaving the negative element in the lower clause — since the highest nonperformative in the
left conjunct contains no negative, the tag is itself negative. In the
derivation of (38d), the optional rule of *negative transportation* has
applied, raising the negative element into the highest nonperformative in the left conjunct — since that clause is negative, the tag is
positive.

The putative case of primary motivation for the cyclic application
of transformational rules arises in the case of an exception to the
generalization stated in ii. Consider the triplet (39):

(39)   a. *I suppose that Pam thinks that Peter doesn't laugh a
            lot, doesn't she?*

b. *I suppose that Pam doesn't think that Peter laughs a
    lot, does she?*
c. *I don't suppose that Pam thinks that Peter laughs a
    lot, does she?*

The derivation of (39a–c) involve zero, one, and two applications
of the transformation *negative transportation,* respectively. The shape
of the tags in (39) is as dictated by i and ii. The shape of the tag in
(39c), however, is well formed with respect to i, but ill formed with
respect to ii. The highest nonperformative in (39c) is positive; thus,
by ii, we predict that the tag will have a negative form; that is, that
the well formed surface realization for (39c) should be (40).

(40) **I don't suppose that Pam thinks that Peter laughs a lot,
       doesn't she?*

As Robin Lakoff points out, if the rule of *tag formation* were to apply
on the cycle on the predicate *think,* the highest nonperformative,
and subsequent to its application, specifically on the next cycle, the
rule of *negative transportation* were to apply lifting the negative element out of that clause, then the correct surface form (39c) would be
generated and the ill formed string (40) blocked. Superficially, then,
the derivation of (39c) has the proper form for a case of primary motivation for the cycle: there is a single derivation d_i, the derivation of
the surface structure (39c), in which two rules have applied, r_i *(negative transportation)* and r_j *(tag question formation)* such that r_i has
applied both before and after r_j. Specifically, r_i applies first to raise
the negative element out of the most deeply embedded clause into
the highest nonperformative. Rule r_j now applies, correctly determining the shape of the tag. Finally, r_i applies lifting the negative
element out of the highest nonperformative into the performative,
yielding the correct surface form (40).

SUBVERSION OF THE TAG QUESTION ARGUMENT

The conclusion that the derivation of the surface structure (39c) is
a case of primary motivation for the cyclic principle of rule application can be nicely avoided. Consider the following noncyclic derivation of (39c). Assume the ordering *negative transportation* > *tag
question formation* in a noncyclic grammar. In the derivation of
(39c), the rule of *negative transportation* applies twice, the negative
element ending up in the performative. The statement i correctly
specifies the shape of the tag excepting the question of negativity.

Now replace the statement ii with iii:

    iii.   The tag question will be positive iff either the performa-
           tive clause or the highest nonperformative clause con-
           tains a negative element; otherwise, the tag will be
           affirmative.

The combination of *negative transportation* and *tag question formation* (as represented by the statements of i and iii) generates the well
formed sequences of (38) and (39) but blocks the ill-formed (40) in
a noncyclic grammar.

    There are several points for discussion here. First, one might object
that formulation iii is more complex than necessary, this complexity
being an artifact of the noncyclic solution to the problem. A serious
discussion of this objection will have to wait until a well defined
deep structure and a well defined cyclic version of the *tag question
formation* transformation are available. Issues such as whether the
tag portion of the underlying structure of tag questions contains
negatives, or whether the negative that appears in sentences such
as (38a and c) is transformationally inserted must be decided before
a comparison of the cyclic and noncyclic solution is possible. Notice
that the generalization stated in iii under the assumption of a noncyclic grammar can be stated in either terms. Under the assumption
that the tag portion of the underlying tag questions contains the
negative, then iii would serve as a surface structure output condition
(cf. Perlmutter, 1968). If, on the other hand, there were some principled reason to believe that the negative element was transformationally inserted, the statement iii would serve as the environment
for the insertion rule. Second, notice that it is possible to state the
negative agreement condition between the tag and nontag portion
of the structures involved in surface structure only because the positions that have to be checked for the presence of a negative element
are bounded; in fact, there will always be exactly two clauses to check,
the performative (if present) and the highest nonperformative. If the
clause that determines the positive–negative agreement, the highest
nonperformative, could be (potentially) an infinite distance away from
the final position of the negative, then a statement such as iii would
not be possible, but rather some recursive procedure would be necessary to check for the presence of a negative element in order to determine the shape of the tag. The incorporation of such a mechanism in
the noncyclic solution would, it seems to me, force one to prefer the
cyclic solution. Notice the fact that, by definition (cf. Ross, 1968, for
discussion), there is at most one performative in the structure of each

surface form that guarantees that the simple nonrecursive statement iii will be adequate.

Third, notice that in the cyclic solution, when determining the positive–negative value of the tag, one must make reference to the highest nonperformative in the left conjunct. That is, in the cyclic solution, one must prevent the application of tag agreement until the rules are applying to the highest nonperformative. In order to determine whether one is cycling on the highest nonperformative, one requires access to information about the elements contained in the domain of application of the cyclic rules *on the succeeding cycle;* specifically, whether the predicate on the next cycle is a performative predicate. Within the cyclic framework, such information is simply not available until the succeeding cycle. But consider the implications of this fact for the ordering of the two rules under discussion, negative transportation and tag question formation. Clearly, *tag question formation* (or minimally, that portion of *tag question formation* contained in the statement iii must be constrained from applying until it is certain that the point in the cycle immediately below the cycle on the performative has been reached. That information is not available until the cycle on the performative itself. Therefore, *tag question formation* must be constrained from applying until the cycle on the performative. On the cycle on the performative, we have the information necessary to decide whether the *tag question formation* may apply. There are two possibilities with respect to the ordering of this transformation and *negative transportation* on the performative cycle:

I.   The order is *negative transportation* > *tag question formation.* Underlying this ordering assumption, there are two ways to state the *tag question formation* rule: the rule is stated to apply between the highest nonperformative and the tag portion, in which case the ill formed (40) is generated; the rule is as stated in i and iii, in which case the well formed sequence (39c) is derived and the ill formed (40) is excluded.

II. The order is *tag question formation* > *negative transportation.* By this ordering assumption, we obtain the correct results; we exclude (40) and allow (39c). This is true whether *tag question formation* is formulated as agreement between the highest nonperformative and the tag or as in the joint statement i–iii. This last appears to be the only difference between the cyclic and noncyclic solutions.

Independent of the final decision of whether the cyclic or the noncyclic solution is to be preferred, it is clear that the *tag question–negative transportation* interaction is not a case of primary motivation. The examples then fail to meet the requirements set up by the schema given at the beginning of this paper as the tree structure involved is properly analyzable with respect to either of the transformations on the last (performative) cycle.

SUMMARY

There are at present no cases of primary motivation for the cyclic principle of rule application in syntax. All cases discussed here have been successfully reduced to cases of secondary motivation; that is, phenomena consistent with the cyclic as well as the noncyclic principle. This successful reduction raises many questions, including:

> Can the cyclic (noncyclic) principle be shown to be preferred on methodological grounds? In other words, is the class of languages generated under the cyclic principle included in the class of languages generated under the noncyclic principle or vice versa?
>
> In the reduction of *three insertion* case, use was made of the principle of partial ordering. What is the relationship between non-cyclic grammars with partial ordering and cyclic grammars with total ordering? Further, while there may be no cases of primary motivation for the cyclic principle, are there second order reasons to prefer the cyclic principle? In this respect, consider the question of extrinsic and intrinsic ordering; that is, the order of application of rules stated for the grammar and the actual order of those rules in well formed derivations in the language. In the case of cyclic grammer, there is always a discrepancy between extrinsic and intrinsic ordering. In a non-cyclic grammar, the two orders necessarily coincide.

Questions such as those above deserve research, especially since, as was noted at the outset, the cyclic principle is always assumed for research conducted within the framework of transformational grammar.

This paper has confined itself to a discussion of the question of whether there are any cases of primary motivation for the cyclic principle. I wish to point out that while there are no such cases, it is not impossible that one could bring forth a number of second order arguments for the cyclic principle of rule application. George Lakoff, for example, has argued (in classes at the California Summer Linguistics Institute, University of California at Santa Cruz), that given the cyclic principle, one can dispense entirely with extrinsic rule ordering. If a number of such arguments could be sustained, their cumulative weight could dictate a relatively unambiguous choice between the two alternatives. Naturally, the less ambiguous situation is one in which a case of primary motivation can be found. By challenging the anal-

yses of the phenomena considered to be cases of primary motivation for the cyclic principle, I hope to have defined the form which
an unambiguous solution to the question of whether the cyclic principle is a necessary component of the grammars of natural languages
will have.

REFERENCES

Bach, E. 1968. Anti-Pronominalization (mimeograph) University of Texas.

Chomsky, N. 1965. Aspects of the Theory of Syntax. MIT Press, Cambridge, Massachusetts.

Chomsky, N. 1969. Some Empirical Issues in the Theory of Grammar. (mimeograph)
MIT, Cambridge, Massachusetts.

Dougherty, R. 1969. An Interpretative Theory of Pronominalization. Foundations of
Language 5. 488–519.

Fauconnier, G. 1971. Theoretical Implications of Some Global Syntactic Phenomena.
Ph.D. thesis, University of California, San Diego, California.

Jackendoff, R. 1969. Some Rules of Semantic Interpretation for English. Ph.D. thesis,
MIT, Cambridge, Massachusetts.

Klima, E. S., and R. Lees. 1963. Rules for English Pronominalization. Language 39.
17–29.

Lakoff, G. 1968. Pronouns and Reference. (mimeograph) Harvard University, Cambridge, Massachusetts.

Lakoff, G. 1970. Global Rules. Language 46. 627–639.

Lakoff, R. 1969. A Syntactic Argument for Negative Transportation. in Papers from the
Fifth Regional Meeting of the Chicago Linguistics Society, University of Chicago,
Chicago.

Langacker, R. 1966. Pronominalization and the Chain of Command. (mimeograph)
University of California, San Diego, California.

McCawley, J. 1970. English as a VSO Language. Language 46. 286–299.

Perlmutter, D. 1968. Deep and Surface Structure Constraints. Ph.D. thesis, MIT, Cambridge, Massachusetts.

Postal, P. M. 1968a. Cross-Over Phenomena. Thomas J. Watson Research Center, IBM.

Postal, P. M. 1968b. On Coreferential Complement Subject Deletion. Thomas J. Watson Research Center, IBM.

Postal, P. M. 1971. Some Arguments for Raising in Random Order. (mimeograph)
Thomas J. Watson Research Center, IBM.

Ross, J. R. 1967. Constraints on Variables in Syntax. Ph.D. thesis, MIT, Cambridge,
Massachusetts.

Ross, J. R. 1968. On Declarative Sentence. (mimeograph) MIT, Cambridge, Massachusetts.

Ross, J. R. 1969a. On the Cyclic Nature of English Pronominalization. (mimeograph)
MIT, Cambridge, Massachusetts.

Ross, J. R. 1969b. Guess Who. in Papers from the Fifth Regional Meeting of the Chicago Linguistic Society, University of Chicago, Chicago.

DISCUSSION

GEORGE LAKOFF
University of Michigan

The principle of the transformational cycle was first suggested by Charles Fillmore (1963) in his classic paper "The position of embedding transformations in a grammar." Fillmore observed that certain transformations could be stated more generally if they applied to embedded sentences before applying to matrix sentences. This conception of grammar antedated the Katz–Postal conception of deep structure, in terms of which Fillmore's "traffic rules" became translated directly into the present-day concept of the cycle.

In 1965, Rosenbaum offered a further argument for the principle of the cycle. based on the assumption of total extrinsic ordering. He observed that sentences like *Boris wants to be beaten by Ursula* would require the ordering *passive* < *equi*, while sentences like *Ursula was persuaded to beat Boris* would require the ordering *equi* < *passive*. Since *passive* applies on the lower S in the first case but on the upper S in the second case, the ordering contradiction can be avoided by the principle of the cycle. In 1966, Ross and I noticed that such an argument could be gotten around by giving up the assumption of total ordering in favor of partial ordering. Then *equi* could be thought of as a rule that was unordered with respect to other rules. The above cases could then be handled if passive were thought of as applying iteratively bottom-to-top. This is essentially the principle Grinder adopts in the preceding chapter.

113

In 1966, I found an argument that seemed to choose between the cyclic principle and the bottom-to-top iterative principle. It was based on the version of the crossover principle held by Postal at that time. The crucial cases were those like *Sheila was believed by herself to have been raped by Irving*. It was assumed that such cases were to be ruled out by the same principle that rules out *Sheila was washed by herself*. At the time, Postal had maintained the following principle: If two NPs are coreferents and clause mates, one cannot be moved over the other. As is discussed in my unpublished 1966 manuscript "Deep and Surface Grammar," the above sentence can be ruled out by Postal's principle if the principle of the cycle is assumed. However, under the bottom-to-top iterative principle, assuming *passive* ordered before *raising* and *reflexive*, both applications of *passive* in the above sentence would precede *raising*, and so at the point in the derivation at which the two coreferential NPs were crossed, they would not be clause mates. Only the subsequent application of raising would make them clause mates. Thus, if the above version of the crossover principle were correct, we would have an argument for the cycle. Unfortunately, that version of the crossover principle has had to be abandoned, and given the current version, this argument would no longer hold.

Subsequent arguments for the cycle have been given by Ross (1967) (the cyclic pronominalization case discussed by Grinder), Ross and Halle (Kimball's *there insertion* case discussed in the previous chapter), Robin Lakoff's *not transportation* argument, and my argument based on the rule of Greek case agreement. Grinder has correctly observed that one can get around these arguments for the principle of the cycle by the following means:

1. Making considerable use of extrinsic rule ordering.
2. Letting *raising* be a copying rule rather than a movement rule.
3. Defining that point in the grammar just after the last rule that forms derived subjects as the point relevant to the statement of such agreement rules as Greek case agreement.
4. Giving up a general rule for the distribution of negatives in tag questions in favor of a disjunctive condition.

It seems to me that if one has to choose between these four propositions and the principle of the cycle, the cycle clearly wins. Just consider 1. Given the principle of the cycle and independently motivated analyses, all known cases of extrinsic rule ordering disappear. If the choice were only between the cycle and extrinsic rule ordering, the cycle comes out ahead because it is a universal principle according to which the application of syntactic rules is determined by independently motivated syntactic structures. Extrinsic rule ordering statements, on the other hand, are ad hoc blocking devices that must be stated in the grammar of each language. Clearly, the cyclic principle is preferable. Moreover, the cyclic principle defines natural levels in derivations (the output of the relevant cycles) for the statement of global agreement rules, which would make 3 unnecessary. Proposition 4 is just a fudge. Whenever you have to give up a general statement in favor of a disjunctive condition, something is wrong. In short, Grinder's paper provides us with some good reasons for maintaining the cyclic principle, though they are not "primary motivations" in his sense.

ACTION AND RESULT: TWO ASPECTS OF PREDICATION IN ENGLISH

MICHAEL B. KAC
University of Minnesota

Details of the current controversy over the nature of lexical insertion are by now generally known. Most discussion has centered on verbs, and a great deal of attention has been devoted to causative verbs in particular, such as *kill*, transitive *melt* and *break*. One of the vintage arguments in favor of a "prelexical" syntactic structure underlying such verbs is presented in a 1969 paper by J. L. Morgan. Morgan claims a three-way ambiguity for sentences like

(1)   *John almost killed Fred.*

In McCawley (1968) the following three paraphrases are given for (1), each said to correspond to one reading:

(2) a. *John almost did something that would have killed Fred.*
     b. *John did something that came close to causing Fred to die.*
     c. *John did something that brought Fred close to death.*

The conclusion drawn from these observations is that the ambiguity is due to differences of scope of *almost* in the prelexical representation. The suggestion is that at this level we would have, corresponding respectively to (2a–c):

(3)   a. *John almost caused Fred to become not alive.*
           b. *John caused Fred to almost become not alive.*
           c. *John caused Fred to become almost not alive.*

At this point it should be stressed that the sentences (3) are not the actual prelexical structures, since those structures contain no lexical items. I will nonetheless, refer to actual sentences throughout this discussion, for clarity and convenience.

This argument has passed into the theoretical canon of one approach to semantic description. And yet, while I feel that the original observations are at least partially correct, I am of the opinion that the inference drawn from them is not the right one. I would like, therefore, to reexamine this particular phenomenon with a view toward making an alternative proposal as to how it is to be explained.

The first point I want to raise is perhaps the least essential but of some importance nonetheless. In Morgan's paper (Morgan, 1969), when he deals with cases like (1) he says:

> The sentence . . . has several readings, due to ambiguity in the scope of *almost*, at least one of which involves the scope of *almost* being internal to *kill* [p. 62].

This assertion is rather troubling, since, as he phrases it, Morgan assumes just what he is out to demonstrate—that it is necessary to acknowledge a structure in which the scope of *almost* is inside a lexical item. He treats the claim that (1) is scope-ambiguous as if that were part of the observation itself, whereas in fact it is merely a possible inference from the observation. I raise this point because, given statements like that above, considerable confusion is introduced as to what we actually know from observation and what we do not. In point of fact, all that is known on observational grounds is that (1) is ambiguous in some way. From there we must proceed, with a certain amount of deliberation and care to a consideration of alternative explanations of this ambiguity, and to adjudicate them on independent grounds.

One possible account is that in which a more complex prelexical structure is assumed, allowing for varying positions and scopes for *almost*. This, however, is immediately suspect, since if the sentences (3) are examined carefully, it becomes evident that they do not show what they purport to show. I mean specifically that while (3b and c) are supposed to correspond to different interpretations of (1), they are themselves not differently interpreted. A number of informants who have been queried on this point have said that they are unable

to see a real semantic distinction between the two (one of the informants, a nonlinguist, nonetheless commented that he prides himself
on his ability to detect semantic subtleties). The situation is no better
in the pseudo-cleft construction, which Morgan offers as a case in
which "the full range of readings becomes more apparent":

(4)   a. *What John almost did was kill Fred.*
         b. *What John did was almost kill Fred.*
         c. *What John did to Fred was almost kill him.*

Once more, my informants see no difference between the (b) and (c)
versions. Indeed, it is difficult to see what the difference is supposed
to be between (2b and c). The first point to be questioned, then, is
the claim that (1) is three as opposed to two ways ambiguous. Examples (2) and (4) are supposed to illustrate the ambiguity, but they
show only the distinction between the (a) sense and the others; even
if these cases did show a difference between the (b) and (c) senses,
this difference could not be accounted for by (3b and c), since these
have identical readings.

At this point, I shall digress briefly to answer an anticipated criticism. In arguing about (3b and c), I am talking about actual sentences, not about the prelexical structures to which they correspond.
It might therefore be argued that what has just been said, while true,
is irrelevant, since the issue is the nature of the prelexical structures
themselves. It might further be maintained, as it sometimes has in
past debate, that the semantic predicates that are terminal items of
the prelexical structures are not exactly equivalent semantically to
such actual lexical items as *cause* or *become*. But this is clearly an
evasion of the issue. All evidence for prelexical structures and the
properties they are to have must come from observable linguistic
entities—sentences. It is meaningless to talk about prelexical structures as if we could actually observe them in the world and thus discern the properties they have or do not have. Indeed, it is precisely
because there are sentences like (3) that the prelexical structure for
kill is said to be CAUSE BECOME NEG ALIVE; consequently, it must be
accepted that the nature of this structure is inferred directly from the
sentences in question.

The assumption to be operated on, then, is that (1) is only two ways
ambiguous, and that the (b) and (c) cases under (2) (4) both represent
the same sense.

A second problem arises with respect to the verb *murder*. This is
obviously a close semantic relative of *kill* and would certainly involve

cause to become not alive as part of its underlying prelexical representation. This information would be supplemented by a succeeding adverbial clause *with malice aforethought* or something similar. But now notice that

(5)   *John almost murdered Fred.*

is unambiguous. For speakers I have consulted, it can only have the (2a) reading. This is further borne out by the fact that these speakers detect a definite difference between the use of *murder* and *kill* in:

(6)   *John fired the bullet at Fred, coming so close that he almost killed/*murdered him.*

(7)   *John wounded Fred so seriously that he almost killed/ *murdered him.*

If we analyze *murder* via the proposed prelexical representation for *kill*, we must deal with a rather puzzling fact, namely, that in this case *almost* is restricted to a single scope external to the verb. Why should this be so? There is no obvious principle that would suggest that the presence of additional information about premeditation, however represented, ought to affect the scope possibilities for *almost*. Therefore, the analysis embodied in (3) leaves many questions unanswered.

I shall now consider an alternative account of the observed ambiguity of (1) which will also be consistent with the observations about (5). Returning to (2), we can see that the basic distinction between the (a) and (b–c) senses is that in the latter case it is understood that John actually did do something; i.e., that he performed some specific act that did not, however, achieve its desired result. On the other hand, in (a) we understand that not even the act took place. This is not made explicit in (3), or even in (2) for that matter. What I should like to suggest, then, is that there is a basic distinction between two ways of construing predicates—as asserting actions or as asserting the achievement of results. This distinction is a real one with systematic properties. If the (2a) sense is elaborated a little, it can be seen that it relates to the kind of situation in which someone is going to do something, and then for some reason decides against it. Notice, however, that the (a) type reading is out for:

(8)   *The bullet almost killed Fred.*

This situation, like the one described for *murder*, is also somewhat strange. On the analysis embodied in (3), it is hard to see why, with such a subject, the scope of *almost* should be restricted to the verb-internal case. But in terms of the action–result dichotomy, the explanation of the fact is clear. An action requires an animate, satient being to perform it, and a bullet is not such a being. Therefore, the action sense, represented by (a) in (2), is not assignable to this sentence. The interaction between action interpretation for a predicate and requirement of an animate subject can be stated as an absolutely general condition in the grammar of English.

Now consider the case of *murder* again. It was noted above that there is a distinct anomaly about (6)–(7) when *murder* is substituted for *kill*. Notice that in these sentences, the nature of the overt action is already understood, so that *kill* or *murder* can only designate the result of the action. But *murder* does not fit the context; we might conclude therefore that *murder* cannot be a result predicate, only an action predicate. Further support for this conclusion comes from the fact that:

(9) **The bullet murdered Fred.*

is definitely ill-formed.

It should be noted in passing that the exact manner in which the term "result" is used is a somewhat specialized one. On the usual reading of this word, it seems somewhat strange to talk about bullets as achieving results, just as it seems strange to talk about them performing acts. Perhaps it would be more appropriate to use a more noncommittal term such as "nonaction." A dispute over nomenclature is somewhat beside the point, though the term chosen is not perhaps the most felicitous. For purposes of this discussion, however, the term "result" will be retained in the knowledge that it is used in a somewhat novel way.

There is a further fact that can be explicated by the action–result dichotomy, but not by the prelexical causative analysis. Consider a sentence like:

(10) *It surprised me that John killed Fred.*

This sentence is also two ways ambiguous: What surprised me is either (a) that John would do such a thing, or (b) that Fred would succumb as a result of John's action. This ambiguity has no accounting whatsoever in the cause-to-become-not-alive analysis, since there is no element like *almost* whose scope can vary. But the ambiguity is directly predicted by the action–result dichotomy. (Indeed, a little reflection will show that *John killed Fred* in isolation is also ambiguous in just this way.)

However, the case of (10) is different from that of, say,

(11)   *John killed Fred, which surprised me.*

where, it is sometimes argued, *which* replaces either the entire VP *cause to become not alive* or *become not alive* only. In (10), there is no replacing element; the pronoun *it*, in particular, is not a candidate since it is not an anaphoric element but a dummy subject associated with the extraposition transformation. If we consider the source of (10):

(12)   *That John killed Fred surprised me.*

it can be seen even more clearly that the ambiguity cannot be represented in terms of scope of replacement. Consequently, though the prelexical causative analysis can, in fact, handle cases like (11), it cannot handle (10) or (12); the action–result dichotomy, on the other hand, allows all cases to be accounted for and on the same grounds.

SUMMARY

   a.   Sentence (1) is two rather than three ways ambiguous.

   b.   There are peculiar restrictions on possible scopes for *almost* in certain situations: *almost* can only be external to *murder* but cannot be external to *kill* if it occurs with an inanimate subject.

   c.   The basic ambiguity of (1) revolves around whether or not it is understood that an act was committed.

   d.   The missing readings for *almost murder* and for *almost kill* with inanimate subject are predicted by the fact that *murder* can only be an action predicate, and that inanimate subjects may not cooccur with action predicates.

   e.   There are parallel ambiguities in sentences with *kill* where scope is not at issue.

Thus, at the very least, the particular prelexical analysis of *kill*, on the basis of which it derives from *cause to become not alive*, has been called into question as providing an insufficiently general account of a variety of clearly related phenomena. The next question we must ask is: What are the implications of these conclusions, if any, for the notion of prelexical structure itself?

The question can be answered in two parts:

First, it can be quite conclusively shown that verbs like *kill* provide no evidence for the reality of prelexical structures. This is not to say that it is impossible in principle to represent these facts in terms of prelexical representations. So, it might be argued, all we have to do is beef up the representations so that every *cause to become* is preceded by *commit the act of* or *achieve the result of*. Thus, the two senses of (1) might be re-represented by

(13)   a. *John almost committed the act of causing Fred to become not alive.*
       b. *John almost achieved the result of causing Fred to become not alive.*

with a restriction, at this level, that *almost* must always precede *commit* or *achieve*. But notice that while this modification is possible, it is not compellingly necessary. The whole reason for wanting prelexical structure is to be able to break up lexical items into smaller units between which it is possible to interpose elements like *almost* to account for ambiguities. But if it turns out in the end that the ambiguity in question is not one of scope after all, then the amount of flexibility that prelexical representation gives us in this regard is not actually needed. There is no empirical difference between representations like (13) and, say, marking verbs in the lexicon as [+Action] or [+Result] (or, in the case of *kill*, as either), and interpreting *almost*-V strings according to the way in which V is specified.

At this moment, one brief remark is in order about what the logical relationship between action and result is conceived to be. When I say, for example, that *murder* can only be an action predicate, I do not mean that in a sentence like *John murdered Fred* no result is to be understood as having occurred. Quite the contrary; in the semantic representation of *murder*, I should expect the information to be incorporated somehow that completion of the action implies a specific result. When *murder* is said to be an action predicate, what is meant is that it asserts an action and implies a result. Similarly, for result predicates, assertion of a result presupposes (rather than implies) an action in at least some instances. Thus if I say *John didn't kill Fred even though he tried, kill* clearly has the result sense and it is presupposed that John undertook some action such as shooting, stabbing, or whatever. However, the relation between action and result will probably have to be stated individually for particular predicates. For example, compare

(14)   a. *John shot Fred.*
           b. *John shot at Fred.*

In both cases we are dealing with action predicates; but *shoot* implies a result, while *shoot at* does not. Whether this means that *shoot* and *shoot at* are to be considered separate lexical items, or whether some further apparatus must be provided for assigning specifications to larger constituents, is a question I will raise but not go into here.

The second part of the answer is a qualification. Although it has been shown that *kill* and other causatives give no evidence in favor of the prelexical hypothesis, this does not in and of itself automatically invalidate the hypothesis. What it does do is establish that proponents may no longer use this particular argument to bolster their claims. A final verdict on the overall question will not be provided for some time, since it is necessary to go through a large number of arguments piece by piece.

REFERENCES

McCawley, J. D. 1968. Lexical insertion in a transformational grammar without deep structure. Papers from the Fourth Regional Meeting of the Chicago Linguistic Society, 71–80.

Morgan, J. L. 1969. On arguing about semantics. Papers in Linguistics 1.1.49–70.

THREE REASONS FOR NOT DERIVING
'KILL' FROM 'CAUSE TO DIE' IN JAPANESE

MASAYOSHI SHIBATANI
University of California, Berkeley

It has been claimed by Lakoff (1970) and McCawley (1968, 1972) that a lexicalized causative verb like *kill* is derived from an embedding semantic structure, which at one intermediate stage of derivation gives rise to a phrase like *cause to die* through successive applications of *predicate raising* and the lexicalization rule. More specifically, McCawley (1968) derives a sentence like (1a) from a semantic structure like (2) by applying *predicate raising* and *lexicalization* in the manner shown in (3) through (6) on page 126.

(1)   a. *John killed Harry.*
        b. *John caused Harry to die.*

Furthermore, it is claimed that *predicate raising* is an optional transformation and that a semantically related sentence like (1b) is derived from the same underlying representation as (1a); the surface difference is interpreted as being due to the failure of the last application of *predicate raising*, that is, the step of (4) to (5) in the derivation.

The proposed analysis is attractive for a number of reasons. For one, it naturally expresses the semantic relation between sentences like (1a) and (1b); for another, it readily accounts for the ambiguity ob-

125

(2)

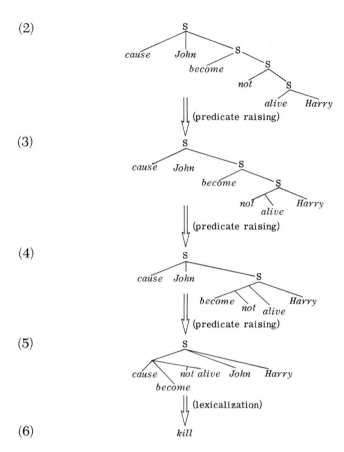

(3)

(4)

(5)

(6)   *kill*

served by Morgan (1970) in a sentence like

(7)   *John almost killed Harry.*

Wallace Chafe (personal communication), however, does not see the three-way ambiguity observed by Morgan. The ambiguity in (7), according to Chafe, is between 'John intended to kill Harry but he changed his mind,' and 'John, without intending to kill Harry, did something which could have killed Harry.' Thus, Chafe thinks the ambiguity of sentence (7) is not captured in McCawley's semantic representation.

Fodor (1970) challenged the proposed analysis by presenting three reasons on the basis of observations made in English. This paper will present somewhat different arguments against the proposed analysis on the basis of Japanese data.

Like the English pair *kill* and *cause to die,* Japanese has quite a number of pairs of lexicalized causative verbs and causative verb phrases as listed in Table I, where the stem of a causative phrase is an intransitive verb, and *sase* is the productive causative morpheme.

TABLE I *Japanese Lexicalized Causative Verbs and Corresponding Causative Verb Phrases*

Lexicalized causative verb		Causative verb phrase	
koros	'kill'	*sin-sase*	'cause to die'
tome	'stop'	*tomar-sase*	'cause to stop'
otos	'drop'	*oti-sase*	'cause to drop'
age	'raise'	*agar-sase*	'cause to rise'
oros	'bring down'	*ori-sase*	'cause to come down'
ire	'put in'	*hair-sase*	'cause to come in'
narabe	'line up'	*narab-sase*	'cause to line up'
nokos	'leave'	*nokor-sase*	'cause to stay'
hiroge	'spread'	*hirogar-sase*	'cause to spread'
mage	'bend'	*magar-sase*	'cause to turn (the corner)'

P-rule: $s \longrightarrow \emptyset/C\text{-}\underline{\quad\quad}$

As in English, two sentences, one with a lexicalized causative verb and another with a causative phrase, (8) and (9) are semantically related and can be used interchangeably in certain contexts. (I will translate *sase* as 'make' instead of 'cause' in order to give more natural English translations.)

(8)   *Taroo-wa musuko-o koros-ta.*
                 son   kill (past)
       'Taroo killed his son.'

(9)   *Taroo-wa musuko-o sin-sase-ta.*
                      die cause
       'Taroo made his son die.'

Furthermore, one will notice that lexicalized causative verbs and related intransitive verbs show a phonological resemblance for most cases. Thus, McCawley's analysis again seems to be attractive. Concerning just the causativization aspect, one may posit underlying representation (10) for both (8) and (9), and account for the surface variation in terms of lexicalization:

(10)

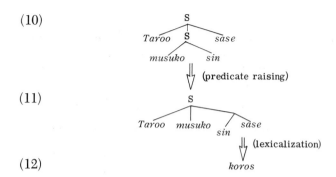

(11)

(12)

ARGUMENTS AGAINST THE ABOVE ANALYSIS

First a reason will be given for not deriving sentence pairs like (8) and (9) from identical underlying representations like (10). There is a semantic constraint in Japanese which says that the subject of the embedded sentence under *sase* must be something which has its own volition. The constraint characterizes the ill formedness of the (b) sentences in (13) through (15).

(13)   a. *Taroo-wa Ziroo-o kuruma-kara ori-sase-ta.*
                       car   get off
          'Taroo made Ziroo get off the car.'

      b. **Taroo-wa nimotu-o kuruma-kara ori-sase-ta*
                  baggage
          'Taroo unloaded the baggage from the car.'

(14)   a. *Taroo-wa Ziroo-o tomar-sase-ta*
                       stop
          'Taroo made Ziroo stop.'

      b. **Taroo-wa enzin-o tomar-sase-ta*
                  engine
          'Taroo made an engine stop.'

(15)   a. *Taroo-wa Ziroo-ni Hanako-o hik-sase-ta*
                                        run over
          'Taroo made Ziroo run over Hanako.'

      b. **Taroo-wa kuruma-ni Hanako-o hik-sase-ta*
          'Taroo made a car run over Hanako.'

However, the (b) sentences become grammatical if we replace the causative phrase by the corresponding lexicalized verb as shown in

(16)   a.   *Taroo-wa nimotu-o kuruma-kara oros-ta.*   (=13b)
            'Taroo unloaded the baggage from the car.'

       b.   *Taroo-wa enzin-o tome-ta.*   (=14b)
            'Taroo stopped an engine.'

Having no corresponding lexicalized verb, the phrase *hik-sase* 'make run over' of (15) cannot be replaced by a lexicalized verb; therefore, one cannot make (15b) grammatical in the same way as (13b) and (14b).

Now notice that if we were to derive sentences (16a) and (16b) from the identical underlying representations as (13b) and (14b), the independently needed constraint would be violated. That is, the constraint is needed in order to characterize ungrammatical sentences (13b) through (15b), but it must be violated in deriving (16a) and (16b). This observation, however, only shows that a sentence with a lexicalized verb and one with a corresponding causative phrase should not be derived from exactly the same underlying representation. And as soon as one admits two types of *sase* in semantic representation, the problem will be resolved. [This does not mean that if we posit two types of underlying causative morpheme, the semantics of the Japanese causative forms is adequately captured. Shibatani (1972) discusses the divergent meanings of Japanese causativization.] Thus, if we represent one *sase* in capital letters and another in small letters, and say that the capital *SASE* requires obligatory applications of *predicate raising* and *lexicalization,* and that the semantic constraint noted above holds only when the small *sase* occurs in semantic representation, the problem would not arise. In other words, (13b) and (16a), for example, should be given different semantic representations; (13b) contains *sase* to which the constraint applies, whereas (16b) contains *SASE* to which the constraint does not apply.

The above observation shows that in addition to the meaning difference noted by Katz (1970), there is good reason for not deriving a lexicalized causative verb and a causative verb phrase from identical representation as McCawley originally claimed. McCawley (1972) no longer derives sentences like (1a) and (1b) from exactly the same underlying representation. But his reason for not doing so is solely based on the difference in meaning. McCawley, moreover, now posits another higher sentence with its predicate *do* over the sentence with the predicate *cause.* Let us, therefore, assume that the underlying representation for a lexicalized causative verb, and that for an unlexicalized causative phrase contain *SASE* and *sase,* respectively.

The remaining cases are specifically concerned with the justifi-
ability of the analysis that posits an embedding structure for a lexicalized causative verb, i.e., the analysis that posits an embedded intransitive sentence beneath *SASE*. The first case argues on the basis
of the *do-so* transformation. As in the English case, the Japanese version of '*do so*' *soo su-ru* replaces an identical verb phrase; therefore,
when there are two verb phrases in an underlying structure the resulting *do-so* sentence becomes ambiguous. This is the case with a
sentence that contains a causative verb phrase as shown in (17b)
through (19b):

(17)   a. *Boku-wa musuko-o gakkoo-ni nokor-sase-ta,*
            I   school   stay

         b. *suruto Hanako-mo soo su-ta.*
            and

            'I made my son stay at the school,
            and so did Hanako.'

(18)   a. *Boku-wa musuko-o kuruma-kara ori-sase-ta,*

         b. *suruto Hanako-mo soo su-ta.*

            'I made my son get off the car,
            and so did Hanako.'

(19)   a. *Boku-wa musuko-o heya-ni hair-sase-ta*
                                room

         b. *suruto Hanako-mo soo su-ta.*

            'I made my son enter the room,
            and so did Hanako.'

Although the English translations do not reveal the ambiguity, sentence (17b), for example, means either 'Hanako also made her son stay
at the school,' or 'Hanako also stayed at the school' (presumably with
my son). The word *soo su-ta* replaces the verb phrase of the matrix
sentence and that of the embedded sentence. The phenomenon argues for an embedding structure with two verb phrases for a sentence
with a surface causative verb phrase.

Now if the same *do-so* operation is performed for the corresponding
sentences with a lexicalized verb, the resulting *do-so* sentences will
not be ambiguous, as observed in (20b) through (22b). Sentence (20b),
for example, uniquely means 'Hanako also made her son stay at the
school,' and one cannot get the reading of 'Hanako also stayed at the
school' from it.

(20)   a.   *Boku-wa musuko-o gakkoo-ni nokos-ta,*

          b.   *suruto Hanako-mo soo su-ta.*

               'I left my son at the school, and
               so did Hanako.'

(21)   a.   *Boku-wa musuko-o kuruma-kara oros-ta,*

          b.   *suruto Hanako-mo soo su-ta.*

               'I put my son down from the car, and
               so did Hanako.'

(22)   a.   *Boku-wa musuko-o heya-ni ire-ta,*

          b.   *suruto Hanako-mo soo su-ta.*

               'I brought my son into the room, and
               so did Hanako.'

If sentences with a lexicalized causative verb were indeed underlain by embedding structures as sentences with an unlexicalized causative verb phrase, we would expect the resulting *do-so* sentences to show ambiguity. However, since this is not the case, the behavior of *soo su-ru* 'do so' thus militates against deriving a lexicalized causative verb from an embedding underlying structure. Notice that one cannot argue here that *predicate raising* and *lexicalization* apply prior to the *do-so* rule, and that as a consequence the *do-so* rule can replace only the lexicalized verbs in (20) through (22). We would not get the ambiguous *do-so* sentences in (17) through (19) either if this were the case, for if the *predicate raising* applied prior to the *do-so* rule collapsing the embedded verb phrase, the latter would no longer refer to the identical subordinate verb phrase. Consequently the resulting *do-so* sentences should not be ambiguous. But since this is not the case, the *do-so* rule must apply before collapsing the embedded verb phrase by *predicate raising*.

In the passive construction of Japanese, which requires an embedding structure similar to the causative construction, *"do so"* can replace only the verb phrase of the embedded sentence as shown in (23a). Thus, it is again necessary that the *do-so* rule apply prior to the *predicate raising*, which destroys the independent status of the identical subordinate verb phrase.

(23)   a. *Taroo-wa kodomo-ni nak-rare-ta, sosite*
                                cry Passive
                Hanako-mo soo su-rare-ta.
                'Taroo was adversely affected by a child
                crying, and so was Hanako.'

            b. *Taroo-wa kodomo-ni nak-rare-ta, sosite*
                *Hanako-mo soo su-ta.

The first argument was based on a transformation that operates on identical verb phrases; now I will give another argument, similar to the first one, on the basis of a transformation that operates on identical noun phrases. The Japanese reflexive pronoun *zibun* 'self,' combined with the possessive affix *no*, means 'one's own.' Furthermore, *zibun* reflexivizes only the noun phrase whose antecedent is a subject; therefore, there is no ambiguity in a sentence like:

(24)   *Boku-wa Taroo-ni zibun-no hon-o yar-ta.*
            'I gave Taroo my own book.'

The fact that sentence (24) is not ambiguous casts a doubt on the analysis that decomposes *give* into 'CAUSE to have' or the Japanese version *yar* into *mot-SASE*. Notice that the following sentence with *mot-sase* 'cause to have' is ambiguous as to which subject *zibun* reflexivizes. The verbs like *kas* 'lend, or *kari* 'borrow' behave in the same way as *yar* 'give' in this respect.

(25)   *Boku-wa Taroo-ni zibun-no hon-o mot-sase-ta.*
            'I made Taroo have my/his own book.'

(However, these verbs, as noted by Kajita, make it possible to attach two tenses as in

(26)   *Boku-wa Taroo-ni hon-o asu-made* $\begin{Bmatrix} kas \\ kari \end{Bmatrix}$ *-ta.*

            'I $\begin{Bmatrix} \text{lent Taroo a book} \\ \text{borrowed a book from Taroo} \end{Bmatrix}$ until tomorrow.'

while *yar* and *moraw* 'receive' do not work the same way.

(27)   **Boku-wa Taroo-ni hon-o asu yar-ta.*
            '*I gave Taroo a book tomorrow.'

(28)   *Boku-wa Taroo-ni hon-o asu moraw-ta.
              '*I received a book from Taroo tomorrow.')

Ambiguity thus arises when there is more than one subject in the underlying representation as in (29), where the phrase *zibun-no isi-de* 'of one's own will' modifies either the matrix sentence or the embedded sentence, reflexivizing either *boku* 'I' or *Taroo*. Thus, the *reflexivization* under discussion concerns identical noun phrases, as the *do-so* rule concerns with identical verb phrases.

(29)   *Boku-wa Taroo-ni zibun-no isi-de tabako-o*
              yame-ru koto-o susume-ta.
              'I advised Taroo to quit smoking volun-

              tarily $\left(\text{of} \begin{Bmatrix} \text{his} \\ \text{my} \end{Bmatrix} \text{own will}\right)$.'

Now if the phrase *zibun-no isi-de* is introduced in sentences with a causative phrase, the same ambiguity arises as observed in:

(30)   a.   *Syusyoo-wa osyoku-su-ta daigisi-o zibun-no*
              isi-de sin-sase-ta.
          (i) 'The prime minister voluntarily (of his own
               will) made a bribed Dietman die.'
          (ii) 'The prime minister brought it about that a
               bribed Dietman died voluntarily.'

         b.   *Hahaoya-wa musume-o zibun-no isi-de*
              zyosidai-ni hair-sase-ta.
          (i) 'The mother voluntarily made her daughter
               enter a women's college.'
          (ii) 'The mother brought it about that her
               daughter entered a women's college
               voluntarily.'

         c.   *Syatyoo-wa munoo-na butyoo-o butyoo-no*
              isu-kara zibun-no isi-de ori-sase-ta.
          (i) 'The president (of a company) voluntarily
               made an incompetent division head step
               down from his position.'
          (ii) 'The president brought it about that an in-
               competent division head stepped down
               from his position voluntarily.'

The ambiguity again shows that a causative verb phrase is derived from an embedding underlying structure.[1] It follows from this that if a lexicalized causative verb were derived from a similar embedding structure with two subject noun phrases, the same ambiguity would again be expected to hold when the phrase *zibun-no isi-de* was introduced. The sentences with a lexicalized verb in (31) correspond to their respective sentences in (30), but the expected ambiguity again does not arise.

(31)   a. *Syusyoo-wa osyoku-su-ta daigisi-o zibun-no isi-de koros-ta.*
            'The prime minister killed a bribed Dietman voluntarily.'

        b. *Hahaoya-wa musume-o zibun-no isi-de zyosidai-ni ire-ta.*
            'The mother enrolled (make enter) her daughter in a women's college voluntarily.'

        c. *Syatyoo-wa munoo-na butyoo-o zibun-no isi-de butyoo-no isu-kara oros-ta.*
            'The president demoted (bring down from the position of division head) an incompetent division head voluntarily.'

Thus, the phenomenon of *reflexivization* gives another piece of negative evidence for the presence of an embedding structure, giving rise to a lexicalized causative verb. [Exactly the same argument against deriving *koros* from *sin-SASE* on the basis of Japanese reflexivization has been independently developed by Susumu Kuno in his paper (Kuno, 1971).]

As alluded to earlier, a major class of evidence for the kind of semantic representation proposed by Lakoff and McCawley comes from the notion of 'modification.' McCawley (1972, p. 3:18) notes: "The existence of a constituent in a semantic representation can be demon-

---

[1] In the Osaka dialect of Japanese, the sentences in (30) are ambiguous in three ways. The reflexive pronoun may refer to the subject of the embedded sentence, that of the matrix sentence, and that of the hypersentence, 'I say to you,' namely the speaker. Take a simplex sentence:

(i) *Taroo-wa zibun-o nagur-ta.*

The sentence means either 'Taroo hit me (speaker)' or 'Taroo hit himself.' The behavior of the reflexive pronoun *zibun* in the Osaka dialect thus supports Ross's analysis of performative sentences. Notice in this connection that Japanese *reflexivization* takes place across clause boundaries.

strated by showing that it is possible for an adverb to modify the piece of semantic structure, e.g. to modify not *John killed Harry* but *Harry not be alive*, or some other part of its meaning." I will now show that in Japanese the notion of 'modification' argues counter to McCawley's case.

The manner adverbs such as *isoi-de* 'hastily' and *mugon-de* 'silently' create ambiguity when introduced in sentences with a causative verb phrase as shown in:

(32)   a. *Taroo-wa Ziroo-o isoi-de tomar-sase-ta.*
            (i) 'Taroo hastily made Ziroo stop.'
            (ii) 'Taroo brought it about that Ziroo stopped hastily.'

         b. *Taroo-wa Ziroo-o mugon-de heya-ni hair-sase-ta.*
            (i) 'Taroo silently made Ziroo enter the room.'
            (ii) 'Taroo brought it about that Ziroo entered the room silently.'

Now if a lexicalized verb were derived from the same type of embedding structure as a causative verb phrase, and if McCawley's conjecture about the scope of modification were correct, we should get the same ambiguous sentences even if we replaced the verb phrases of the sentences in (32) by their corresponding lexicalized causative verbs. But if we actually replace the causative phrases *tomar-sase* 'make . . . stop' and *hair-sase* 'make . . . enter' by their corresponding lexicalized verbs *tome* 'stop(tr.)' and *ire* 'bring in' the expected ambiguity does not arise as shown in

(33)   a. *Taroo-wa Ziroo-o isoi-de tome-ta.*
            'Taroo stopped Ziroo hastily.'

         b. *Taroo-wa Ziroo-o mugon-de heya-ni ire-ta.*
            'Taroo brought Ziroo into the room silently.'

The time adverbs such as *sibarakusi-te* 'after a while' and *zyuuzi-ni* 'at ten o'clock' argue against McCawley's hypothesis in Japanese as well as in English. Thus, while (34a) and (35a) are ambiguous as to which event the time adverbs modify, the corresponding sentences with a lexicalized causative verb are not, as shown in (34b) and (35b).

(34)   a. *Taroo-wa Hanako-o sibarakusi-te sin-sase-ta*
            'Taroo caused Hanako to die after a while.'

         b. *Taroo-wa Hanako-o sibarakusi-te koros-ta.*
            'Taroo killed Hanako after a while.'

(35)   a. *Taroo-wa Hanako-o zyuuzi-ni sin-sase-ta.*
            'Taroo caused Hanako to die at ten o'clock.'

        b. *Taroo-wa Hanako-o zyuuzi-ni koros-ta.*
            'Taroo killed Hanako at ten o'clock.'

Moreover, we can construct a sentence that becomes well formed
only when an adverbial phrase in it is interpreted as modifying the
embedded sentence, and see how this argues for McCawley's claim.
Sentence (36a) is well-formed, for the adverbial phrase *ryo0ude-o
tukaw-te* 'using both arms' can be interpreted as modifying the embedded sentence namely, *Taroo-ga ki-kara ori-ru* 'Taroo comes down
from the tree,' and *ryooude* 'both arms' referring to both of Taroo's
arms. The corresponding sentence with a lexicalized causative verb
(36b), however, turns out to be ill formed, which means the adverbial
phrase in question cannot be interpreted as modifying anything but
the matrix sentence, that is, it denies the presence of the putative embedded sentence:

(36)   a. *Ryooude-no nai otoko-ga Taroo-o ki-kara
            ryooude-o tukaw-te ori-sase-ta.*
            'An armless man brought it about that Taroo
            came down from the tree using both arms.'

        b. **Ryooude-no nai otoko-ga Taroo-o ki-kara
            ryooude-o tukaw-te oros-ta.*
            '*An armless man brought Taroo down from the
            tree using both arms.'

Since McCawley believes that the notion of modification gives a
major class of supporting evidence for his analysis, the preceding
cases must be considered to be serious counterevidence against his
claim. In conclusion, let me stress that I by no means deny the need
for relating such lexical items as *dead, die,* and *kill* in semantic terms.
The question raised is whether it is justifiable to derive a lexicalized
causative verb from an embedding semantic structure with a higher
verb, say capital *CAUSE* (or *SASE* in Japanese) and an intransitive
sentence beneath it. Three pieces of negative evidence have been
given for the presence of an embedded sentence beneath *SASE* in
Japanese. Now the burden of proof rests on those who claim that there
is such an embedding semantic structure that gives rise to a lexicalized
causative verb.

ACKNOWLEDGMENT

The preparation of this paper was in part supported by a Grace W. Drake scholarship of the University of California. I am grateful to Wallace L. Chafe, John Crothers, Richard Stanley, and Leonard Talmy for discussing the topics covered in this paper. Special thanks are due to my wife Noriko Shibatani for helping me compile example sentences.

REFERENCES

Fodor, J. A. 1970. Three reasons for not deriving 'kill' from 'cause to die.' Linguistic Inquiry 1/4.429–438.

Katz, J. J. 1970. Interpretive semantics vs. generative semantics. Foundations of Language, 6.220–259.

Kuno, S. 1971. The reflexive pronoun and the passive and causative constructions. Unpublished: Harvard University.

Lakoff, G. 1970. Irregularity in Syntax. Holt, New York.

McCawley, J. D. 1968. Lexical insertion in a transformational grammar without deep structure. Papers from the fourth regional meeting, Chicago Linguistic Society. Pp. 71–80 (B. J. Darden et al., eds.)

McCawley, J. D. 1972. Syntactic and logical arguments for semantic structures. Proceedings of the Fifth International Seminar on Theoretical Linguistics. Tec Co., Tokyo. In press.

Morgan, J. L. 1970. On arguing about semantics. Papers in Linguistics 1/1.49–70.

Shibatani, M. 1972. Semantics of Japanese causativization. Foundations of language. In press.

KAC AND SHIBATANI ON THE GRAMMAR OF KILLING

JAMES D. MC CAWLEY
University of Chicago

Kac argues that the ambiguity of

(1)   *John almost killed Fred.*

is not an ambiguity of scope; that is, it is not an ambiguity as to what constituent of the logical structure of (1) *almost* applies to, but an ambiguity in the word *kill* between an action sense and a result sense. His chief piece of evidence for this conclusion is that

(2)   *That John killed Fred surprised me.*

which contains no element such as *almost* whose scope might be varying, is ambiguous in the same way as is (1): it might express either surprise that John did what he did or surprise that John's action accomplished what it did. The analysis that has a single complex *kill* would thus provide only one source for (2); the analysis that has two different simple *kill*s would provide two sources for (2), whence Kac rejects the former analysis in favor of the latter.

I maintain, however, that *John killed Fred* in (2) behaves exactly the same as syntactically complex unambiguous sentences do. For example,

(3)   *That John forced Shirley to polish his shoes surprised me.*

is ambiguous as to whether it refers to surprise at John's doing what he did, or surprise at John's forcing Shirley to do what he forced her to do. I would indeed maintain that the complement of *surprise* involves an element whose scope can vary, namely topicization — in one interpretation of (2), the topic of the embedded sentence is "what happened," and in the other it is "what John did". The action–result ambiguity Kac sees in

(4)   *John killed Fred.*

appears also to be an ambiguity as to what the topic is, not an ambiguity in the verb *kill*.

Kac also claims that (1) is only two ways ambiguous, not three ways, citing as evidence that his informants could not detect any meaning difference between the second and third of three sentence that match the trees I had suggested (McCawley, 1968) as underlying (1):

(5)   a. *John almost caused Fred to become not alive.*
           b. *John caused Fred to almost become not alive.*
           c. *John caused Fred to become almost not alive.*

In proposing the structure:

(6)

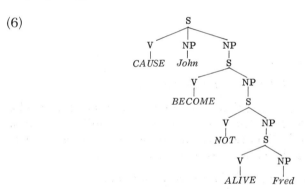

I was guilty of gross inconsistency, since the paraphrases that I had given for the three senses of (1):

(7)a. *John almost did something that would have killed Fred.*
   b. *John did something that came close to causing Fred to die.*
   c. *John did something that brought Fred close to death.*

in fact do not match the three possible scopes for *almost* in (6). In McCawley (1972), I argue for an underlying structure matching (7), that is, one involving a notion of "doing," which is a relation between a person and an action, and a notion of "causation," which is a relation between an action or event and an event — not between a person and an event as in (6):

(8)

```
                        S₀
              ┌─────────┼─────────┐
          V      NP         NP
          │      │        ╱    ╲
         DO    John    NP      S₁
                        │    ╱    ╲
                        x   V    NP      NP
                            │     │      │
                          CAUSE   x      S₂
                          effect      ╱    ╲
                                     V      NP
                                     │      │
                                  BECOME    S₃
                                         ╱    ╲
                                        V      NP
                                        │      │
                                       NOT     S₄
                                            ╱    ╲
                                           V      NP
                                           │      │
                                         ALIVE   Fred
```

It is not clear whether (8) commits me to the claim that (1) is not three but four ways ambiguous, since

(9)   *John almost died last night.*

appears to refer only to John's becoming almost dead, not to something happening that was close to an event of his dying (such as a bullet just barely missing him); it may be that S_2 is not a possible scope for *almost* in (8), in which case there would be only three possible scopes for *almost* [see below for why S_4 is not a possible scope for the *almost* of (1)]. If so, that would explain why Kac's informants could not distinguish between the senses of (5b) and (5c); they would then correspond to the same semantic structure and would differ only to the extent that in (5b) raising of *almost* would have taken place.

In addition, sentences such as

(10)   *John almost almost killed Fred.*

are possible, though admittedly not elegant, in describing John's being on the verge of beating Fred to within an inch of his life. If the scope of *almost* must be a clause, then (10) requires an embedded sentence to provide the scope of the second *almost*.

The lack of ambiguity in

(11)   *John almost murdered Fred.*

can probably be explained within this theoretical framework in terms of the semantic structure of *murder* and the conditions under which Morgan's *adverb-raising* rule applies. Morgan has noted that in any case, *almost* cannot be moved over negatives and that such a restriction on its movement explains why (1) cannot be understood as meaning "John caused Fred to cease to be almost alive" (for plausibility, replace *John* and *Fred* by *Dr. Frankenstein* and *the monster*, respectively). The case of *assassinate* is discussed in McCawley (1972), where it is noted that:

(12)   *John almost assassinated Spiro.*

unambiguously refers to John's almost committing the act and that

(13)   **FDR was miraculously brought back to life, and then George Wallace assássinated him agàin.*

is ungrammatical, as contrasted with

(14)   *Franz Liszt was miraculously brought back to life, and then Karlheinz killed him agàin.*

which indicate that *almost* and *again* cannot be raised over the higher predicate that links the "John kill Spiro" part of *John assassinated Spiro* to the reason clause, which is incorporated into *assassinate* [see Gallagher (1970) and McCawley (1972) for observations on the semantic structure of *assassinate*]. One piece of evidence supporting the claim that (14) has an underlying structure in which *again* modifies a clause such as "Franz Liszt die," is that the destressing of *again* in (14) — note that if *again* were stressed, it would refer to a second killing, whereas (14) merely refers to a second death — is matched by destressing in parallel sentences, in which the hypothesized subordinate clause is actually manifested in surface structure as in

(15)   a.   *Franz Liszt was miraculously brought back to life, and then Karlheinz caused him to die agáin.*
        b.   *Franz Liszt was miraculously brought back to life, and then Karlheinz caused him to die again.*

The *again* of (15a) is ambiguous as to whether it refers to *die* or to *cause to die*, but the *again* of (15b) unambiguously refers to *die*. This is exactly the paradigm predicted by the assumption that stress is assigned by the *nuclear stress* rule, but raised adverbs are destressed; the two interpretations of (15a), which have different immediate constituent structures, as evidenced by possibilities of making pauses, correspond to *again* originating in either of the two clauses and not being raised.

Finally, I maintain that the notions of action and result that Kac uses are not appropriately represented in semantic structure by features on a verb, since they are in fact relations rather than simple properties; an action is what an agent does and a result is what results from an action. A tree representation such as (8) indicates in a natural way the manner in which agent and action, and cause and effect fit into the meaning of clauses with *kill*. The use of feature representations in syntax, while remarkably ubiquitous, has never been given anywhere near adequate justification, and until such justification is given, their use should be regarded as suspect. Kac has not demonstrated any advantage of his proposal over an alternative which appears to provide a reasonably simple and coherent account of the phenomena in question in terms of descriptive devices whose necessity in grammatical theory is beyond question.

Shibatani (in this volume) argues that derived causative verbs and lexicalized causative verbs in Japanese display radically different behavior: that the differences indicate in every case that underlying structures of clauses containing the former have embedded clauses, but underlying structures of clauses containing the latter do not. On the contrary, there are cases where clauses with lexicalized causatives show evidence of a complex source; they allow adverbs that modify not the entire clause but part of the complement of a hypothetical verb of causation. This gives reason for setting up such underlying structures, but does not in itself provide any answer to the question of why the various adverbs discussed by Shibatani can in fact only modify the main and not the hypothesized subordinate clause. A partial answer to this question will emerge from the following argument that the relation between a lexicalized causative (such as *nokos-* 'leave behind') and a corresponding intransitive (*nokor-* 'remain') differs from that of a derived causative (such as *kir-ase-* 'cause to cut') and the corresponding simple verb (*kir-* 'cut').

In the following examples,[1] various lexicalized causatives discussed by Shibatani are combined with adverbs that modify not them but a part of their meanings:

(16)   a.   *Boku wa musuko o gakkoo ni **sibaraku** nokosita.*
            'I left my son at the school **for a while**.'

       b.   *Saibantyoo wa Ari o **ninenkan** rooya ni ireta.*
            'The judge put Ali in prison **for two years**.'

       c.   *Boku wa **yuubinkyoku e iku aida** musuko o kuruma
            kara orosita.*
            'I let my son out of the car **while I went to the post
            office**.'

[1] I am grateful to Noriko Akatsuka, Masako Inoue, Masaaki Yamanashi, and Naomi Hanaoka for providing me with examples and valuable discussion of the matters treated here.

    d. *Nakasima wa battingu-abereezi ga warukatta no de*
        *rain-appu kara **issyuukan** orosareta.*
        'Nakashima was dropped from the lineup **for a week**
        because his batting average was bad.'

Sibaraku 'a while' in (16a) gives the length of time that the son is to be
in school, not the length of time over which my action of leaving him
there takes place; and similarly with (16b–d). Note, however, that
except possibly in the case of (16a), what is being said to be for "a
while," "two years," etc. is not describable with the corresponding
intransitive verb *hair-* 'enter,' *ori-* 'get off, step down'; one week is not
the length of time for which the manager's dropping Nakashima from
the lineup takes place, but rather the length of time for which his
being out of the lineup takes place. Thus, (16) provides reason for
deriving clauses containing *nokos-*, *ire-*, and *oros-* from structures
containing "x be in y" or "x not be in y," which are of course part of
the meaning of clauses with *nokor-*, *hair-*, and *ori-*, but they do not
provide support for the proposal Shibatani was arguing against,
namely, that they are derived from structures containing all of what
goes into the meanings of *nokor-*, *hair-*, and *ori-*. Shibatani has provided examples that show that many of the intransitives have something in their meaning that is not in the meaning of a corresponding
lexicalized causative; for example, the embedded clause in Shibatani's
*-ed (13b):

(17)   *Nimotu ga kuruma kara orita.*
            'The baggage got out of the car.'

illustrates the fact that *ori-* refers to the subject not merely ceasing to
be in the vehicle (or role or job) but doing something that results in his
ceasing to be in the vehicle or job.[2] Note also that there is more here
than just a restriction that the subject of *ori-* be animate; it is inap-
propriate to say

(18)   *Tatibana-san ga kuruma kara orita.*
           'Mr. Tachibana got out of the car.'

if Mr. Tachibana is paralyzed and has to be lifted out of the car. Two
further differences between lexical causative *oros-* and derived causative *ori-sase-*, which Shibatani cites, follow from an analysis in which
ori- is derived from a structure whose main verb is "do" and *oros-* is
derived from a structure containing some causative verb plus a com-

---

[2] One exception to this for which I have no explanation is that *Nimotu ga orite imasu*
is appropriate if said of baggage being brought from a plane to waiting passengers.

plement that consists of the content of *ori-* minus the higher "do" clause. First, the impossibility of the *soo* of

(19)   *Boku wa musuko o kuruma kara orosita, suruto Hanako*
         mo soo sita.
         'I let my son out of the car and Hanako did so, too.'

referring to "Hanako get out of the car" follows from the above proposal provided that *soo suru* 'do so' is derived from pronominalization of the complement of *suru* 'do.' Such a treatment of *soo suru* appears to be both feasible and necessary, since (just as in English; see Ross, 1972) this *suru* appears only in sentences derived through pronominalization or deletion in a clause that refers to an action:

(20)   a.   **Taroo wa kega o sita, suru to Ziroo mo soo sita.*
            'Taro received an injury and Jiro did so too.'

       b.   *Hanako ga sita no wa todana o katazukeru koto da.*
            'What Hanako did was to clean out the cupboard.'

       c.   **Hanako ga sita no wa kega o suru koto da.*
            'What Hanako did was received an injury.'

Since the hypothesized embedded sentence in (19) does not contain *suru*, it could not yield *soo sita*. Second, *zibun no isi de* 'by (self)'s own will' can only be combined with a clause of the type that would be analyzed as having the main verb *suru*:

(21)   a.   **Taroo wa zibun no isi de kega o sita.*
                'Taro willingly received an injury.'

           b.   **Taroo wa zibun no isi de gan de sinda.*
                'Taro willingly died of cancer.'

Hence, my suggestion for the analysis of *oros-* would involve an embedded sentence that would not provide the conditions for the use of *zibun no isi de*, from which follows the fact noted by Shibatani that in

(22)   *Syatyoo wa munoo na butyoo o butyoo no isu kara*
         zibun no isi de orosita.
         'The president willingly removed an incompetent divi-
         sion head from his position.'

zibun refers unambiguously to *syatyoo* '(company) president,' whereas in a sentence with *orisaseta* in place of *orosita*, it is ambiguous as to whether it refers to *syatyoo* or to *munoo na butyoo* 'incompetent division head.'

However, there are better examples for making the point that Shibatani was making with (22). The explanation of why (22) does not allow *zibun* to refer to *munoo na butyoo* is based on facts about *isi*, not on facts about *zibun*, and examples can be constructed in which this revised analysis appears to give spurious applications of *zibun-pronominalization* (*reflexivization*). For example, *zibun* in

(23)   *Boku wa Taroo o zibun no kuruma kara orosita.*
         'I let Taro out of (self)'s car.'

cannot refer to Taro, but since this analysis has an embedded sentence "Taro not be in Taro's car" and *reflexivization* is a cyclic rule involving a condition of identity with the subject of the clause to which it is applying, *reflexivization* appears to be applicable to that clause in the derivation of (23). There is no explanation at present of why *reflexivization* is not applicable here, but there exists a recently discovered and as yet poorly understood class of facts in Japanese for which an attractive but programmatic analysis has been suggested. If this can be made precise, it may provide an explanation for the non-application of *reflexivization* here. Kuno (1972) discusses cases where sentences of apparently identical syntactic structure differ in the applicability of *reflexivization*, the difference correlating with whether the NP to be pronominalized originates in a clause which reflects the point of view of the person referred to by the antecedent NP; for example,

(24)   a.   *Zyon wa, zibun ga komatta toki dake, boku ni*
              denwa o kakete kuru.
              'John calls me up only when he is in trouble.'

         b.   **Zyon wa, zibun ga sinda toki, issen mo motte*
              imasen desita.
              'John didn't have a penny when he died.'

An especially clear case of such a difference is provided by sentences with an embedded benefactive construction. The benefactive construction involves a verb of giving, whose choice depends on the identities and relative status of the benefactor and recipient. In a simple sentence describing a favor done by someone for a person of equal status, *kure-* is used if the recipient is the speaker, *yar-* if the recipient is someone else. In a complex sentence, it is sometimes possible to choose the verb of giving from the point of view of either the speaker or some person mentioned in the sentence, as in the following example:

(25)   *Taroo wa Ziroo ga kakumatte kureta/yatta ie o syuuzen*
         site iru.

'Taro is repairing the house which Jiro did him the favor
of sheltering him in.'

In (25), the object of *kakumaw-* is deleted by a pronominalization
rule, which is seen to be applicable regardless of whether the relative
clause is presented from Taro's point of view (*kureta*) or the speaker's
(*yatta*). However, only in the former case can the object of *kakumaw-*
be reflexivized:

(26)   *Taroo wa Ziroo ga zibun o kakumatte kureta/*yatta ie o
         syuuzen site iru.*
        'Taro is repairing the house which Jiro did him the favor
        of sheltering him in.'

When this vague notion of point of view is made precise, will it preclude the possibility of the hypothetical embedded sentence in (23)
expressing the point of view of its (nonagent) subject? This I cannot
yet answer; not enough is known at present about reflexives and point
of view even to say whether that conjecture is plausible. If it does not
pan out, then Shibatani has a good argument against my proposals.

I have so far treated mainly *ori-*. Not all the other intransitives that
are paired with lexicalized causatives involve a semantic structure
with "do," for example, *tomar-* 'stop' can take such subjects as *enzin*
'engine.' A detailed enough study of the other verbs in Shibatani's list
(8) has not yet been made to determine the extent to which they provide problems. Contrary to what Shibatani states, not all derived
causatives require "that the subject of the embedded sentence under
Sase . . . be something which has its own volition":

(27)   a.   *Taroo wa enzin o tometa.*
             'Taro stopped the engine.'

        b.   *Taroo wa enzin o tomaraseta.*
             'Taro made the engine stop.' (*-ed by Shibatani)

are both grammatical, and they differ in meaning in an interesting way.
Tomar- refers to a "normal" way of stopping something and *tomar-ase-*
is required for stopping something by force. For example, while:

(28)   *Kagi de enzin o tometa/tomaraseta.*
        '(He) stopped the engine with the key.'

are both possible, *tometa* would be appropriate only for turning the
engine off with the key, and *tomaraseta* only for throwing the key into
the engine so as to jam the machinery. Similarly, *tomaraseta* and not
tometa would have to be used in describing someone's applying a
tourniquet to stop the flow of blood from a wound. These facts indicate

that different notions of causation are involved in lexicalized causatives than in derived causatives; the little that I have to say about
such notions of causation is presented in McCawley (1972).

One fact worth citing in support of the claim that there is some relationship between intransitives and associated lexicalized causatives
(albeit not a relation of inclusion) is the existence of pairs of idioms
such as:

(29)   *kado ga tatu*   'a difficulty arises'
       kado o tateru   'cause a difficulty'
       ki ga tuku   'notice'
       ki o tukeru   'pay attention'
       bake no kawa ga hageru 'be exposed (as a fraud)'
       bake no kawa o hagu   'expose (as a fraud)'
       yori ga modoru   'be reunited'
       yori o modosu   'reunite'

in which the idiom with the lexicalized causative verb is a causative
of the other idiom. If there is in fact a systematic relationship between
such pairs of idioms, one way to build it into the grammar is to allow
lexical insertion to insert an idiom when the cycle applies to one
clause, after which *predicate raising* could adjoin the verb of the idiom
to the predicate of the next higher clause. I have suggested such an
interpretation of the parallelism between idioms with *come* and *bring*
(discussed in Binnick, 1971). *Bring* replaces a combination of an abstract causative verb plus the English word *come* derived by *predicate
raising*. However, I have not been able to reconcile this suggestion
with what I said above about not all of the meaning of *ori-* being contained in the meaning of *oros-*, and hence of *oros-* not being equal to
CAUSE + ori-.

Finally, regarding the word *koros-* 'kill,' I have not been able to
construct Japanese analogs to the two good arguments that I know for
lexical decomposition of *kill*, which involve *almost* and *again* modifying pieces of its meaning. The chief conclusion arrived at after some
examination of Japanese translations of sentences with expressions
like *almost kill* is that the supposed equivalent of *almost* is not really
equivalent to it. The supposed Japanese translation of *John almost
died:*

(30)   *Zyon wa moo sukosi de   sinu tokoro datta.*
       more a little with   die place   was

is appropriate to describe a situation in which nothing actually happens to John, but he might very well have died (that is, a bullet misses

him), whereas *John almost died* is not appropriate to express that. Thus, for the time being, there are no arguments for lexical decomposition of *koros-*. However, a syntactic theory involving lexical decomposition seems to have stood up sufficiently well so far in the analysis of English and Japanese, which suggests that further examination of Japanese will produce such arguments.

REFERENCES

Binnick, Robert I. 1971. *Bring* and *come*. Linguistic Inquiry 2:260–265.

Gallagher, Mary. 1970. Does meaning grow on trees? Studies presented to Robert B. Lees by his students (J. Sadock and A. Vanek, eds.), Linguistic Research, Inc., Edmonton and Champaign. 79–93.

Kuno, Susumu. 1972. Pronominalization, reflexivization, and direct discourse. Linguistic Inquiry 3:167–195.

McCawley, James D. 1968. Lexical insertion in a transformational grammar without deep structures. Chicago Linguistic Society 4:71–80.

McCawley, James D. 1972. Syntactic and logical arguments for semantic structure. Proceedings of the Fifth International Seminar on Theoretical Linguistics. TEC Co., Tokyo.

Ross, John Robert. 1972. Act. Semantics of natural language (D. Davidson and G. Harman, eds.), Reidel, Dordrecht, Netherlands. Pp. 70–126.

REPLY TO McCAWLEY

MICHAEL B. KAC
University of Minnesota

McCawley presents three major substantive arguments against my
claims: (a) that it can indeed be demonstrated that scope is involved
in the ambiguities observed; (b) that phenomena involving the use
of *again* suggest the reality of an underlying embedded source for
kill; and (c) that in any event the prelexical proposal operates "in
terms of descriptive devices whose necessity in grammatical theory
is beyond question," whereas my proposal does not. I will deal with
these claims in order.

THE QUESTION OF SCOPE

McCawley first suggests that the ambiguity of:

(1)   *That John killed Fred surprised me.*

is, contrary to my argument, one of scope. He notes, first, that the
complement of (1) behaves "exactly the same way that syntactically
complex unambiguous sentences do." He points out, for example,
that in:

(2)   *That John forced Shirley to polish his shoes surprised me.*

what is surprising is either (a) that John would do what he did or
(b) that Shirley would do what he forced her to do. He proposes to

151

account for this fact by introducing an element he calls topicization (henceforth "TOPIC") into the underlying representation. Then, depending on whether it is associated with a higher or lower sentence, the appropriate sense is marked. Thus, he concludes, the ambiguity of (1) can be appropriately handled in terms of scope variation of some terminal element.

But the logic of this claim is not valid. All McCawley in fact shows is that **if** there is a prelexical element TOPIC, then (1) is indeed scope-ambiguous. But in the absence of any independent justification for the claim that this element exists, the argument is vacuous. That is to say, the only motivation given so far for a treatment in terms of scope of TOPIC is just the desire to claim that (1) shows ambiguity of scope. So in essence, no claim is made at all.

Not that this is the only problem. What is this thing "TOPIC"? On what basis could any independent evidence be provided as to its existence or syntactic properties? Note also, that in cases like the original *almost* example,

(3)   *John almost killed Fred.*

McCawley's proposal has rather peculiar consequences. If (1) and (3) are to be given a uniform account, then we would expect (3) also to have underlying sources showing variation in the scope of TOPIC. But in this case, we also have parallel variation in the scope of *almost*, so that inclusion of TOPIC is redundant in this instance. And yet to exclude TOPIC from (3), or from its underlying representations, would preclude just the uniform account we want. Then we would also need some kind of special machinery to exclude configurations like the following:

(4)

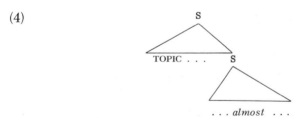

since the position of *almost* determines that of TOPIC. Finally, there was an argument in my original paper, which McCawley chose to ignore, but which has some importance relative to this question. I pointed out that:

(5)   *The bullet killed Fred.*

is unambiguous and that this has a natural explanation under the action–result analysis, since inanimate subjects cannot be said to perform actions. In the prelexical analysis we would need some crazy restriction on the scope of *almost* in such situations. But clearly there is an analogous argument with respect to TOPIC. Thus, for the sentence

(6)   *That the bullet killed Fred surprised me.*

we would have to have a similar arbitrary scope restriction, prohibiting TOPIC from occuring outside the lower sentence of the prelexical complement source.

It is possible that (6) might seem ambiguous on the grounds that the speaker could be expressing surprise because of the extremely small caliber of the bullet involved (or some other property specifically associated with the weapon) or because Fred's death was unlikely because of his known constitutional strength. Thus, it might be claimed, no restriction on TOPIC would be required in the case of (6). But this is not quite right. One could, for example, translate the first sense cited into the terms of the second. Thus, surprise could be due to such a small bullet causing such a strong man to die. It is, in other words, still the result (or the effect) that is at issue. I would prefer to say, therefore, that (6) is vague as to what the basis of the result/effect might be, but unambiguous on the side of the result rather than the action sense of *kill*.

The question remains as to how the action–result analysis would deal with cases like (2). The answer seems straightforward enough. I would maintain that the verb *force* (and the verb *cause* as well) can have both action and result interpretations. This is supported by the fact that both of the following are indeed ambiguous:

(7)   *John almost forced Shirley to shine his shoes.*

(8)   *John almost caused Fred to die.*

If this is so, notice that it is thus possible to account for the parallelism between sentences with *kill* and sentences with *cause to die* without recourse to a transformational derivation of the latter from the former.

The major advantage I would claim for the action–result analysis, then, is that it is both comprehensive and natural. McCawley's attempt to save the prelexical analysis by means of the arbitrary element TOPIC nonetheless fails to produce an analysis having these properties. In short, the facts point to a semantic phenomenon not reducible to a purely syntactic treatment (via arbitrary terminal elements in syntactic trees), and the action–result analysis is consistent with this irreducibility.

CASES WITH *AGAIN*

McCawley then proceeds to an argument involving sentences like:

(9) *Franz Liszt was miraculously brought back to life, and then
     Karlheinz kílled him agàin.*

The claim here is that the unstressed *again* can only refer to a second
death, not a second killing. A parallel claim is made for the putative
underlying structure:

(10) *Franz Liszt was miraculously brought back to life, and
      then Karlheinz caused him to díe agàin.*

It is observed that:

(11)   a. . . . kílled him agáin.
                      b. . . . caused him to díe agáin.

show parallel ambiguities. It is then noted that the unstressed *again*
in (9)–(10) can be accounted for by the part of the *nuclear stress rule,*
which destresses raised adverbs if it is assumed that it has been
brought up out of a lower sentence.

The claim that *again* is a raised adverb requires both that we have
a clear conception of what an adverb is and that *again* be known to
belong in the class. Both of these matters are currently problematical,
and hence, the claim, while interesting, can hardly be considered
conclusive.

More significantly, it does not seem to me to be the case that an
unstressed *again* need always have the significance McCawley asso-
ciates with it. Thus the following conversation is wholly plausible:

(12) *Did you hear about what happened when Abraham Lin-
      coln was resurrected?
      Nope. What happened?
      That SOB Booth kílled him agàin.*

It is possible in this context to interpret the contour / ´ ` / as expressing
the fact that the speaker does not necessarily find it surprising that
Booth should still be up to his old tricks. But it is also quite clear
that the speaker can be understood to be talking about a second killing. The difference between this case and McCawley's has to do with
an irrelevancy, namely, that we know that Franz Liszt died of natural
causes while Lincoln did not. Consequently, I do not see that the
stressing or destressing of *again* has any direct relation to the issue
at hand. This is not to deny, incidentally, that there is an important
question buried in all this. Compare the sentences:

(13)   a.   *Fred opened the door and then John clósed it agàin.*
       b.   *Fred opened the door and then John clòsed it agáin.*

In (13b), it is presupposed that John has closed the door at least once previously, whereas no such presupposition is made by (13a). Superficially, this suggests that there are two items both represented on the surface by *again*, one of which is associated with repetition of actions, the other denoting reattainment of some previous state. But clearly these two senses can be reduced to one if there is machinery for showing that *again* is either associated directly with the action part of the statement or with the state part. An opponent of the prelexical analysis must be able to show how, if *close* is assumed to be a simple predicate, this fact is to be captured. A proposal as to how this might be done is presented in Kac (1972).

THE ISSUE OF REPRESENTATION

McCawley's concluding remarks make three basic points:

1.   He claims that since the notion of "action" is relational, it is not appropriately represented as a feature on a single lexical element. I agree that the notion involves a relation but contend that nothing follows concerning my suggestion. A feature specification [+Action] would mean only that a verb so specified enters into that relation with its subject, the relation itself being characterized universally as one obtaining between subject and verb. I assume that this is what is generally true in systems where relations are indicated by labeling. Thus, it seems reasonable to suppose that in case grammar, for example, the case names are meant to refer to relations entered into by nominal elements and defined in universal linguistic theory.

2.   He also claims that the notion of "syntactic feature" itself has never been given adequate justification. This claim is somewhat remarkable in view of the motivating arguments that have been with us since 1965. (I cannot resist, in this regard, bringing up the matter of TOPIC again.) But the question is really beside the point in any event. It is ultimately of no importance whether action and result valences are represented by binary features, by Chafe's (1971) system (in which there are minuses but no pluses), by Katz–Fodor (1963) semantic markers, or by any of a number of other systems that might be created for the purpose. What is at issue is the question of whether or not we want to treat verbs like *kill* in "transformationalist" or "lexicalist" terms. Just what formalism a proponent of the lexicalist alternative chooses is a subsidiary question of no apparent major import.

3. Finally, McCawley defends the prelexical hypothesis on the grounds that it makes use only of devices which are known to be needed in linguistic descriptions anyway, such as phrase structure rules and transformations. Hence, he finds it preferable to my proposed alternative. But this kind of criterion is only valid if the approaches being compared are equal in other respects. It is just this situation that I deny exists, claiming empirically that it is the action–result analysis that is the preferable alternative. The entire point of my paper was to show that the empirical consequences of the prelexical explanation of the facts were in certain respects undesirable and that the problems could be obviated by adherence to a different approach. I still feel that this position is justified, whence I conclude that however necessary syntactic rules are to grammatical description, they do not provide the appropriate mechanism for dealing with the phenomena under consideration.

REFERENCES

Chafe, W. 1971. Meaning and the Structure of Language. Chicago: University of Chicago Press.

Kac, M. B. 1972. Formal aspects of semantic representation. Doctoral Dissertation, University of California, Los Angeles.

Katz, J. J. and Fodór, J. A. The structure of a semantic theory. Language 39:170–210.

DOUBL-ING[1]

JOHN ROBERT ROSS
Massachusetts Institute of Technology

In this paper, I will investigate a type of grammatical ill-formedness that is traceable to the repetition, under certain specified conditions, of present participles. Thus we find that the verb *continue*, which normally admits both infinitival and participial complements (1a, b), cannot occur with participles if it is in the present progressive — cf. the contrast between (1c) and (1d).

(1) a. *It continued to rain.*
     b. *It continued raining.*
     c. *It is continuing to rain.*
     d. **It is continuing raining.*

I will attempt to show that what accounts for this violation is a global rule, in the sense of Lakoff (1970a), a rule which must be formulated in such a way as to link certain features of remote structure (this term is from Postal, 1970a) to certain features of surface structure. The

[1] This work was supported in part by a grant from the National Institute of Mental Health (Number 5-PO1-MH 13390-05) and by a grant from the National Science Foundation (Number GS-3202). A version of this paper was presented at the Conference on the English Verb, organized by the Center for Applied Linguistics, at Harper's Ferry, West Virginia, Mary 1969.

I would like to thank a number of friends for their criticisms and suggestions: Bruce Fraser, Ken Hale, George Lakoff, and Paul Postal. Any errors that may remain are due to sunspots.

157

relevant rule thus has as a component an output condition, in the sense of Perlmutter (1970a) and Ross (1967). In the next section, I will give a brief demonstration of the necessity of providing sufficient apparatus in the theory of grammar so that such static templates as output conditions can be stated in a grammar, as well as the more familiar syntactic transformations. In the following, I will show that doubl-ing violations of the sort exemplified in (1d) are not characterizable in terms of restrictions on transformations, but rather must be stated (in part) as a static filter on the output of the syntactic component. I will then attempt to refine and to state formally the requisite global rule in such a way that it is not too powerful; i.e., so that it does not stigmatize as ungrammatical a wide class of sentences containing sequences of present participles which are in fact perfectly natural. Finally, I will examine the consequences for linguistic theory of postulating such a global rule.

NECESSITY OF PROVIDING SUFFICIENT APPARATUS

There are a number of ways of showing that some grammatical violation is best accounted for by setting up an output filter, leaving all transformations unconstrained. One kind of motivation, the kind I first suggested in connection with characterizing the possible postverbal sequences of constituents in English (Ross, 1967, §3.1.1.3), consists in showing that what can be treated as a unitary phenomenon, if stated in terms of output, must be stated many times, if formulated as conditions on syntactic transformations. Put more simply, if a grammar is only a sequence of transformations, what is intuitively a unitary phenomenon must be fragmented so as to appear as a scattered set of conditions throughout the syntax. Only if a grammar can contain both static filters as well as transformations can the relevant generalization be captured.

As a case in point, let us consider the interaction of possessives and demonstratives in English. Note first that there are at least three distinct transformational sources for the possessive morpheme. These are shown in abbreviated form in (2).

(2) a. *One petal which this tulip has* ⇒ *one petal of this tulip's*
     b. *the execution of it* ⇒ *its execution*
     c. Poss + ing: *That it is unprovable* ⇒ *Its being unprovable.*

In 2(a), I have stated in abbreviated form an analysis of possessives that is at least as old as Harris (1957). While it is not necessary to accept the claim that all possessor-possessed constructions have this source, it does seem likely that at least some do. Some examples of this construction that seem likely not to derive from *have* sentences are *my lap* (cf. **the lap which I have*), and *my sister*.

Another source, at least as old as Lees (1960), and accepted by transformational grammarians of all persuasions, is illustrated schematically in (2b). The rule in question merely possessivizes and preposes to the left of certain abstract nominals any NP in an *of*-phrase that follows the nominal.

The final source, (2c), is the rule that, in the complements of certain predicates, possessivizes the subject and participializes the main verb of the complement clause. (These are largely factive predicates, in the sense of Kiparsky and Kiparsky (1970), though not exclusively these, contrary to their claim. Compare such sentences as *His having been there alone is possible/likely/doubtful.*) In Rosenbaum (1967), this process is referred to as poss + ing complementation, a usage I will adopt here.

What is important for my present purposes is the fact that none of these three processes may operate in such a way as to produce an output in which one of the demonstratives (*this, that, these, those*) is followed by the possessive morpheme, as is shown by the ungrammaticality of the examples in (3).

(3)   a.   **One petal of this's fell off.*
       b.   **That's execution was flawless.*
       c.   **These's being unprovable made Euclid cry.*

In order to capture the fact that these sentences are all deviant for the same reason, I propose the following restriction:

(4) Any surface structure analyzable as $\quad X - \begin{Bmatrix} this \\ that \\ these \\ those \end{Bmatrix} - Poss - Y$

      is ungrammatical.

There is a very interesting sense in which the constraint stated in (4) can be said to be "stupid". (This necessary terminology was discovered by Dave Perlmutter.) Namely, (4) is structure-independent. In the examples of (3), it is always the case that the demonstrative and the following constituent form an NP, but this is an accidental property of the examples. It would be incorrect to limit the applicability of (4) by requiring the second and third terms of the condition to be analyzable into an NP, as the impossibility of converting the sentences in (5) to the corresponding sentences in (5′) shows.

(5) a. *The manner which an advocate of this had was irritating.*
    b. *The discovery of a paper about that preceded my coronation.*
    c. *That proofs of these are impossible made Euclid cry.*

(5') a. **The manner of an advocate of this's was irritating.*
     b. **A paper about that's discovery preceded my coronation.*
     c. **Proofs of these's being impossible made Euclid cry.*

The ungrammaticality of these sentences shows the necessity for casting the net wide. It appears to be true that any sequence of demonstrative and possessive, no matter what its source or parsing, produces a violation. Thus, condition (4) is stupid, obtuse, scattershot. We shall see below, however, that not all output conditions have the wholesome crudeness of this one. The condition necessary to exclude violations caused by doubl-ing is refined, sophisticated, and intelligent.

Jim Herringer (personal communication) has brought to my attention evidence that even (4), alas, is not entirely stupid. Thus note that (6a, b) are both well-formed.

(6)   a. *The spelling of this is regular.*
               b. *This's spelling is regular.*

Similarly with many other examples, such as *These's being plural means further debugging, That's vowel is lax.* What this means is that some conditions must be placed on (4) to the effect that the elements in its second term must be being used demonstratively, and not metalinguistically. Thus even (4) must be a global rule, since its correct reformulation would link semantics and surface structure.

Actually, it may be possible to use Herringer's observation to cast some light on the source of such linguistically puzzling NPs as the object of *of* in (6a), if my intuitions about the grammaticality of (7) are correct.

(6')   *The word this's spelling is regular.*

That is, if (6') is grammatical, and if (6b) derives from something like (6') by way of a rule of *metalinguistic noun deletion*, then the fact that both (6b) and (7) are exceptions to (4) can be stated once—in a static stupid template, ordered before the metalinguistic noun that *this* must be assumed to modify in remote structure has been deleted.

CHARACTERIZATION OF DOUBL-ING VIOLATIONS

As a first step toward seeing that the condition involved in doubl-ing violations is connected with surface structure, observe that there are a number of distinct sources for the morpheme ing. These are summarized in (8).

(7)   a. Poss + *ing* complementation.
        b. Tense → *ing* in exclamations
        c. Tense → *ing* in relative clauses.

An example of the first type of *ing* is (1b). Examples of the second type can be seen in (8c), which must be related to (7a) by some rule that marks the subject with the oblique case, and either deletes the tense entirely, as in (7b), or replaces it with *ing*.[2]

(8)   a. *He likes blintzes.*
        b. *Him like blintzes!?*
        c. *Him liking blintzes!?*

It is possible, though I have no proof of this at present, that the *ing* of sentences like (8c) will eventually be reducible to the *ing* of Poss + *ing* complementation, if it can be demonstrated that a deeper, performative analysis of such sentences as (8b) and (8c) is independently necessary. (CF. Ross, 1970b, for an exposition of the performative analysis of declaratives.) That is, since the verb *exclaim* is a verb that takes Poss + *ing* complementizers, as (9a) shows, the underlying structure of (8b) and (8c) may be roughly that shown in (9b). One fact, in addition to complementizer choice, that supports this proposal, is that just as *exclaim* is a factive predicate, so exclamations presuppose the truth of the state of affairs they describe, instead of asserting it. This would follow automatically if (9b) underlay the exclamations of (8).

(9) a. *We exclaimed (to Shel's mother) at him liking blintzes.*
     b. *I exclaim to you at him liking blintzes.*

However, whether or not (7b) can be reanalyzed as a subcase of (7a), it seems to me unlikely that (7c) can be.

In asserting that some relative clauses are converted by rule to *ing* clauses, I have in mind such sentences as those in (10).

---

[2] In addition, the rule deletes *be* obligatorily, and *being* optionally. Thus, the exclamation corresponding to *He is flatulent* is either *Him flatulent!?* or possible *Him being flatulent!?*, but not °*Him be flatulent!?* The existence of such a deletion rule lends support to Fillmore's analysis of *have* as deriving from *be* + *with*, for the exclamation corresponding to *He has a Caddy* is *Him with a Caddy!?* For some reason unknown to me, there are no exclamations corresponding to sentences with expletive subjects. Note the ungrammaticality of °*It (being) muggy in Fresno!?* °*It (being) possible that one of my features is ad hoc!?*

A number of interesting properties of exclamations were brought to my attention by an interesting unpublished paper by a Cornell student, Philip Cohen.

(10)   a. *Men **sharpening knives** were leering at us.*
            b. *Men **sharpening knives** leer at us.*

Intuitively, the italicized postnominal modifiers in (10a) and (10b)
differ in meaning. The most plausible sources for (10a) and (10b)
would be (11a) and (11b), respectively.

(11)   a. *Men **who were** sharpening knives were leering at us.*
        b. *Men **who** sharpen knives leer at us.*

There is a well known and uncontroversial rule, which I will refer to
as *whiz deletion*, that could be used to convert (11a) into (10a) by
deleting the boldface portion of (10a). It is this rule that accounts for
the deletions suggested in (12).

(12)   a. *Tell me something (which is) valid.*
            b. *I giggled at a man (who was) in the fishbowl.*

However, there is no generally accepted analysis under which (11b)
is converted into (10b). I propose that a transformational rule, which I
will refer to as *stuff-ing* (a preliminary version of which is formulated
below), is the mechanism which should be postulated to account for
the synonymy of (10b) and (11b).

> *Stuff-ing*
> $$X - [_{NP} \text{ NP} - [_S \text{ NP} - V - Y]_S]_{NP} - Z$$
> SD: 1   2   3   4 $\overset{\text{OPT}}{\rightarrow}$
> SC: 1 ϕ 3 # *ing* 4

This rule, as formulated here, Chomsky-adjoins *ing* to the right of the
highest verb of a relative clause whose subject has been relativized,
and deletes the relative pronoun. The rule thus presupposes the correctness of the analysis of the English auxiliary that I suggested in
Ross (1969), under which all auxiliaries are main verbs; otherwise,
such NPs as *men being photographed* could not be generated. A
possible alternative analysis was suggested in Hall (1964). Under this
analysis, all stative verbs would derive from progressives by an obligatory deletion of a preceding *be* + *ing* at some late stage of derivations; thus, (13a) would underlie (13b):

(13)   a. **Jim is resembling Quang in accent.*
            b. *Jim resembles Quang in accent.*

This alternative seems to provide a plausible source for such otherwise troublesome modifiers as the boldface phrase of (14b), which
would in this analysis be derived by *whiz deletion* from (14a).

(14) a. *Linguists who are resembling Quang should be
           denied the right to disseminate their smut.
      b. Linguists **resembling Quang** should be denied the
           right to disseminate their smut.

However, as Kenneth Hale (personal communication) has brought to
my attention, this alternative runs into difficulties when such sentences as (15) are considered.

(15)   Anyone having been wounded should report at once to
       the infirmary.

If (16) were to be considered as a possible source for (15),

(16)   *Anyone who is having been wounded should report at once
       to the infirmary.

it would entail postulating two underlying be + ings, so that (17a) can
be whiz deleted into (17b).

(17) a. *Anyone who is having$_1$ been working$_2$ on this for more
           than one year should resign.
     b. Anyone having been working on this for more than one
           year should resign.

Presumably, then, since the first be + ing would somehow have to be
deleted if the relative clause of (17a) stood in isolation, all sentences
such as those in (18) would be ambiguous, having been derived either
with or without this first be + ing.

(18)   a. He has been coughing.
                            b. He is coughing.

It seems to me that this analysis does not hold much promise of over-
coming the above technical problems. Also, one of Hall's original
motivations for postulating a rule that deletes be + ing, namely the
fact that present adverbs like now, at this instant, and so forth, could
appear with true progressives and statives, is not paralleled by the
behavior of adverbs in sentences like Hale's; note that (15) becomes
ungrammatical if at this instant is inserted into the ing phrase. Thus,
it appears that sentences like (15) provide fairly strong support for
stuff-ing.
  Another piece of evidence in favor of this rule derives from such
sentences as those in (19), which (though bookish) are certainly grammatical, in my speech.

(19)   *These two examples, neither of which proving much in
        isolation, combine to make an iron-clad argument for
        Precyclic Buttering.*

Actually, this sentence provides evidence for a slightly modified version of *stuff-ing* in which the *ing* would be inserted without the relative pronoun being deleted. Only later, if the relative pronoun constituted the entire subject of a verb followed by *ing*, would this pronoun be deleted. Thus, (15) would pass through a stage containing . . . *who having been wounded* . . ., which would obligatorily lose its pronoun. In contrast, the relative pronoun *which* in (19), which constitutes only part of the subject NP *neither of which* could not be deleted. It is possible that this relative pronoun deletion rule could be extended by making it obligatory before any nonfinite verb form, thus accounting for the contrast between *a razor with which to shave,* and *a razor (*which) to shave with.*

Some speakers reject sentences like (19), but all I have asked accept it if *which* is replaced by *them.* The resulting clause is just as good as that in (19) for my present purposes; it could not have resulted from a Poss + *ing* complement. Since no possessive morpheme can follow the subject in (19) (cf. * . . . *neither of which's* . . ., *. . . neither of whose* . . .), it seems obvious that the *ing* in the subordinate clause here is not the result of Poss + *ing* complementation.

There are a number of problems that remain, but all in all, it does not seem unreasonable to postulate the existence of some rule like *stuff-ing* to convert finite to nonfinite relative clauses. Such an analysis allows an easy explanation for the second meaning of the phrase *sharpening knives* in (10), a meaning not accounted for if postnominal *ing* phrases are only derived by *whiz deletion,* and it accounts readily for such otherwise problematic sentences as (15) and (19).

If, in fact, there are two (or possibly even three) sources for *ing,* then note that there will have to be a condition upon each of the rules introducing this morpheme forbidding its insertion if certain doubl-*ing* sequences would result, for all the sentences of (20) must be marked as deviant.

(20) a.   **His keeping chanting ads bugs me.*
     b.   **Him keeping chanting ads!?*
     c.   **Anyone keeping eating swordfish will regret it briefly.*

The rule, whether phrase structural or transformational, that introduces the complementizers Poss and *ing,* will have to be restricted to block (20a) and (20b) [or, if (20b) is not analyzed as a deep complement of an exclamatory verb, then (20b) will have to be stopped by a condition on the rule that forms exclamations]. And in addition, an exactly parallel constraint will have to appear on the rule of *stuff-ing* to keep this rule from converting the well-formed clause *who keeps eating swordfish* into the ungrammatical postnominal modifier of (20c).

Thus one argument for the correctness of the claim that doubl-ing violations are to be characterized, at least partially, in terms of an output condition, has the same logical form as the argument I presented in Ross (1967) to the effect that the order of postverbal constituents in English is only to be described by an output condition. There I showed that the ungrammaticality of both the sentences in (21) could be easily accounted for by an output condition which throws out any tree in which any constituent intervened between a verb stem and a following pronoun.

(21) a. *I thought up it.
      b. *I handed Frederika it.

Without output conditions, it would be necessary to place essentially identical constraints on two separate rules — in this case, on the rules of particle movement and dative. In the case of (21), then, as in the case of (20), the availability of output conditions as part of the theoretical apparatus with which particular grammars are stated allows an otherwise uncapturable generalization to be stated. What is intuitively one fact must be stated several times in a theory that only provides transformations and conditions on transformations as types of theoretical machinery. This type of argumentation in favor of output conditions is also that which was used above in establishing the correctness of (4). Below (pp. 166–171) I will use a different kind of argument to show that doubl-ing violations are due in part to a violation of an output condition.

Additional Arguments for an Output Condition

In this section, I will present a number of additional arguments for an output condition on doubl-ing clauses — arguments that have a different logical form than those cited so far in support of output conditions. These are based on sentences that allow one to infer that earlier stages of a derivation must have contained subtrees that would have eventuated in violations if some other rule had not applied to destroy the output sequences in question. This type of argumentation is developed extensively in Perlmutter (1970). I will refer to it as the *necessary intermediate stage* type of argument, to distinguish it from the previous type of argument, which I will refer to as the *condition duplication* type.

FIRST ARGUMENT

As the first case of an argument of the necessary intermediate stage type, let us consider the rule of *topicalization*, a rule which optionally preposes NPs to the front of certain clauses, converting the sentences of (22) to the corresponding ones in (23).

(22) a. *Richard has never seen **Giselle**.*
      b. *They didn't realize that we knew them.*
      c. *I've never tried kissing this moray eel.*

(23) a. ***Giselle** Richard has never seen.*
      b. *That we knew them they didn't realize.*
      c. *Kissing this moray eel I've never tried.*

Now note that this rule can apply to (24a) to convert it to (24b).

(24) a. **I'm not particularly keen on trying kissing this moray eel.*
      b. *Kissing this moray eel I'm not particularly keen on trying.*

But (24a) is an instance of a doubl-ing violation, as is indicated by the asterisk preceding it. Topicalization, however, can rescue this structure by breaking up the sequence of present participles. Thus, it must be the case that the cause of the ungrammaticality of (24a) is not that the rule inserting the complementizers Poss + *ing* has been violated, but rather that a certain configuration has been allowed to persist to surface structure. Obviously, therefore, it would be totally mistaken to attempt to block (24a) by anything but an output condition; the ancestors of (24a) must be inferred to be grammatical, because they are needed to provide the source for (24b). This is a paradigm case of the necessary intermediate stage type of argument.

SECOND ARGUMENT

Another set of facts that allows the drawing of exactly the same conclusions is provided by a consideration of the rule of pseudo-cleft formation, the rule that "converts" the sentences of (25) into the corresponding ones of (26).[3]

---

[3] I have put "converts" in quotes, because it has been obvious for some time to workers in generative grammar that the underlying structure of pseudo-cleft sentences like those in (26), while it may contain as a subpart such simple sentences as those in (25), is in reality far more complex. In fact, I suspect that the underlying structure of a sentence like (26a), rather than being like the one underlying (25a), is really more like the structure that underlies: *The answer to the question as to what Ultraman replaced in the light socket is that he replaced the banana in it.* For some research leading along essentially identical lines, cf. Faraci (1970).

(25)   a. *Ultraman replaced the banana in the light socket.*
         b. *Kong realized that the IRT would demand
             reparations.*
         c. *I'm going to attempt playing the "Minute Waltz"
             with my nose.*

(26)   a. *What Ultraman replaced in the light socket was the
             banana.*
         b. *What Kong realized was that the IRT would demand
             reparations.*
         c. *What I'm going to attempt is playing the "Minute
             Waltz" with my nose.*

Just as was the case with (24), this rule can rescue sentences. Thus,
note that while (27a) is ungrammatical, the related (27b), which has
been produced by pseudo-cleft formation, is all right.

(27)   a. **I was attempting playing the "Minute Waltz" with
             my nose.*
         b. *What I was attempting was playing the "Minute
             Waltz" with my nose.*

Again, the inference is clear; the doubl-ing sequence that produces
the deviance of (27a) is part of a necessary intermediate stage. Hence,
it must be thrown out only on the basis of an output condition.

THIRD ARGUMENT

A third argument of this type is provided by the rule of *anaphoric
complement deletion*, which converts the structures underlying (28)
into the corresponding ones in (29).

(28)   a. *Fritz suggested growing a beard, and I approved of*
             $\begin{Bmatrix} it \\ growing\ a\ beard \end{Bmatrix}$.
         b. *Jezebel was watching me as I entered, and she con-
             tinued* $\begin{Bmatrix} it \\ watching\ me \end{Bmatrix}$ *as I sat down.*
         c. *You can go on working if you want, but I've got to*
             stop $\begin{Bmatrix} it \\ working \end{Bmatrix}$.

(29)   a. *Fritz suggested growing a beard, and I approved.*
         b. *Jezebel was watching me as I entered, and she con-
             tinued as I sat down.*
         c. *You can go on working if you want, but I've got to
             stop.*

It is at present unclear to me whether this rule deletes the repeated complement directly, or whether the complement must first have been converted to *it*. Also, while the small class of verbs to whose complements this rule applies (the class includes, in addition to the three verbs in (28)–(29), such verbs as *begin, finish, start, commence, agree, insist, keep on, cease, reconsider, persist, try* (but not *endeavor* or *attempt*); this last contrast between what seem to be near synonyms (i.e. *try* and *attempt*) appears to mean that the rule must be lexically governed—that is, that it can have exceptions) can all appear with present participle complements, I have not investigated this phenomenon thoroughly enough to know whether this constitutes a necessary condition for the rule to apply (the impossibility of **I avoided, *I kept,* and so on indicates that it is not a sufficient one). However these questions are resolved when this process has been studied further, it seems clear that enough is known about the process for us to be able to use it to cast some light on the doubl-ing phenomenon. For consider the sentences in (30).

(30)   a. **You can go on watching this if you want, but I'm stopping watching it.*
        b. *You can go on watching this if you want, but I'm stopping.*

As in the preceding sections, we see that a rule, here *anaphoric complement deletion,* can repair the unacceptability of (30a). Thus, *if* cannot be unacceptable for deep reasons, but must rather be rejected because it fails to satisfy an output condition.

FOURTH ARGUMENT

Yet a fourth argument of this type is provided by the rule of *being* deletion, which is possibly the same rule as that discussed in footnote 2 above. This is the rule that obligatorily [cf. **(31b)] deletes *being* after *stuff-ing* has applied. Thus, (31c) would be derived from (31a).

(31)
        a. *Anyone who is undernourished will be treated.*
        b. **Anyone being undernourished will be treated.*
        c. *Anyone undernourished will be treated.*

But if *being* is obligatorily deleted, how can such sentences as (32) be derived?

(32)   *Anyone being sassy will be horsewhipped.*

I claim that (32) has indeed undergone *being* deletion—that its history is that shown in (33).

(33) a. *Anyone who is being sassy will be horsewhipped.*
b. **Anyone being being sassy will be horsewhipped.*

That is, the *being* that deletes by this rule contains the *be* of the progressive, not that of the copula. This means that it would be wrong to constrain *stuff-ing* so that it would not convert (33a) into (33b), despite the fact that in doing so, it produces a doubl-ing sequence that would produce a violation if it made it to surface structure. The rule must be free to apply to (33a) in the most general way, because (33b) is needed as an intermediate source for (32).

FIFTH ARGUMENT

Another argument of the same type is provided by Klima's rule of negative incorporation (Klima, 1964). Briefly, this rule moves a negative element to the right, attaching it to an element like *any* or *ever*. Thus, the sentences in (34) would be converted to the corresponding ones in (35).

(34)   a. *I won't ever go there.*
b. *I won't force you to marry anyone.*
c. *He hasn't signed any radical petitions.*

(35)   a. *I will never go there.*
b. *I will force you to marry no one.*
c. *He has signed no radical petitions.*

For our present purposes, it is immaterial whether the first or the second set of sentences is regarded as more basic; the only necessary assumption is that some rule moves the negative element either onto or away from the main verb. For notice that if the negative intervenes in a doubl-ing sequence, the strength of the violation is greatly reduced. Thus compare the sentences in (36).

(36) a. *?He is beginning not signing any radical petitions.*
b. **He is beginning signing no radical petitions.*

I am at present unable to account for my feeling that (36a) is slightly odd, but the contrast between (36a) and (36b) is surely clear, and this contrast can be accounted for by formulating the doubl-ing constraint in part as an output condition.

The arguments in the five preceding sections seem to me to be compelling; the correct way to characterize doubl-ing violations is in part by means of an output condition. Forbidden sequences of present participles must be granted a transitory existence, for otherwise, independently motivated rules could not retain their maximally general formulation.

I might mention in passing two more partial arguments of the necessary intermediate stage type. I say "partial" because the facts on which these arguments rest are unclear. First, note that the output condition must mention immediate contiguity of the *ing* forms; if a particle, for instance, intervenes, then no violation ensues. Thus consider the following paradigm:

(37) a. *She's taken up knitting sweatshirts.*
     b. *?She's taken knitting sweatshirts up because she has nothing better to do.*
     c. *She's taking up knitting sweatshirts.*
     d. *??She's taking knitting sweatshirts up because she has nothing better to do.*

Sentences in (37b) and (37d) are worse than (37a) and (37c), because a sentential object intervenes between verb and following particle. But if my (very weak) intuitions to the effect that (37d) is slightly worse than (37b) are right, then presumably, this extra dollop of deviance is to be attributed to the violation of the doubl-ing constraint.

Another possible argument might be derivable from some paradigm like (38).

(38)   a. *He began his polishing of the yoyo.*
         b. *He began polishing the yoyo.*
         c. *He was beginning his polishing of the yoyo.*
         d. **He was beginning polishing the yoyo.*

If it could be shown that (38b) arose optionally from (38a), via the rule of *equi* (see Postal, 1970b, for an extensive study of this rule) then the output of this rule could violate the doubl-ing restriction, as is the case in (38d). Since, however, (38c), the putative source of (38d) is grammatical, we would have one more case of a necessary intermediate stage type argument.

As the provisory tone of these last sentences indicates, I am extremely doubtful that (38a) is the source of (38b), and I have not been able to find a truly convincing case of optional *equi* with a verb like *begin.*

A Sixth Argument

In conclusion, let me cite one more set of facts that enables one to construct an argument that is roughly the converse of the necessary intermediate stage type. In all the sections immediately above, I gave cases in which structures were necessary that would result in unacceptable surface structures unless some optional rule intervened to "rescue" them. The case below is one in which a structure containing two noncontiguous *ing* forms becomes ungrammatical by virtue of the application of a rule which brings the two forms together.

Consider the verb *watch*. It can take either *ing* forms or uninflected stems in its complement, as shown in (39).

(39)   a.   *I like watching those girls crochet doilies.*
         b.   *I like watching those girls crocheting doilies.*

But when the object NP of *watch* is extracted (by some rule such as *question formation, relative clause formation, topicalization*) then the contiguity of the two *ing* forms produces, for many speakers, a slightly deviant string.

(40) a.   *?Which girls do you like watching crochet doilies?*
     b.   *??Which girls do you like watching crocheting doilies?*

I have no explanation for the fact that such sentences, whose doubling sequence has arisen via the extraction of a previously intervening constituent, are systematically better, for many speakers, than such sentences as (1d), in which this was not the case. Nor do I understand why (40a) itself is somewhat odd. Possibly this oddness means that the doubl-ing constraint must be formulated in more general terms, than I have attempted in this paper. Further research is needed here. Obviously, then, excluding (40b) by virtue of its superficial doubl-ing sequence is preferable to trying to append some ad hoc condition to the rule that inserts the complementizers Poss and *ing*.

Summary

Arguments of both types—condition duplication and necessary intermediate stage—can be adduced to support the contention that doubl-ing violations are not to be accounted for by restricting some transformational rule(s), but rather by stating an output condition, or filter, which will throw out any derivation terminating in a tree with certain types of sequences of present participles. The question as to exactly what sequences produce doubl-ing violations is the topic of the immediately following section.

THE NECESSITY OF POSTULATING A GLOBAL RULE

Lest it be suggested that what is involved in all doubl-ing violations is merely a phonetic dissatisfaction with strings ending in the
same phonetic subsequence (thus parallel to *rummy, ginny, winy,
beery,* but not **whiskey-y, *sake-y*) let us consider an often cited
example.

(41)   *The police stopped drinking on campus.*

This sentence is ambiguous; it can mean that the police ceased to
drink on campus, or that they prevented others from doing so. Now
let us examine what happens when (41) is made into a progressive.

(41')   *The police are stopping drinking on campus.*

This sentence is perfectly grammatical, but it has only one reading:
that the police are stopping other people from drinking on campus.
The fact that (41') is well-formed on one reading, however, is enough
to shoot down any suggestion that what is involved in doubl-ing violations is merely phonetic.

Presumably, what produces the ambiguity of (40) is the fact that the
word *drinking* can either be taken as a participle or as a noun. That is,
(40) can be read as parallel to the sentences in (42), or those in (42').

(42)   a.   *The police stopped drinking beer on campus.*
          b.   *The police stopped punching students out.*

(42')   a.   *The police stopped beer-drinking on campus.*

          b.   *The police stopped* $\left\{\begin{array}{l} \textit{fornication} \\ \textit{drug abuse} \\ \textit{lasciviousness} \\ \textit{debauchery} \\ \textit{bribery} \\ \textit{blackmail} \\ \textit{etc.} \end{array}\right\}$ *on campus.*

The reason that (41') has an acceptable reading, apparently, is that the
doubl-ing constraint must be stated in such a way as to be sensitive
to the syntactic categories of the two ing forms, such that while . . .
$[Ving]_V[Ving]_V$ . . . subsequences can yield violations, subsequences
like . . . $[Ving]_V[Ving]_N$ . . . cannot. This is presumably the reason

that sentences like *He is going (shark)-fishing* are acceptable. That is, as the incorporability of the object of *fishing* suggests, the word *fishing* is probably a noun when it follows *go*. This impression is confirmed by the impossibility of **He is going drinking beer*. However, as the two examples in (43) show, limiting the doubl-ing restriction to sequences of *ing* forms, while necessary, is not sufficient.

(43)   a.   *Waldo keeps **molesting sleeping** gorillas.*
       b.   *I watched a man who had been **flying describing** it to some chicks.*

Obviously, therefore, it is necessary not only that the second *ing* form be a verb, but that it be in the complement of the first verb.

However, even this latter restriction on the power of the output constraint does not yield a sufficient condition for doubl-ing deviance. For consider the pair of sentences in (44).

(44)   a.   *He expects that breathing deeply will benefit us.*
       b.   *He expects breathing deeply to benefit us.*

I assume that the arguments to the effect that the superficial object of *expects* in (44b), the phrase *breathing deeply*, originates in a lower clause and is removed by a rule of *(subject) raising*, are familiar enough not to require recapitulation. What is important about these two sentences for our present concerns is that even the second one cannot produce a doubl-ing violation. Thus, both of the sentences in (45) are well formed.

(45)   a.   *His expecting that breathing deeply will benefit us is hopelessly naive.*
       b.   *His **expecting breathing** deeply to benefit us is hopelessly naive.*

Apparently, what is necessary is to limit the doubl-ing constraint so that only superficially contiguous verbs *which were in immediately adjacent clauses in remote structure* will be subject to the constraint. In other words, the doubl-ing constraint is a global rule, in the sense of Lakoff (1970), because it links remote and surface structure. That is, since the deep structure of the subject clauses of (45b) is that shown in (46),

(46)

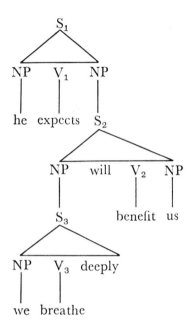

the fact that *expecting* (=V_1) and *breathing* (=V_3) can end up as surface structure neighbors is irrelevant for the doubl-ing constraint,
which must be stated in such a way as to ensure both remote structure
and surface structure adjacency.

Two other constructions that show the necessity of mentioning remote structure adjacency in the statement of the doubl-ing constraint
are shown in (47) and (48).

(47) a.   *He has$_1$ to consider$_2$ getting$_3$ into college.*
      b.   *He has$_1$ getting$_3$ into college to consider$_2$.*
      c.   *His having$_1$ getting$_3$ into college to consider$_2$ is a drag.*

(48) a.   *There is$_1$ getting$_3$ into college for Matt to consider$_2$.*
      b.   *There being$_1$ getting$_3$ into college for Matt to consider$_2$
           is an unexpected difficulty.*

While the complete remote structure of (48a) is opaque, to say the
least, I think it can be argued with a fair degree of certainty that the
NP *getting into college* must appear as the direct object of *consider* in
some prior stage of derivation, in part so that the controller NP, *Matt,*
for the application of the rule of *equi,* which deletes the subject of
getting, can command the deleted element, a condition shown in
Postal (1970b) to be necessary for *equi* to apply. That is, there must be
some rule that uproots the object of *consider* so that it follows *there is.*

I believe that the analysis of such sentences as (47b) must closely parallel that of (48a); again, though I will not argue extensively for the correctness of this claim here (though the above remarks about *Equi* are equally relevant here) it seem to me that the superficial direct object of *has* in (47b) must have appeared as an object of *consider* at a deeper level of the derivation, and that some rule, quite possibly the same rule that is operative in forming (48a), takes this object out of a lower clause and inserts it into a higher one. That is, the remote structure of (47b) is probably something that contains (47a) as a subtree. The only other alternative that I can conceive of, namely that the remote structure of (47b) is roughly that shown in (49) —

(49)

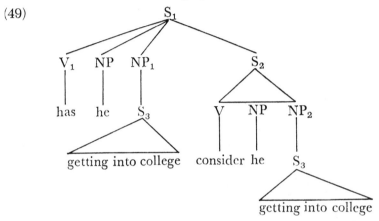

I accept McCawley's argument that all verbs are initial in remote structure in English (McCawley, 1970) — with a deletion rule deleting NP_2 under identity with the higher NP object of *has*, NP_1, is probably to be ruled out of independent grounds. That is, for all other verbs which, like *has* in (49), take NP + S objects, the object NP must be animate. A few examples of such verbs are *bribe, compel, motivate, get, make*. All of these require their direct objects to be animate (*I bribed the table to fall on Judy*). But NP_1 in (49) is not animate. Thus, assuming (49) to be a possible remote structure would entail abandoning an otherwise valid generalization.

It seems to me, therefore, that the assumption is a justified one that neither of the occurrences of *getting* — [that is, neither the one in (47c) nor the one in (48b)] — is in a clause adjacent to *having* or *being* in remote structure, and that these two sentences are merely additional cases of the type of evidence provided by (45b) to the effect that only verbs adjacent in remote structure can cause doubl-ing violations when contiguous in surface structure.

I am aware of one final set of facts that must be taken into account in finding a not-too-restrictive statement of the doubl-ing constraint. Consider the grammaticality of the sentences in (50), all of which, in their versions without parentheses, contain doubl-ing sequences of verb followed by complement verb, where these verbs were adjacent in remote structure.

(50)   a.   *Ed's resenting (Ann's) getting photographed drunk is just too funny.*
        b.   *I am hating (your) wanting to participate in rigged elections more and more these days.*
        c.   *Disliking (my) drinking vodka with only her cats for company, Griselda reached for the telephone.*

As far as I know, no verb that allows the present participle of its complement to be preceded by a possessive NP will produce doubl-ing violations. These verbs seem to be factive predicates (cf. Kiparsky and Kiparsky, 1970). Other examples of such verbs are: *regret, protest, defend, prefer, adore, accept, admit, contemplate.* Thus, apparently the global rule, which the discussion above has indicated is necessary to account for the doubl-ing phenomenon, must be restricted along the lines of (51):

(51)   The only verbs that can produce doubl-ing violations are either equi-subject verbs or intransitive verbs that have undergone *raising*.[4]

The surface structure of (1b) would be derived from (i) by inserting Poss + *ing* complementizers, and then by raising NP_2 to become the superficial subject of *continued.*

As George Lakoff (personal communication) has pointed out to me, however, to state anything like (51) as a restriction on the *doubl-ing* global rule would be to miss an important generalization. Namely, it is not an accident that it is *raising* verbs that behave like *equi-subject* correctly is the fact that *no other possessive NP could intervene between the two ing forms.*

But no global rule could capture this generalization, which is a transderivational one. That is, what is necessary to exclude such cases as those in (50) from those that the final form of the doubl-ing con-

---

[4] An equi-subject verb is a verb that requires in remote structure that the subject of its complement clause be identical to either its direct object (i.e., *I bribed Harry [sfor {Harry/*Sandra} to leave]s*) or to their subject (i.e., *Pauline struggled [sfor {Pauline/ *Rafe} to remove the slimy tentacle from her heaving bosom]s*). For a discussion of the

straint will stigmatize is a statement that no sequence of the form . . . $[Ving]_{V_1}[Ving]_{V_2}$ . . . produces the violation if a possessive NP could intervene between V_1 and V_2 in another derivation from essentially the same remote structure. Obviously, since it requires quantifying over possible "parallel" derivations, such a condition is beyond the power of even a derivational constraint, unless we are to settle for something on the lines of (51). However, accepting (51) would leave us without any explanation for the fact that it is equi-subject verbs and those that have undergone Raising that are linked, instead of equi-subject verbs and those subject to *dative or anaphoric complement deletion.*

It seems to me that a strong case can be made on grounds independent of these for the necessity of broadening linguistic theory so that such transderivational constraints are formulable in particular grammars. (For a pioneering paper in this important new area of linguistic theory, cf. Lakoff, 1970b.) However, such a demonstration would not be germane to the point at hand, so I will not pursue this issue here. I make no assumptions as to the correct form for stating transderivational constraints, and so I will leave the transderivational addendum that sentences like those in (50) show to be necessary out of the formal statement of the doubl-ing constraint, in (52) below.

Summary

What the above discussion has indicated is (minimally) necessary to correctly characterize the class of doubl-ing violations is a global rule such as the one in (52).

---

necessity of allowing such constraints on remote structure, see Perlmutter (1968). One intransitive verb having undergone raising is *continue* in some uses (see Perlmutter, 1970b). That is, the remote structure of (1b) would be, schematically, that shown in (i).

(i)

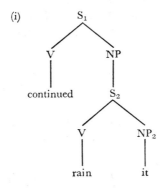

(52) *The Doubl-ing Constraint*

All surface structures containing a subtree of the form shown here in which the
node corresponding to V_a in remote
structure was immediately dominated
by S_i, and the node corresponding to V_b
in remote structure was immediately
dominated by S_j, and in which no S node
intervened in remote structure between
S_i and S_j, are ungrammatical.

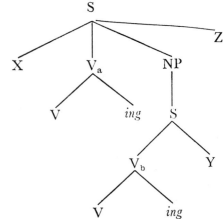

CONSEQUENCES FOR LINGUISTIC THEORY

Before beginning to investigate the consequences of (52) for other areas of English and for linguistic theory in general, let me reformulate (52) as the two halves of a biconditional:

(53) a. All surface structure subtrees of the form specified in (52)
          produce doubl-ing violations.
      b. No surface structure subtrees which are not of the form
          specified in (52) produce violations.

At present, the first of these two implications (53a)—and of course (52) itself, for (53a) merely recapitulates (52)—is too strong. There are some verbs that mysteriously do not occasion doubl-ing violations— *avoid* is one. More importantly, (53a) seems to be wrong in a far more serious way, because it cannot account for the fact that there is a hierarchy of unacceptability for doubl-ing violations. That is, I imagine most speakers would perceive the sentences in (54) as decreasing in grammaticality, even though they might not agree with the absolute values of grammaticality that the prefixes I have used indicate are correct in my speech.

(54)   a. *His avoiding contacting Harriet is understandable.*
        b. ?*Red's attempting breathing without a snorkel
            was ill considered.*
        c. ??*Red's trying swimming back alone was probably
            due to all that ale he drank.*
        d. ?*Harold's continuing fondling Astrid did not
            produce the desired sensations.*
        e. *Her keeping resisting him didn't help much, though.*

[Some Southern speakers have informed me that they can find no doubl-ing violations in their speech except for the verb *keep* (and the *be* of the progressive, see immediately below).]

Apparently, there are additional factors, at present unknown, at work here that interact with (52) and that have the effect of producing such a hierarchy. Exactly what factors, however, must be left as a problem for future research. Nevertheless, for what follows, it is not necessary that we accept (53a). The weaker (53b) will suffice. And to the best of my knowledge, it is entirely accurate: there are no doubl-ing violations that can be traced to phrase structural or derivational properties other than those specified in (52).

Assuming, then, in the absence of counterevidence, the correctness of (53b), consider the following pairs of sentences:

(55)   a.   *That Tillie is working on presentences is tragic.*
          b.   **Tillie's **being working** on presentences is tragic.*

(56)   a.   *That Al is being arrested I find extremely comical.*
          b.   **Al's **being being** arrested I find extremely comical.*

(57)   a.   *That Cat is being adamant complicates things.*
          b.   **Cat's **being being** adamant complicates things.*

(58)   a.   *That Alice is going to vote is doubtful.*
          b.   **Alice's **being going** to vote is doubtful.*

Briefly, (53b) states that it is only possible for the boldfaced sequences of *ing* forms to produce violations if they are instances of a complement-taking verb followed by the verb of its complement. That is, at least one of the remote structures of each of the subject clauses of (55)–(58) must be as shown in (59)–(62), respectively.

(59)   *Progressive*

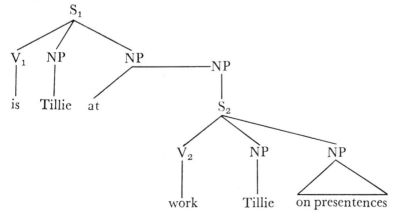

(60) *Passive*

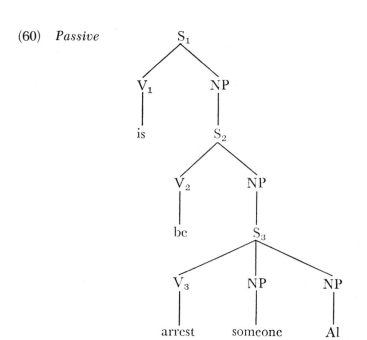

(61) *Copula*   (62) *be going to*

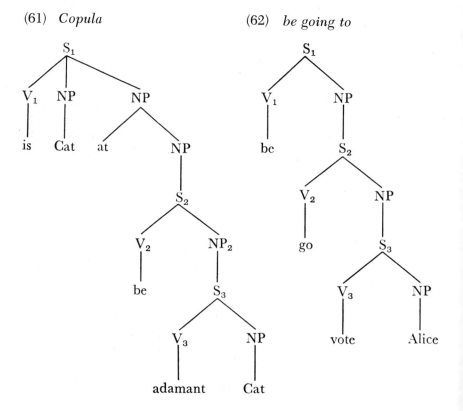

As (59) shows, in order for (53b) to characterize the deviances of (55b), what has previously (e.g., Chomsky, 1957, 1965) been analyzed as being not a true verb, but rather as an auxiliary, namely the *be* of the progressive, must be analyzed as a verb, in consonance with my claim — see Ross (1969) and Ross (in preparation) — that all so-called auxiliaries must be analyzed as main verbs.[5]

The situation is the same with (56b). The *is* of (56a) is the *be* of the progressive, in an intransitive alloform,[6] and (55b) has already indicated this form to be a main verb. However, for (52) to be triggered, both *ing* forms must be verbs in surface structure — recall the discussion of (39)–(42) above. This means that the *being* of (56a), a form of the passive "auxiliary", must also be a main verb.

Exactly the same is true in the case of (57). Again, since the *is* of (57a) is the progressive main verb, the *being* that follows must be a main verb, in order for (53b) to allow (57b) to be excluded. Thus the *be* of the copula must also be a main verb. The progressive main verb is probably the transitive alloform, if my intuition is correct that *Cat may be being adamant now, but I'll be surprised if he's still at it tomorrow* is grammatical.

This conclusion was argued for independently in Ross (1970a). When that paper was written, I believed it to be necessary for the *be* of the copula to be a transitive main verb. I now see no reason for such an assumption. All the evidence presented in Ross (1970a) to the effect that adjectives must, at some stage of derivation, be embedded in an NP following a main verb *be* is consonant with the structure dominated by S_2 in (61), under the quite reasonable assumption that raising will produce such a structure as (63) (and eventually (64)) when applied to the complement of *be*. It is to NP_2 in (63) that all the rules mentioned in Ross (1970a) is requiring NPs to follow *be* refer.

Notice that I am assuming here (although nothing rests on this assumption) that *raising* is effected by a process of copying the subject NP of the complement, with subsequent deletion of a doomed proform

---

[5] One reason for assuming an underlying *at* in (some) progressive sentences can be seen from the grammaticality of such sentences as *He was whistling in the dark as Vice President and he's still at it now.*

[6] See Perlmutter (1970b) for a discussion of such transitive–intransitive complement verb pairs. The source for my claim that the progressive *be* of (55) is transitive and associated in remote structure with *at*, as suggested in (59), while the progressive *be* of (56) is not, is the ungrammaticality of *°Al was being arrested when I left, and he was still at it at suppertime.*

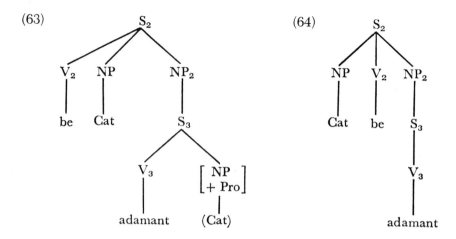

(63)   (64)

left behind (presumably by the same late deletion rule which Postal shows to be necessary for *equi* (Postal, 1970b). There is independent support for the assumption that *raising* involves a copying process, but I will not go into this tangential matter here.

Finally, the same is true of the form *go* in the idiomatic phrase *be going to*. The *is* of (58a) is again the intransitive form of the progressive,[7] and the ungrammaticality of (58b) argues that here *going* must also be analyzed as a main verb. This is a matter of some interest, for it indicates that upward selection for verbs is possible. The *go* of (62), a complement-taking verb that has an infinitival complement and a meaning of futurity, never appears except when embedded in remote structure as the complement of the intransitive progressive. Thus, this type of selection, which in my view is fairly clearly necessary here, becomes available in other areas of grammar as well. Another case where upward selection appears necessary is discussed in Ross (1972).

Thus, one consequence of (53b) is that the "Syntactic Structures" (Chomsky, 1957) analysis of the auxiliary must be abandoned. The reason is that this analysis forms such a tight system that one loophole

---

[7] This is argued for not only by the impossibility of (i), but by the fact that *be going* to can be preceded by *there*, as in (ii).

(i)   °*Alice was going to vote when I left, and she's still at it.*

(ii)   *There is$_1$ going$_2$ to be$_3$ a full scale investigation of perversion by the FBI.*

This *there* must have originated on the cycle whose main verb is *be$_3$* of (ii), and must have been successively moved up to become the derived subject first to *go$_2$*, and finally of *is$_1$*, the intransitive progressive.

in one part of it renders the rest of it untenable. That is, it is not possible to accept the conclusions of the preceding argument to the effect that the *be* of the progressive, the *be* of the passive, and the *be* of the copula are all main verbs, while still maintaining the claim that other "auxiliaries," such as *have, do,* and the modals, are to be analyzed as in "Syntactic Structures." To see this, consider the phenomenon of *subject verb inversion.* In "Syntactic Structures," it was observed that certain sentences with *have* have two inverted forms. An example is (65):

(65) a. *Have you any reason to distrust the government?*
      b. *Do you have any reason to distrust the government?*

Chomsky observed that this was an automatic consequence of the structural description of this rule, which would resemble that shown in (66).[8]

(66)
$$Q - NP - Tns \begin{Bmatrix} \text{Modal} \\ \text{have} \\ \text{be} \end{Bmatrix} - X.$$

Since, in Chomsky's analysis, the structure of the sentences in (65) would be that shown in (67),

(67)

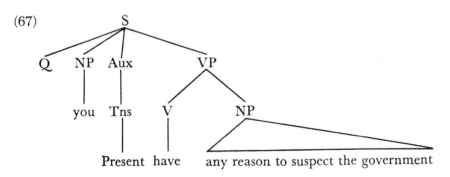

the structural description in (66) could choose to regard *have* as part of the term to be inverted, producing (65a), or as the main verb, with only the tense morpheme inverting, producing (65b).

What is problematic for this analysis is that given the correctness of structures like (55)–(58), it would predict exactly the same double

---

[8] He did not observe the magnitude of the problem occasioned by a rule which inverts all instances of *have.* Some of the many sentences that any analysis must exclude are: °*Had you the valet press your pants?* ?°*Has there to be an investigation?* and °*Has the IRS you by the short hairs?*.

questions for progressives (and passives and copulas). That is, if anything like (66) is right, it will generate not only the desired (68), but also the ill-starred (69).

(68)   a.   *Are you thinking about Precyclic Buttering?*
        b.   *Were they searched?*
        c.   *Is Fred sallow?*

(69)   a.   **Do you be thinking about Precyclic Buttering?*
        b.   **Did they be searched?*
        c.   **Does Fred be sallow?*

If structures like (55)–(58) are necessary, then it is a fact about English that some main verbs invert in forming questions and others do not (e.g., **Liked you my term paper?*). I propose to mark those that can invert with the feature [+Aux], a feature that must be given a universal definition. That is, while verbs meaning futurity, desire, ability/ possibility, need, intent, inception (and other aspects), and so forth can have the feature [+Aux] in some language, presumably no verb that meant, for instance, *condescend to, avoid, abhor, insist on,* could. The matter is an extremely complex one, but I believe that it is already possible to make a number of nontrivial observations about the universal content of the feature [+Aux]. Only when this has been achieved, however, will it be possible to overcome the inadequacy of all analyses that include rules with structural descriptions resembling that of (64). Such analyses, which merely list elements that behave similarly together [as is the case of the terms in the braces in (64)], can never explain why some elements can function together but others cannot. What must be appended to any such analysis is a theory of possible and impossible lists. To postulate a universal feature like [+Aux] and to restrict its content as narrowly as possible is in effect to provide such a theory. This problem requires a far lengthier discussion than I can devote to it here. I will return to the matter in Ross (in preparation).

Two other consequences of accepting the *doubl-ing constraint,* as formulated in (52), are possibly obvious, but they should probably be noted in passing here. The first is that (52) is an excellent example of a global rule; that is, of a grammatical process linking noncontiguous levels of derivations. Some linguists dispute the existence of such processes (e.g., Chomsky, in press), so the existence of the *doubl-ing constraint* constitutes one of a number of to my mind compelling arguments that no theory that does not make such grammatical devices available can attain adequacy. Similar remarks apply, of course, in connection with the fact that, as was observed above (p. 177), a more adequate statement of the *doubl-ing constraint* than (52) would require the power of a transderivational constraint. Finally, to return to the topic broached at the beginning of this chapter, it is clear that that part of the *doubl-ing constraint* that could be called an output condition is not "stupid" as (4) was (but see p. 160). Thus, the need to state a condition for English that is at least as complex and structure-specific as (52) implies that Chomsky's claim (Chomsky, 1970) to the effect that the only kinds of possible output conditions are "stupid," i.e., structure-independent, ones is incorrect.

REFERENCES

Bierwisch, M., and Heidolph, K. 1971. Progress in Linguistics. Mouton, The Hague.

Chomsky, N. 1957. Syntactic Structures. Mouton, The Hague.

Chomsky, N. 1965. Aspects of the Theory of Syntax. MIT Press, Cambridge, Massachusetts.

Chomsky, N. (in press). Some empirical issues in the theory of transformational grammar. IN Goals of Linguistic Theory (S. Peters, ed.). Prentice-Hall, Englewood Cliffs, New Jersey.

Faraci, R. 1970. On the deep question of pseudo-clefts. Unpublished mimeograph. MIT, Cambridge, Massachusetts.

Fodor, J. A., and Katz, J., eds. 1964. The Structure of Language: Readings in the Philosophy of Language. Prentice-Hall, Englewood Cliffs, New Jersey.

Hall, B. 1964. Adverbial subordinate clauses. Working Paper W-07241, MITRE Corporation, Bedford, Massachusetts.

Harris, Z. 1957. Cooccurrence and transformations in linguistic structure. IN Fodor and Katz (1964).

Kiparsky, P., and Kiparsky, C. 1970. Fact, IN Bierwisch and Heidolph (1971).

Klima, E. 1964. Negation in English. IN Fodor and Katz (1964).

Lakoff, G. 1970a. Global rules. Language 46.3, 627–639.

Lakoff, G. 1970b. Some thoughts on transderivational constraints. Unpublished multilith, University of Michigan, Ann Arbor, Michigan.

McCawley, J. 1970. English as a VSO language. Language 46.2, 286–299.

Perlmutter, D. 1970a. Surface structure constraints in syntax. Linguistic Inquiry 1, 2, 187–255.

Perlmutter, D. 1970b. The two verbs *begin* IN Readings in English Transformational Grammar (R. Jacobs and P. Rosenbaum, eds.). Blaisdell, Waltham, Massachusetts.

Perlmutter, D. 1971. Deep and Surface Structure Constraints in Syntax, Holt, Rinehart and Winston, New York.

Postal, P. 1970a. On the surface verb *remind*. Linguistic Inquiry 1, 1, 37–120.

Postal, P. 1970b. On coreferential complement subject deletion. Linguistic Inquiry 1, 4, 439–500.

Rosenbaum, P. 1967. The Grammar of English Predicate Complement Constructions, MIT Press, Cambridge, Massachusetts.

Ross, J. R. 1967. Constraints on Variables in Syntax. Unpublished doctoral dissertation, MIT, Cambridge, Massachusetts.

Ross, J. R. 1969. Auxiliaries as main verbs. IN Studies in Philosophical Linguistics, Series One (W. Todd, ed.), Great Expectations Press, Carbondale, Illinois.

Ross, J. R. 1970a. Adjectives as noun phrases. IN Modern Studies in English, (D. Reibel and S. Schane, eds.), Prentice-Hall, Englewood Cliffs, New Jersey.

Ross, J. R. 1970b. On declarative sentences. [IN Readings in English Transformational Grammar (R. Jacobs and P. Rosenbaum, eds.). Blaisdell, Waltham, Massachusetts.]

Ross, J. R. 1972. Act. IN Semantics of Natural Languages, (D. Davidson and G. Harman, eds.). D. Reidel, Dordrecht, Holland.

Ross, J. R. (in preparation). "Why helping verbs don't."

WHERE DO RELATIVE CLAUSES COME FROM?

JUDITH AISSEN
Harvard University

INTRODUCTION

Relativization applies to an NP which is contained in a clause embedded under a coreferent NP. It is generally accepted that *relativization* operates on sentences that are embedded as a result of two distinct processes.

Restrictive relatives are derived by *relativization* operating on an S which is embedded under an NP by a rule of the base which has the following formulation:

(1)   NP → NP   S

Nonrestrictive relatives are derived by the same rule of *relativization*. However, in this case, at least for English, the clause that undergoes *relativization* is not generated as an embedded S by the base. It has been reasonably suggested that it is embedded by a transformational rule operating on the second of two sentences conjoined by *and*. Thus, for example, (2) is postulated to underlie (3), which arises by the embedding transformation and *relativization:*

(2)   *My brother$_i$ smokes three packs a day and my brother$_i$ is a heart surgeon.*

(3)   *My brother, who is a heart surgeon, smokes three packs a day.*

187

It is clear that in order to account for the fact that non restrictive relatives differ in phonological, syntactic, and semantic ways from restrictive relatives, the two must be derived from different sources. There is some evidence that the source for nonrestrictive relatives is the second of two conjoined sentences. Notice the ungrammaticality of (4) and (5):

(4)   *I won't vote for a man, who wears red suspenders.*

(5)   *John will settle for any two books, which are about wine-making.*

The ungrammaticality of these sentences correlates with the ungrammaticality of (4') and (5'):

(4')   *I won't vote for a man and he wears red suspenders.*
(5')   *John will settle for any two books and they are about wine-making.*

If nonrestrictive relatives are derived from the second of two conjoined sentences, then the ungrammaticality of (4) and (5) is explained by the ungrammaticality of (4') and (5').

Other evidence in support of this derivation is the synonymy of nonrestrictive relatives and conjoined sentences, and the existence of a plausible intermediate stage in the derivation after *embedding*, but before *relativization*. Namely,

(6)   *My brother, and he is a heart surgeon, smokes three packs a day.*

I will present evidence here from Attic Greek that will provide additional evidence for the derivation of nonrestrictive relatives from conjoined sentences, and more generally, will indicate that embedding of an S conjoined by *and* in English is only one manifestation of a more general universal process of embedding one sentence in another to which it is connected by a conjunction or complementizer, when there are coreferent NPs in the two sentences. I will henceforth use the term "conjunction" to cover both conjunctions and complementizers.

RELATIVE CLAUSES IN ATTIC GREEK

In addition to restrictive and nonrestrictive relatives, there is in Greek what I will refer to here as a third class of relative clauses. It will be shown later that this class actually includes the nonrestrictives.

It has a number of types called, for example, relative purpose clause, relative result clause, and so on. For example:[1]

(7) Relative causal:

> *dóksas   amathéa   eînai **hòs** . . . ekéleue*
> believing (him) unlearned to be who . . . commanded
> [HERODOTUS 1.33]
>
> 'Believing him to be unlearned because he commanded'

(8) Relative result:

> *tís   hóutō maínetai **hóstis** ou boúletai soi phílos   eînai*
> who so   mad   who not wants to you friend to be
> [XENOPHON Anabasis, ii, 5[12]]
>
> 'Who is so mad that he doesn't want to be your friend?'

(9) Relative conditional:

> *talaipōros eî   **hôi**   méte   theoì patrōîoi eisi*
> wretched you are to whom neither gods ancestral are
>
> *méth' hierá . . .*   [PLATO Euthydemus. 302 B]
> nor   rites
>
> 'You are wretched if you have neither ancestral gods nor rites.'

(10) Relative purpose:

> *presbeían pémpein **hétis** taût'   ereî*
> embassy to send   which these things will say
> [DEMOSTHENES 1.2]
>
> '. . . to send an embassy to say these things.'

These clauses are formally like restrictive and nonrestrictive relatives, being introduced by a relative pronoun (boldface in the examples), coreferent with an antecedent NP. However, they differ from restrictives and nonrestrictives in two important ways.

Semantic Differences

As a class, these clauses bear a different semantic relation to the antecedent than that borne by either restrictives or nonrestrictives. As seen in the examples, each subtype as well bears a distinctive semantic relation to the antecedent. I do not know how to state this differ-

---

[1] All Greek examples in this paper are from W. W. Goodwin (1968).

ence, except to say that these clauses express a relation that cannot be translated into English by a relative, but must rather be translated by a conjunction-introduced clause. The semantic representation of the sentence will have to account somehow for the purpose, causal, result, or conditional reading.

Syntactic Differences

As a class, these clauses also differ syntactically from the other two types of relatives. In order to characterize this difference, it is necessary to discuss two aspects of Greek syntax. In brief, the structure of the argument is that certain aspects of Greek syntax — namely mood and negation, which need to be accounted for in these relatives — are predictable in terms of structure present before but not after embedding of the clause and deletion of the conjunction have occurred. Thus I conclude that these relatives must be derived from clauses that are not embedded under the coreferent NP, but from clauses that originate outside the sentence containing the antecedent NP. These clauses are introduced by a conjunction. Mood and negation must be assigned before *embedding–deletion* has occurred.

MOOD

There are three finite moods in Greek — indicative, subjunctive, and optative. Although these are usually characterized in semantic terms in Greek grammars, it is clear from the distribution of mood in terms of syntactic structure that there is a good deal of purely syntactic conditioning as well. In particular, independent clauses and NP-complements take a range of mood distinct from that which occurs in S- and VP-complements. The subjunctive does not occur in an independent clause or in the topmost S of an NP-complement. In addition, aside from its use in the expression of wishes and as an automatic alternate to the subjunctive in certain environments, the optative only occurs in independent clauses and is always accompanied by a particle adverb *an*. The optative plus *an* expresses contingency. The optative plus *an* never occurs in S- or VP-complements. The subjunctive only occurs in S- and VP-complements. The indicative occurs in structures of all types. The distribution of mood is represented in (11). I am ignoring certain occurences of the subjunctive in superficially independent clauses. It can be argued that at the time of mood and negation assignment, these clauses are dominated by an S which is later deleted.

(11)	Independent clauses, NP-complements	S-, VP-complements
	optative + *an*	subjunctive
	indicative	indicative

This distribution only holds good if we leave aside the third class of relatives. Whereas restrictive and nonrestrictive relatives allow the moods indicated for NP-complements, there are some relatives of the third class that only allow the moods indicated for VP- and S-complements. For example, a conditional relative of a certain type — a general conditional — takes the subjunctive:

(12)   hó   ti àn boúlētai,   dṓsō.
         which something he wants I will give
                        (subj.)
         'I will give him whatever he wants.'

This counterexample will force us either to give up the characterization of mood distribution in (11) or seek another explanation for the presence of the subjunctive in the relative clause.

The presence of the subjunctive would be explained if this relative clause were derived from the synonymous *if* clause of a conditional sentence, where the subjunctive regularly occurs. For instance, from:

(13)   eán ti boúlētai, dṓsō.
         if something he wants I will give
                     (subj.)
         'If we wants something, I will give (it to him).'

Since the *if* clause is almost certainly either an S- or VP-complement, this derivation would allow us to maintain (11).

NEGATION

The second fact about Greek syntax to be noted is that there are two distinct forms of the negation: *ou* and *mē*. Their distributions are also predictable and can be described as follows: *mē* occurs in embedded clauses other than restrictive and nonrestrictive relatives. Other NP-complements are negated by *mē*. The negation *ou* occurs in main clauses, and in restrictive and nonrestrictive relatives. This distribution is represented in (14).

(14)   *ou*   *mē*
----
       main clauses   other embedded clauses
       restrictive and nonrestrictive relatives

What is the form of the negation found in the third class of relatives? In some it is *ou*, in others it is *mē*, depending superficially on the semantic reading of the clause. Thus, purpose relatives and conditional relatives are negated by *mē*; causal and result relatives, by *ou*. This again raises a problem for the characterization of negative distribution indicated in (14), for all restrictive and nonrestrictive relatives are negated by *ou*.

It must be noted at this point that an important question has been begged in the preceding discussion of mood and negation. I have made reference to the notion of embedded clause. In order for the descriptions of mood and negation distribution to be adequate, it is necessary that some conjunctions introduce embedded clauses, while others introduce nonembedded clauses. Thus, since *ei* 'if' allows the subjunctive, but never the optative plus *an*, it must be the case, according to my characterization, that *ei* introduces an embedded clause. Similar arguments cause us to recognize the causal and result conjunctions as introducing nonembedded clauses and the purpose conjunction as introducing an embedded clause. The only way I know of to formalize this is by subcategorizing the conjunctions. This is ad hoc. Perhaps a richer semantic theory would be able to account for these syntactic facts in a non-ad hoc manner. There are empirical facts of the distributions of mood and negation that need to be explained. An explanation in terms of embedded versus nonembedded clauses is assumed here.

We have observed that there are certain distributions of mood and negation that need explanation. We have suggested that these facts can be accounted for, or at least described, in terms of syntactic structure. However, it has been noted that there is a class of exceptions to both of these characterizations, namely the third class of relatives. We now have the problem that we must either provide another explanation for the behavior of these relatives or give up the proposed characterizations of mood and negation distribution.

There is another explanation for the behavior of these relative clauses. As noted before, these clauses differ in semantic relation to the antecedent from restrictive and nonrestrictive relatives. Namely, they had to be translated into English by complement-introduced clauses. In Greek, there are complement-introduced clauses corresponding to each of the relatives of the third type. Thus, for example:

(15) Causal clause:

> *hoi Athēnaîoi enómidzon hēssâsthai   hóti   ou*
> the Athenians thought   to be defeated because not
>
> *polù   enikōn.*   [THUCYDIDES vii, 34]
> much they were victorious
>
> 'The Athenians thought they were defeated because they were not signally victorious.'

(16) Result clause:

> *Bébēken,   hóste   pân en hēsúkhōi éksesti   phōneîn.*
> he has gone so that all   in   quiet   it is possible   to say
> [SOPHOCLES O.C. 82]

'He has gone so that we can say everything in quiet.'

(17) Conditional clause:

> *polù àn thaumastóteron   ên   ei etimônto.*
> much   more wonderful been if they were honored
> [PLATO Republic 489B]

'It would be much more wonderful, if they were honored.'

(18) Purpose clause:

> ⌈they were ⌉ *éprasson hópōs tis   boḗtheia   héksei.*
> |bringing it| that   some assistance will come
> ⌊about   ⌋
> [THUCYDIDES 3.4]

'They were trying to effect (this) that some assistance should come.'

It is in terms of such structures as these that mood and negation are predictable. The mood and negation for a conjunction-introduced clause is the same mood and negation that turns up in the synonymous relative clause, in terms of which it is not possible to predict correctly the mood and negation that occur. This is strong evidence that the third class of relatives should be transformationally derived from conjunction-introduced clauses. Such a derivation will, in addition, account for the semantic relation of the relative clause to the antecedent.

The existence of sentences like (7)–(10) raises questions about the nature of the embedding required by the relativization transformation. Note that in all but (9), the relative clause is not adjacent to the antecedent, but rather follows the clause containing the antecedent, apparently remaining in the same position as the conjunction-introduced clause from which it was derived. The relativization transformation, as usually formulated, requires that the NP to be relativized be in an S which is Chomsky-adjoined to the antecedent. The only way to accomodate the facts of (7)–(10) to this formulation of *relativization* is to assume that the embedding transformation Chomsky-adjoins the S to the antecedent NP, that *relativization* applies, and that *extraposition* then applies, apparently obligatorily, to move the relativized S out of the NP back to the position of the original conjunction-introduced clause.

This would require a global formulation of the extraposition transformation, since it would have to distinguish relatives coming from conjunction-introduced clauses from restrictive relatives, since restrictive relatives usually remain next to the antecedent NP. In addition, the extraposition rule would have to know where the original clause came from, since it would not suffice to simply move the relativized S to the end of the clause, since other clauses might intervene.

It seems intuitively more correct to assume that the relativized clause was never moved from its original position. If *relativization* is formulated universally, however, and if the same relativization transformation operates to derive all relative clauses, then the Greek evidence will require that Chomsky-adjunction of the S to the antecedent NP not be part of the universal structural index of *relativization*. The fact that English does require the relativized S to be adjacent to the antecedent NP would then be a language-particular fact.

Although I do not assume that the S to be relativized is embedded in the NP, I do assume that it is a subordinate clause and in addition that it is subordinate to the S that dominates the NP. What seems to be crucially interdependent with *relativization* in these cases is deletion of the conjunction. Apparently, then, the notion of subordinate or embedded clause, at least as it pertains to *relativization*, is related to the deletion of the conjunction.

The same notion of embedded clause is operative in participle formation in both Greek and English. Independent clauses do not become participles (e.g., in Greek only the *if* clause of a conditional and never the *then* clause can become participle). In general, the same range of conjunction-introduced clauses that allow relativization in each language also allows participle formation. Thus, Greek has participle phrases that can be shown to derive from conjunction-introduced clauses by arguments similar to those given for relative clauses, and these participles are from the same conjunction-introduced clauses that yield relative clauses.

There is however, at least one participle construction in English that does not have a corresponding relative clause. In addition to participle phrases corresponding to nonrestrictives, English has participle clauses that are clearly causal:

(19)   *Being a gentleman, John paid the bill.*

which must come from a sentence like:

(20)   *Since/because he was a gentleman, John paid the bill.*

Note that *participle formation* is not crucially dependent on deletion of the subject of the participle phrase. This only occurs when the subject of the participle phrase is coreferent with the subject of the main clause:

(21)   *The time having come, they all said their good-byes.*

I will refer to the transformational process by which an S becomes embedded and the conjunction deleted, as *embedding–deletion.* The proposed embedding transformation will have the following effect. Given two sentences connected by a conjunction of a specified class, if there is an NP in the second clause coreferent to one in the first clause, subordinate the second clause to the first. Delete the conjunction. Once the clause is embedded, *relativization* can apply.

Having posited this transformation for Greek, note that the same transformation can be used in Greek to derive nonrestrictive relatives from sentences conjoined by *and.* In Greek, the mood and negation found in nonrestrictives is the same as that found in a sentence introduced by *and.* As in English, the two are also synonymous. We see now why, in Greek, restrictives and nonrestrictives have the same negation, namely *ou,* and the same range of mood – the indicative, and the optative plus *an.* Clauses introduced by *and* are not embedded, and, as we have seen, restrictive relatives are treated as independent clauses for the purpose of mood and negation assignment.

Having syntactically motivated this transformation for Greek, I suggest that the same transformation be used to derive nonrestrictive relatives in English. The justification for extending this transformation to English rests on the principle that the power of particular grammars is to be minimized, and the power of universal grammar maximized; that is, if one explanation can explain two facts in two different languages, it is to be preferred to two explanations that explain the same two facts.

Thus, there are not really three classes of relatives, but two, distinguished by whether the embedding required for *relativization* results from a rule of the base, as in restrictive relatives, or from an embedding transformation as in English nonrestrictives and the class of relatives in Greek discussed here.

On the basis of these facts, I propose that the embedding transformation be formulated universally, roughly as follows:

(22) $[W \; NP_i \; X]_{S_1}$ conjunction $[Y \; NP_i \; Z]_{S_2} \rightarrow [W \; NP_i \; X + S_2]_{S_1}$

where '+' stands for sister-adjunction. I leave open the question of what the relation of the conjunction deletion is to the embedding and subsequent relativization.

RECOVERABILITY

There is now an interesting problem to be faced. The embedding transformation as stated in (22) is not sufficient to account for the facts of Greek or English. It cannot apply to every pair of sentences conjoined by a conjunction in either language. In English, in fact, this conjunction is limited to *and*. In Greek, a considerably larger range of conjunctions allows *embedding–deletion*. How are we to formulate this restriction? There are several alternatives.

One would be to posit a universal transformation like (22), but in addition, to constrain it with a language-particular list of conjunctions that allow *embedding–deletion*. Although this is not particularly satisfying, in the absence of any more general restriction, it will be necessary to so restrict the transformation if it is to be formulated universally. Even a language-particular formulation of the transformation will require a list of eligible conjunctions if there is no other way to predict them. Thus, if there is some universal aspect of the embedding–deletion transformation, it is worth capturing this degree of generality.

Another possibility is that the list of eligible conjunctions in a given language might follow from some other fact in the language that had to be somewhere stated, so that an explicit list would not be necessary. If this were so, linguistic theory, at present, would allow this other fact to be either universal or one that was language-particular. In this case, a universal constraint that makes reference to language-particular facts is, I think, the correct one.

If one looks at English and Greek for some explanation of the significant difference in number of conjunctions that allow deletion, the most obvious one is that Greek has additional means for allowing recovery of the deleted conjunction, namely, the mood and negation (if there is one) in the remaining clause. Of the five types of derived relatives, including now nonrestrictive relatives in this class, all but causals and nonrestrictive relatives have sufficient syntactic information remaining after deletion of the conjunction to recover the conjunction. In the case of causals, although these are cited in grammars with no mention of possible ambiguity, they appear to be indistinguishable from nonrestrictive relatives. Both take *ou* as negation and both take the same range of mood: that allowed in an independent clause. A sentence like:

(23) *dóksas   amathéa   eînai,   hòs . . . ekéleue* [HERODOTUS 1.33]
     believing (him) unlearned to be who . . . commanded

may be vague in the same way that the English sentence

(24)   *John, who was the only boy in the group, paid the bill.*

is vague or indeterminate as to whether the relative has any causal force. Surely, the relative in (24) should not be derived from a clause introduced by *because* or *since*, and perhaps (23) should not either.

In English however, there are no such means for assuring recoverability of the conjunction once deleted. A clause which follows any conjunction in English can also occur after *and;* thus, any conjunction that was deleted would not be recoverable. *And* is apparently the unmarked conjunction in English, since it is the one that permits deletion. It seems likely that *and* is universally the unmarked conjunction. This predicts that any language that allows deletion of a conjuction other than *and* also allows deletion of *and*. We predict further that any language that has relative clauses derived from clauses introduced by conjunctions other than *and* also has nonrestrictive relatives.

In addition to a recoverability condition constraining the generally formulated embedding–deletion transformation it will also be necessary then to specify somehow a hierarchy of conjunctions dictating which may be deleted in cases of potentially ambiguous outputs.

If we can account for the facts with a very generally formulated embedding-deletion transformation and a recoverability condition, then it is the case that the recoverability condition is of a different type than that proposed by Chomsky in *Aspects*. He restricts the form of deletion transformations themselves to the effect that nothing can be deleted unless it is specifically mentioned in the structural index, or under identity with another element in the sentence. Given the output and the rule, the input is thus always determinable.

Such constraints on the form of deletion rules will not assure recoverability in the case of the embedding–deletion transformation if we state it in its most general form. Rather, some sort of transderivational constraint appears to be necessary, which would block all but one output when the embedding–deletion rule produced identical outputs from distinct inputs. As noted above, some hierarchical list is necessary to dictate which derivations are blocked.

SUMMARY

I have presented evidence from classical Greek that there is a class of relative clauses in that language that must be derived from conjunction-introduced clauses. This evidence was based on the predictability of mood and negation in terms of syntactic structure present before embedding of the clause and deletion of the conjunction, but not after.

I suggested that the same embedding–deletion transformation be used to derive nonrestrictive relatives in English from conjoined sentences. Thus, the transformation will be formulated universally. It is necessary, then, to account for the difference in range of conjunctions that allow deletion from language to language. A recoverability condition, transderivational in nature, was suggested as the appropriate device to account for this difference.

REFERENCE

Goodwin, W. W. 1968. A Greek Grammar. London: Macmillan.

ON THE NONEXISTENCE OF MIRROR IMAGE RULES IN SYNTAX

JORGE HANKAMER
Massachusetts Institute of Technology

The rules discussed in this chapter are universally formulated rules. Since the notion of universal rules is relatively new in linguistic theory, a word on the nature of such rules and the empirical claims implicit in the universal formulation of rules is in order.

In giving a rule a universal formulation, we make a powerful restricting claim about the grammars of natural languages. We claim that for a given universal rule, a given language may or may not have the rule; but, if it does, the rule will be formulated exactly as in any other language. In the case of the particular universal rules discussed here, a stronger claim can be made: that they are universal in the sense that every language has them.

I consider here two rules that have been proposed in universal formulations—the rule of *gapping* proposed by Ross (1971) and the rule of *conjuction reduction* proposed by Ross and Lakoff (Ross, 1967). These rules have a common formal property: They are mirror image rules. A mirror image rule is a rule that has one structural effect when applying to elements on left branches and the mirror image structural effect when applying to elements on right branches. For example, the

199

gapping rule converts (1a) into (1b):

(1)   a. *John cooked the rice, and Harry cooked the eggplant.*
      b. *John cooked the rice, and Harry the eggplant.*

But the same rule in Japanese converts (2a) into (2b):

(2)   a. *watakusi wa sakana o tabeta, Biru wa gohan o tabeta.*
              I   fish   ate   Bill   rice   ate
      b. *watakusi wa sakana, Biru wa gohan o tabeta.*
              I   fish   Bill   rice   ate.

This rule deletes from conjoined sentences all but one occurrence of an identical verb. Under Ross's proposed formulation of *gapping* as a mirror image rule, the directionality of the deletion operation is determined by the input structure: if the identical items are on left branches, as in English, the nonleftmost ones are deleted; if the identical items are on right branches, the nonrightmost ones are deleted.

The rule of *conjunction reduction* as proposed by Ross and Lakoff likewise has a mirror image formulation. This rule converts (3a) into (3b):

(3)   a. *Peter Piper was picking peppers and Susan was*
          picking peppers.
      b. *Peter Piper and Susan were picking peppers.*

The operation specified for this rule can be informally stated as follows [for a more explicit statement and some discussion see Ross (1967)]:

> Identical elements on rightmost branches of conjoined sentences are copied and Chomsky-adjoined to the right of the node immediately dominating the conjunction, and the original identical elements are erased.

But if the identical elements are on leftmost branches of the conjoined structures, the mirror-image structural effect is specified:

> Identical elements on leftmost branches of conjoined structures are copied and Chomsky-adjoined to the left of the node immediately dominating the conjunction, and the original identical elements are erased.

Thus, the same rule of conjunction reduction converts (4a) into (4b):

(4)   a. *Peter Piper picked a peck of pickled peppers and Peter*
          Piper ate himself sick.

b. *Peter Piper picked a peck of pickled peppers and ate
    himself sick.*

I will argue that the mirror image formulation of both of these rules
is wrong. Since there are no other syntactic rules clearly requiring mirror image formulation, I propose that the following principle be added
to linguistic theory as a constraint on the formulation of rules:

There are no mirror image rules in syntax.

GAPPING

The first step in the argument is to show that *forward* and *backward
gapping* (exemplified by the *gapping* rules of English and Japanese,
respectively) cannot be conflated into a single mirror image rule as
Ross proposed. This formulation has already been attacked in Maling
(1972). The evidence presented by Maling indicates that *forward* and
backward gapping in German subordinate clauses have different conditions of application. Similar evidence is to be found in every language that has both forward and *backward gapping*.
    It has been noted (see Ross, 1971; Jackendoff, 1971) that there is a
restriction on *gapping* in English to the effect that *gapping* cannot
occur if identical verbs are preceded by nonidentical adverbs or
auxiliaries:

(5)   *Peter Piper rapidly finished off the pickled peppers,
        and Susan eventually the dandelion heads.*

And if the verbs are preceded by identical adverbs or auxiliaries,
gapping deletes these elements along with the verb:

(6)   *Peter Piper rapidly finished off the pickled peppers,
        and Susan rapidly the dandelion heads.*

Forward gapping in Turkish, as in English, has a like-adverb condition. Gapping cannot occur if there are unlike adverbs immediately
before the verbs; and like adverbs are obligatorily gapped along with
the verb:

(7) *Ahmet cabuk suyu içti,   Mehmet yavaşça şarabi.*
     Ahmet quickly the water drank, Mehmet slowly the wine.

(8) *Ahmet çabuk   suyu içti,   Mehmet çabuk şarabi.*
     Ahmet quickly the water drank, Mehmet quickly the wine.

But there is no such restriction on backward gapping:

(9) *Ahmet çabuk suyu, Mehmet yavaşça şarabi içti.*
     Ahmet quickly the water, Mehmet slowly the wine drank.

(10) *Ahmet cabuk suyu,   Mehmet çabuk şarabi içti.*
     Ahmet quickly the water, Mehmet quickly the wine drank.

Under Ross's hypothesis, these sentences must be derived by *forward gapping* from an underlying SVO order. The surface order results from an obligatory rule placing the verb in final position.

Thus, *forward gapping* is blocked by some condition in cases where *backward gapping* is not. Similar evidence is to be found in other languages. Japanese and Korean, for example, which have only *backward gapping*, have no like-adverb restriction on the *gapping rule*. English, French, German (main clauses), and other languages that have only *forward gapping*, have the *like-adverb restriction*. Languages like Russian and Persian, which are like Turkish in having both *forward* and *backward gapping*, have the *like-adverb restriction* on *forward gapping* but not on *backward gapping*.

Furthermore, there is evidence that the structure resulting from *backward gapping* is not that predicted by Ross's rule, but rather that which would be assigned by *conjunction reduction;* that is, the structure after *backward gapping* is not (11), but (12).

(11)

(12)

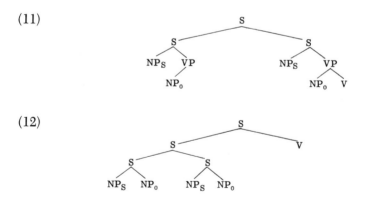

Ross (1967a) considers this possibility, noting that for some speakers of Japanese there is phonological evidence that the major constituent break in such a sentence is immediately before the verb. He rejects it, however, on the grounds that languages with *subject–verb agreement*

show agreement between the verb and the nearest subject. This would be an argument against the derivation of these sentences by *conjunction reduction* only if the rule that derives conjoined subjects, which must precede the rule of *agreement,* is the same as the rule which reduces final constituents. Below, I will argue that these are two different rules, and that the rule that derives conjoined constituents must precede the rule that reduces identical final constituents. Therefore, there is no reason the rule of *agreement* cannot intervene between them.

Note that in (11) the verb is in a coordinate structure, whereas in (12) it has been raised out of the coordinate structure. I will refer to structures such as (11) as gapped structures, and structures such as (12) as reduced structures. Note, also, that *forward gapping* necessarily produces a gapped structure:

(13)

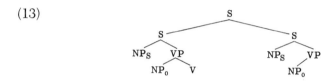

If we can find a rule that refers to V, we can test whether *backward gapping* assigns a gapped or a reduced structure by making use of the *coordinate structure constraint;* such a rule should not be applicable to a verb in a backward-gapped conjunction if the structure assigned by *backward gapping* is a gapped one, as Ross's rule predicts. But if the structure assigned by *backward gapping* is a reduced one, as in (12), the coordinate structure constraint should not apply and the application of the rule should not be blocked.

Such a rule in Turkish is the rule of *nominalization,* which converts the verb of an embedded sentence into a participle or verbal noun and puts the subject of the embedded sentence in the genitive case:

(14)   *Hasan, Ahmed-in   suyu   içme -si -ni   istiyor.*
       Hasan Ahmet (gen)   water   drinking (poss)   wants
       'Hasan wants Ahmet to drink the water.'

This rule can apply to nominalize the verb in a backward-gapped conjunction:

(15) *Hasan,   Ahmedin suyu,   Mehmedin şarabı içmesini istiyor.*
     Hasan Ahmet's the water Mehmet's   the wine drinking wants
     'Hasan wants Ahmet to drink the water, and Mehmet the wine.'

But it cannot apply if *forward gapping* has occurred:

(16)   *Hasan, Ahmedin suyu icmesini, Mehmedin şarabı istiyor.*

If, as Ross's formulation of the *gapping rule* claims, *forward* and *backward gapping* are the same rule, it is difficult to see how *forward gapping* is to be blocked in (16) while *backward gapping* is allowed in (15), or alternatively, how *nominalization* is to be blocked in (16) when it must be allowed to occur in (15). If, on the other hand, *backward gapping* is not *gapping* at all, but rather *conjunction reduction* applying to identical final elements, the grammaticality of (15) and the ungrammaticality of (16) are automatically explained by the *coordinate structure constraint.* There are parallel facts in other languages that have *backward gapping* and a *nominalization* rule like that of Turkish (e.g., Japanese and Korean).

These facts are in accord with the hypothesis that the rule effecting *backward gapping* is simply the rule of conjunction reduction applying to identical final constituents, and thus a totally different rule from that effecting *forward gapping.*

This hypothesis also accounts for another otherwise unexplainable fact. One of the necessary components of Ross's *gapping* hypothesis was that *gapping* must be an "anywhere" rule; in particular, it must be able to apply both before and after *scrambling.* However, in order to account for the gapping patterns in various languages, it is necessary to postulate another hypothesis, which has the effect of making it impossible for *backward gapping* ever to apply before *scrambling* or for forward gapping ever to apply after *scrambling.* This hypothesis is as follows:

> Any language that has verb/object scrambling is SVO in underlying order (verb-initial languages being left out of consideration).

This is required, in Ross's theory, to account for the fact that the *gapping* pattern SO SVO never arises; if an underlying SOV language had both verb/object *scrambling* and an anywhere *gapping* rule, the application of *gapping* followed by *scrambling* would yield the forbidden pattern.

This means that languages with underlying SOV order never have *forward gapping;* languages with underlying SVO order can gap forward, but only before the application of *scrambling,* if the language has *scrambling* at all; and languages with underlying SVO order can gap backward, but only after the application of *scrambling* or some rule that permutes verb and object.

Thus, although *gapping* is formulated in Ross's hypothesis as a mirror-image anywhere rule, it in fact never gets a chance to apply forward except before *scrambling* and never gets a chance to apply backward except after *scrambling* in any language that has *scrambling*.

This appears to be a queer accident under Ross's hypothesis; the whole point of making *gapping* an anywhere rule is to allow its application both before and after *scrambling*. There is no reason whatever to expect that some independent factor should restrict the application of *forward* and *backward gapping* in this manner. If, however, *forward* and *backward gapping* are effected by two entirely different rules, and if the ordering relation between these rules is universally that which is required (apparently accidentally) by Ross's hypothesis, it is no longer an unexplained accident that *forward gapping* invariably precedes *backward gapping*.

Since *forward* and *backward gapping* have different entry conditions, result in different derived structures, and cannot apply at the same point in derivations, it is difficult to see how they can be maintained to be the same rule. If they are different rules, one effecting deletion of constituents whether on right or left branches under identity with a constituent in the preceding conjunct, and one effecting *conjunction reduction* of final identical constituents, these facts are automatically explained.

This hypothesis also automatically accounts for one of the universal peculiarities of *gapping*, which Ross's hypothesis was intended to explain — the fact that in no language does the pattern SO SVO occur. If *backward gapping* is really *conjunction reduction*, so formulated that it can only apply to constituents in initial or final position, it clearly cannot apply to produce the pattern SO SVO, since the identical verbs are in neither initial nor final position. The rule of *conjunction reduction* can produce no pattern other than SO SOV. If the rule of *conjunction reduction* is universally ordered after *scrambling* (and note that under Ross's hypothesis *backward gapping* is universally ordered after *scrambling*), the pattern SO SVO can never be derived.

The notion of a universal rule ordering is a new kind of constraint on grammars, the implications of which cannot be gone into here. [The empirical and theoretical consequences of this proposal are investigated in detail in Hankamer (1971).] But in the case of universal constraints, novelty is no counterargument. Such an ordering constraint would severely restrict the class of possible grammars, and thus contribute to a stronger linguistic theory.

CONJUNCTION REDUCTION

I have suggested that *backward gapping* should be identified with *conjunction reduction* operating on the right. I will now consider the mirror image formulation of *conjunction reduction* and argue that *right conjunction reduction* is in fact not the same rule as *left conjunction reduction*.

It has been assumed that the rule of *conjunction reduction*, as outlined above, reduces identical elements on the rightmost or leftmost branches of conjoined sentences. Thus, it applies not only to derive conjoined subjects and conjoined VPs, as in (3) and (4), but also to reduce final constituents of the VP, such as objects:

(17)   *Peter Piper picked, and Susan ate, the pickled peppers.*

The pronounced and obligatory pauses, indicated by commas, in sentences like (17) are unaccounted for under this assumption; they do not appear in such sentences as (3) and (4).

I will argue that the rule involved in the derivation of (17) is not the same rule as that involved in the derivation of (3) or (4); that conjoined constituents are derived by one rule, which I will continue to call *conjunction reduction,* and that final constituents of the VP are reduced by a different rule, which I will refer to as *delay.*

Note that in (17) the conjoined segments are nonconstituents. The structure assigned by *right conjunction reduction,* as formulated by Ross and Lakoff, is the following:

(18)

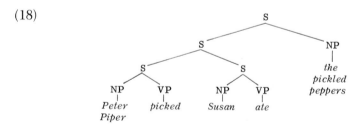

Such a structure containing a conjunction of nonconstituents also appears when *right conjunction reduction* is applied to derive reduced verbs in verb-final languages. But note that only when applying to final subconstituents of VP does the rule produce such a conjunction of S fragments. I suggest that there is a rule (*delay*) that applies only to final subconstituents of the VP and results in this structure, and that conjoined constituents—whether subjects, verbs, objects, or VPs—are derived by a different rule.

Under the Ross–Lakoff formulation, the rule of *conjunction reduction* must be able to apply to its own output in order to derive conjoined verbs and conjoined objects. Thus, (19) is converted into (20) by two successive applications of *conjunction reduction:*

(19)   *Alvin cooked the peppers and Alvin cooked the beans.*

(20)   *Alvin cooked the peppers and the beans.*

The first application of conjunction reduction reduces the identical subjects, producing the intermediate stage (21) with conjoined VPs:

(21)   *Alvin cooked the peppers and cooked the beans.*

The second application of *conjunction reduction* reduces the identical verbs, yielding (20).

Now observe that *right conjunction reduction* cannot, at least with the same felicity, reapply to its own output:

(22)   *John wrote a letter to his congressman, and Albert*
            sent a telegram to the newspaper, protesting
            the publication of NSF26.

(23)   **John wrote a letter, and Albert sent a telegram, to the*
            newspaper protesting the publication of NSF26.

Sentence (22) is perfectly good, but (23), in which *right conjunction reduction* has applied twice to reduce both the final and prefinal constituent, is terrible.

Furthermore, although final subconstituents of the VP can be reduced even when the VP containing them is deeply embedded, as in

(24)   *John swore that Kathy was, and Albert succeeded in*
            proving that Sally had never been, a virgin.

the entire VP of an embedded sentence cannot be reduced:

(25)   **John swore that Kathy, and Albert succeeded in proving*
            that Sally, was a virgin.

There is no way the Ross–Lakoff *conjunction reduction* rule can be prevented from applying to the embedded VPs in (25) and at the same time be allowed to apply to the embedded subconstituents of VP in (24); and also be allowed to derive conjoined subjects by reducing identical VPs in nonembedded clauses. The conclusion is inescapable that the rule that derives conjoined subjects by reducing identical VPs is not the same as the rule that effects the reduction in (24) and is blocked in (25).

There are cases where, in the derivation of a single sentence, the *conjunction reduction* rule as formulated by Ross and Lakoff must apply both on the left and on the right, as in the derivation of a sentence with conjoined verbs:

(26)   *Alvin cooked and ate the potatoes.*

Presuming that the underlying structure is that of

(27)   *Alvin cooked the potatoes and Alvin ate the potatoes.*

(26) can be derived by first applying *conjunction reduction* on the left to yield

(28)

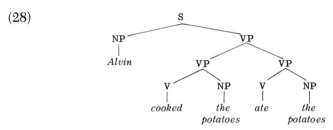

A subsequent application of conjunction reduction applying on the right yields:

(29)

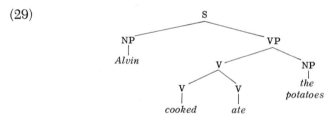

And this is correct. However, if *conjunction reduction* is a Ross–Lakoff mirror image rule, there is nothing to stop the rule from applying first on the right in (27) to yield:

(30)

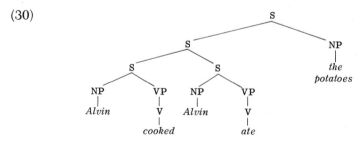

and subsequently on the left to yield:

(31)

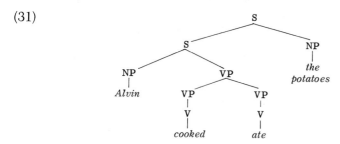

This is clearly wrong. The derived structure claims that the major constituent break in the sentence is immediately before *the potatoes* and that *Alvin cooked and ate* is a constituent.

Thus, not only do *right conjunction reduction* and *left conjunction reduction* have different conventions of application, so that *left conjunction reduction* can reapply to its own output whereas *right conjunction reduction* cannot, but *right conjunction reduction* must not be permitted to apply until after *left conjunction reduction* has had a chance to apply. This would be a natural consequence of the formulation of these as two separate rules ordered with respect to one another.

There are other formal problems with the formulation of *conjunction reduction* as a single mirror image rule. Ross (1967) notes that *right conjunction reduction* fails to obey one of the constraints on pied piping:

(32)　*I am confident of, and my boss depends on, a successful*
　　　　outing at the track.

Here, according to Ross, an NP has been moved to the right out of a prepositional phrase, in violation of one of the pied piping constraints, namely, that the preposition must obligatorily pied pipe under such a movement.

Ross cites this as an unexplained quirk of *conjunction reduction* requiring that a rider be placed on the pied piping constraint to the effect that it does not apply to *conjunction reduction*. This ad hoc rider is necessary, Ross claims, because *conjunction reduction* in general does obey the constraints on pied piping. However, the example he provides to demonstrate this conclusion involves not *right conjunction reduction* but *left conjunction reduction*. He notes that (33) cannot be converted to (34):

(33)　　*The university's students are intelligent and the*
　　　　university's faculty is committed to freedom.

(34)   *The university's students are intelligent and faculty is
       committed to freedom.

Here, according to Ross, the application of *conjunction reduction* is
blocked by the left branch constraint, a condition that makes pied
piping obligatory if the constituent affected by a movement rule is on
the left branch of a higher NP.

That it is not the left branch constraint that blocks (34), however, is
shown by the grammaticality of

(35)   The university's students and faculty are intelligent.

Here, *conjunction reduction* has applied to constituents on the left
branches of higher NPs, and the application of the rule is not blocked.
Ross notes this, and proposes another ad hoc rider to the effect that the
left branch constraint fails to apply to *conjunction reduction* when the
NPs affected are directly conjoined.

However this problem is to be solved, it is clear that *left conjunction reduction* cannot apply to reduce elements of constituents that are
not directly conjoined; *right conjunction reduction*, as we have seen,
is not so restricted. If *conjunction reduction* is formulated as a mirror
image rule, there is no way out but to place an hoc riders on the pied
piping conditions or on the rule itself, referring specifically to one or
the other of its directions of application. The evidence indicates, however, that *left* and *right conjunction reduction* are two different rules
with different formal properties.

CONCLUSION

These conclusions raise the question as to what exactly is claimed
by mirror-image formulation of a rule. The evidence clearly indicates
that any generalization captured by the mirror-image formulation of
gapping and *conjunction reduction* is spurious. In this section I will
discuss a proposal by Langacker (1969) that a notational device be incorporated into linguistic theory specifically for the purpose of formulating such rules.

Langacker's major examples of rules requiring mirror image formulation are *gapping* and *conjunction reduction*. He also cites the rule of
relative clause formation, which, if given a universal formulation,
must be able to effect a deletion or movement operation to the right in
some languages and to the left in others. He also includes as mirror
image rules such rules as *pronominalization*, *right* and *left disloca-
tion*, and *indefinite incorporation*, all of which seem to be capable of

applying either to the left or to the right, although with different conditions of application in each case being in effect for the different directions of application.

It is clearly necessary, in spite of Langacker's contrary assumption, to distinguish between devices allowed for the formulation of rules in particular grammars, and devices allowed for the formulation of universal rules, whose language-specific realizations may be determined by other factors in the particular languages. There is no language in which the *relative clause formation* rule is bidirectional. The direction of application of the deletion or movement involved is determined by the position of the relative clause with respect to the head, which is fixed in every known language.

Without *gapping, conjunction reduction,* and *relative clause formation* in the list, we are left with the question of whether such rules as *pronominalization,* which can operate either to the right or to the left, require mirror image notation for their statements. It should be clear that these rules are not mirror image rules in the sense that the position of the affected constituent on a right or left branch determines the direction of application of the rule. If the device required to formulate such rules is to be called "mirror image" notation, it is at least not the same device which would be required in the statements of *gapping* and *conjunction reduction* as mirror image rules. What these rules require is rather some form of directionless notation, if they are to be collapsed at all.

In conclusion, on the basis of currently available evidence, and employing the sense of mirror image rule adopted above, the following constraint on rule formulation in particular grammars can be added to linguistic theory:

> There are no mirror image rules in syntax.

Alternatively, this can be formulated as a negative constraint on notation:

> No notational device such as that proposed by Langacker, which could have the effect of allowing mirror image formulation of rules, may be employed in the formulation of any rule in the grammar of any language.

Such a universal constraint would prevent, in principle, the formulation of *gapping* and *conjunction reduction* as mirror image rules, which has been shown on empirical grounds to be incorrect. It would thus constitute a significant and empirically justified restriction on the notion "possible rule of grammar."

REFERENCES

Hankamer, J. 1971. Constraints on Deletion in Syntax. Ph. D. Thesis, Yale University.

Jackendoff, R. 1971. Gapping and related rules. Linguistic Inquiry II/1.21–35.

Koutsoudas, A. 1970. Gapping, Conjunction Reduction, and Coordinate Deletion. Indiana University Linguistics Club, Bloomington, Indiana.

Langacker, R. 1969. Mirror image rules I: Syntax. Language 45.575–598.

Maling, J. 1972. On "Gapping and the order of Constituents." Linguistic Inquiry III/1.101–108.

Ross, J. R. 1967. Constraints on Variables in Syntax. Indiana University Linguistics Club, Bloomington, Indiana.

Ross, J. R. 1971. Gapping and the Order of Constituents. Recent Developments in Linguistics. (Bierwisch, M. and K. E. Heidolph, eds.). Mouton, The Hague, The Netherlands.

THE VP-CONSTITUENT OF SVO LANGUAGES

ARTHUR SCHWARTZ
University of California, Santa Barbara

TWO SETS OF FACTS

The First Set—A

Some languages can be characterized by a basic organization of the sentence in terms of predicate first (the so-called VSO type), and some by predicate last (the so-called SOV type). Among the VSO group are Samoan, Berber, Squamish, Chinook, and Kalispel; among the SOV are Telugu, Japanese, Basque, Amharic, Hindi, and Turkish. This chapter deals with the constituency relation that may or may not obtain between the VS elements of VSO languages, and the OV elements of SOV languages. We will take Samoan as representative of the first type, and Turkish as representative of the second.

The normal order of elements in Turkish is subject first, predicate last, and "complements" intervening: roughly, *The boy a book reads; the boy to-school goes.* "Any element which is to be emphasized may be placed immediately before the verb" (from Lewis, 1967, pp. 240–241):

Base *Ressam geçen hafta Bebek'te bize resimlerini gösterdi.*
     artist   last   week Bebek at us   pictures his showed
     'The artist showed us his pictures last week at Bebek.'

*Geçen hafta Bebek'te bize resimlerini **ressam** gösterdi.*
'It was the artist who showed us his pictures. . .'

*Ressam Bebek'te bize resimlerini **geçen hafta** gösterdi.*
'It was last week that the artist showed. . .'

*Ressam geçen hafta bize resimlerini **Bebek'te** gösterdi.*
'It was at Bebek that the artist showed. . .'

Unless we are to imagine all unemphatic material brought forward so as to leave the emphatic element immediately before the verb, we conceive of this positioning as a movement of the focussed element from its basic position in the sentence toward the predicate.

The normal order of elements in Samoan is predicate first, subject next, complements following. There is apparently considerable freedom of order, although the basic arrangement in a transitive expression seems to be predicate–agent–patient. Adverbials are positioned basically in clause final position. However, alternations do occur:

> *Sa   togi   e   le   tama le ma'a lelei*
> past throw by the boy   the rock good
> 'The boy threw the rock well'

> *Sa   togi   lelei e   le   tama le   ma'a*
> past throw good by the boy   the rock
> 'The boy threw the rock well'

But this movement is strictly in terms of "toward the predicate" since a movement resulting in

> *Sa   togi   e   le   tama lelei le   ma'a.*
> past throw by the boy   good the rock

is ungrammatical if intended as 'The boy threw the rock well'; it can only mean 'The good boy threw the rock' (Pizzini, 1969, pp. 82 and 102).

Turkish and Samoan might be conceived as shown in (1),

(1)

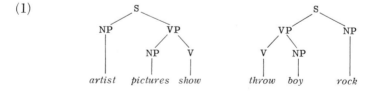

in which case, any constituent brought toward the predicate will have to intervene between the predicate and its co-constituent. The move would result in a tripartite constituency relation in the representations above. I have argued elsewhere for a general constraint on movement transformations (Schwartz, 1972) that would rule out lowering of phrases; in particular, it would rule out the merger of sister phrases, as in (2):

(2)

Intuitively, the constraint expresses the empirical observation that, in the unmarked situation, transformations do not increase structure (depth of branching). If the constraint is right, and the facts in Samoan and Turkish are right, then the notion of VP in representation (1) is wrong.

We now consider three languages that fall into the SVO class— Mandarin, Tera, and Indonesian. In Mandarin, time adverbials have two positions:

> Last week my friend gave me the ticket.
> My friend last week gave me the ticket.
> *My friend gave last week me the ticket.
> *My friend gave me last week the ticket.
> *My friend gave me the ticket last week.

The two acceptable constructions in themselves do not show that the time adverbial is positioned basically in clause initial position, and optionally moved so as to intervene between the subject and the rest of the sentence. However, the positioning of the negative *bu* can only be given as

> My friend *bu* gave me the tickets.
> *Bu* my friend gave me the tickets.
> *My friend gave *bu* me the tickets.

and so on. This unique position is particularly instructive when we find that locative expressions precede the main verb, and that the negative of such a construction has only one possibility:

> My friend in-the-city lives.
> *My friend lives in-the-city.

> My friend *bu* in-the-city lives.
> *My friend in-the-city *bu* lives.

The impression one receives from such an array of facts is that *bu* marks the beginning of the predicate, and not simply the main verb.

The kind of evidence brought forward in Mandarin assumes that a feeling for interruptability (more accurately, a resistance toward interruptability) can be used as evidence for constituency relations. Such evidence has been used in the past (Maclay and Osgood, 1959; Johnson, 1965; Fodor and Bever, 1965) in support of major constituency breaks. However, it is at best a weak argument. Notice, for example, that in the Samoan case, one could argue for a constituency relation between *tama* 'boy' and *ma'a* 'rock' as to explain why *lelei* 'good' cannot intervene. The explanation seems to be simple enough; the movement is toward the predicate, and so any other positioning is ungrammatical. To interpret that constraint as evidence for constituency would lead us to suppose that the ungrammaticality of *Sa lelei togi e le tama le ma'a* — in which the adverb *lelei* intervenes between the tense marker *sa* and the verb *togi* — indicates a constituency relation between *sa, togi, tama,* and *ma'a*. True enough, they form an S constituent, but it is difficult to see how the *lelei*-interruptability test shows anything more than that the adverb is strictly positioned.

To use interruptability as a criterion for constituency, we must be able to show that an element that is otherwise freely positioned is excluded from the context that interests us. For example, time adverbials in Indonesian do have considerable freedom:

> **Yesterday** the patient died.
> The patient **yesterday** died.
> The patient died **yesterday.**

With this observation as background, we feel justified in interpreting facts like

> Yesterday the patient wrote a letter.
> The patient yesterday wrote a letter.
> *The patient wrote yesterday a letter.
> The patient wrote a letter yesterday.

as indicating some special relation between *wrote* and *a letter*, since no other principle would seem to explain the inability of the time adverbial to occur in just that position. That transitivity has nothing to do with the constraint is evident from other facts:

> Yesterday the patient went to the hospital.
> The patient yesterday went to the hospital.
> *The patient went yesterday to the hospital.
> The patient went to the hospital yesterday.

Thus, the intuitive sense of a bond or valence between these predicates and their complements is substantiated by a probing of constituency breaks; the stronger the bond, the worse the violation. Interruptions like *to yesterday the hospital* and *to the yesterday hospital* are worse than *went yesterday to the hospital* (in Indonesian, as in English).

In Tera, the normal order of a transitive expression is subject–verb–object. There is a particle *ku* that marks a nominal phrase as plural. "If a sentence has either a plural noun or conjoined nouns as subject, and if the predicate is either verbal or existential, the plural marker [*ku*] is added to the end of the predicate [Newman, 1970, p. 49]":

> A and B learn reading *ku*
> Children learn reading *ku*
> *A and B learn *ku* reading
> *Children learn *ku* reading

The notion "end of the predicate" is corroborated by the effect of sentence-level time and place adverbials. These normally are in clause final position:

> A learns reading tomorrow.
> A learns reading at-school.

Ku placement is dictated quite strictly by the facts:

> A and B learn reading *ku* tomorrow.
> A and B learn reading *ku* at school.
> *A and B learn reading tomorrow *ku*.
> *A and B learn reading at school *ku*.

which support a feeling that the sentence has as its major constituents "A and B," "learn reading," and "tomorrow/at school."

Another aspect of Tera confirms the need for this end of predicate notion. In sentences with conjoined nominals as subject, one member of the conjunction can be shifted away:

> a. A and B learn reading   ⇒
> b. A   learn reading and B

Type (b) might be thought of as a reduced S conjunction: *A learn reading and B learn reading* ⇒ *A learn reading and B ∅ ∅*. But the evidence of the plural marker militates against this alternative:

> a. A and B learn reading.   ⇒
> b. A and B learn reading *ku*.   ⇒
> c. A   learn reading *ku* and B.

That is to say, the manifestation of *ku* in sentence (c) shows that *A and B* were a compound subject at some point in the formation of the sentence. Now, in order to state the shift of *and B* precisely, we have to allow for the same strictness as in *ku*-placement; the conjunct must be positioned before time and place adverbials:

A and B	learn reading tomorrow.
A and B	learn reading *ku* tomorrow.
A	learn reading *ku* and B tomorrow.
*A	learn reading *ku* tomorrow and B.
*A	learn and B reading *ku* tomorrow.

These facts, like those originally cited for Mandarin, rest on the placement of certain elements; in order to say where the material is to be positioned, it is convenient to establish a boundary point (as in phonology, we posit word boundaries for stress placement, devoicing phenomena, and cluster reduction). Tera does not indicate whether *ku* and the shifted member of the compound subject are part of the predicate or simply follow the predicate; the facts do suggest that a major constituent break occurs between *learn reading* and clause final adverbials like *tomorrow* and *at market*. But neither placement nor interruptability constitute hard evidence for constituency. As far as I can see, the only clear test is based on the unit-movement constraint; if two or more constituents can be shown to move simultaneously, then we must assume that they themselves form a constituent.

Indonesian has a way of forming emphatic questions by attaching an enclitic -*kah* to the emphasized element, thereby bringing that element to clause initial position. Thus,

Base	The patient went to-the-hospital yesterday.
	Yesterday-*kah* the patient went to-the-hospital?
	To-the-hospital-*kah* the patient went yesterday?
	Went to-the-hospital-*kah* the patient yesterday?

Given the *unit-movement constraint*, the sequence "went to-the-hospital" must form a constituent, since there is no evidence that motivates two movements—one of "to-the-hospital," the other of "went."

The Second Set—B

Some languages manifest a transitive expression that has come to be called the ergative construction. Essentially, an ergative construction treats the patient nominal as its subject, much as an intransitive predicate would treat its subject. The agent nominal in an ergative construction is usually marked by some particle. In rough English translation, we might contrast active, passive, and ergative forms in the following way:

Active:	*the girl*	*sews the shirts*
Passive:	*the shirts are-sewn by the girl*	
Ergative:	*the shirts*	*sew*	*by the girl*

Languages that have only the active type, or only the active and passive types, are commonly called accusative systems. Languages that have active and ergative, or active, passive, and ergative, are commonly called accusative–ergative systems. Languages that have only the ergative as a basic transitive expression are called ergative systems.

By "basic," I mean that an ergative construction is the unmarked member of a pair of constructions expressing a transitive relationship (e.g., that obtaining between *girl, shirt,* and *sew*). By unmarked, I mean essentially the same kind of evidence that would distinguish active and passive in, say, Indonesian:

Anak itu mem-batja buku ini.
boy   the   read   book this
'The boy read this book.'

Buku ini di-batja (oleh) anak itu.
book this be-read (by) boy   the
'This book was read by the boy.'

The fact that both nominals are unmarked in the active while the agent is marked in the passive suggests that the active is primary. In another language (e.g., Hebrew), the verbal form itself might show increased complexity in the passive. In this sense, an ergative system might have an alternative transitive construction (e.g., active) as derivative. However, this development in an ergative system is rare (but see Dyirbal in Dixon, 1969:36-7).

Considering the three elements in a transitive network—the predicate, the patient, and the agent—there are six possible basic orders:

I	II	III
Pred–pat–ag	Pat–pred–ag	Pat–ag–pred
Pred–ag–pat	Ag–pred–pat	Ag–pat–pred

But as has been observed (Greenberg, 1966), the only types that show up significantly are pred–ag–pat, ag–pred–pat, and ag–pat–pred. In other words, there is a prevailing tendency to announce the agent nominal before the patient, regardless of the basic position of the predicate. We will refer to these three types by their by now familiar rubrics VSO, SVO, and SOV — bearing in mind that S = agent and O = patient, not subject and object.

Accusative systems can be found in all three types, as indicated by the following:

VSO: Berber, Hawaiian, Squamish
SVO: Nguna, Indonesian, Yoruba
SOV: Japanese, Telugu

Accusative–ergative systems can also be found in all three types:

VSO: Samoan, Tongan
SVO: Sikaiana, Luangiua
SOV: Hindi, Georgian

But true ergative systems are not distributed as generally:

VSO: Chinook, Niuean
SVO: —
SOV: Basque, Dyirbal

The question, then, is are the above two sets of facts related? That is, is the nonoccurrence of SVO–ergative systems in any way connected to the fact that SVO systems seem distinct in other respects from both VSO and SOV systems, and what is that connection?

FOUR HYPOTHESES

At the beginning of this chapter, it was suggested that a Samoan transitive construction might be represented by a structure like

(3)

But if the notion VP is to have any interesting value, it should be regarded as a general (constant) relation — such as that between the predicate and the patient nominal, as is usually assumed. I take it, then, that the notion VP means, in the transitive case, a constituent whose head is a predicate and whose complement is a nominal in the patient relation to it.

A number of hypotheses with respect to the distribution of the VP constituents are possible, including (1) all systems have VP (2) only SOV and SVO systems have VP, (3) no systems have VP, (4) only an SVO system has VP. With regard to hypothesis (1), then, we see that in order to account for VSO systems that seem to prefer the order agent–patient, allowance will have to be made for a maneuver like (a) or (b):

(4)

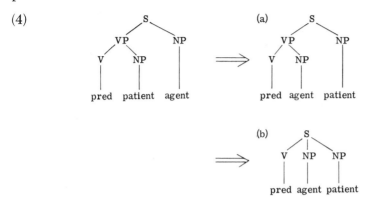

Before examining each hypothesis more carefully, let us list some of the general principles or constraints that one or more of them presupposes with respect to notions like agent, patient, subject, and predicate:

I. Agent to precede patient in the unmarked transitive construction.
II. "Subject" to be a nominal immediately dominated by S node.
III. "Subject" to have a uniform time orientation with respect to predicate.
IV. Only one nominal to be immediately dominated by S node.

Constraint (I) has already been introduced and is reflected in the fact that we have typed all possible systems in terms of (a) the position of the predicate; and (b) the universal requirement that agent precede patient. This constraint will not be discussed further here.

Hypothesis (1) is a universalistic statement and requires that all systems assume a certain structure fundamentally. The prime advantage resulting from such a thesis is that a general definition of "subject" can be obtained—that is, hypothesis (1) is based on constraints I–IV:

(5)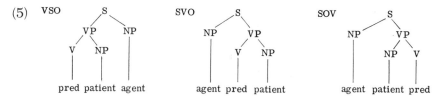

Constraint IV is critical to the value of hypothesis (1), for the effect of positing the VP-construct is to remove the patient nominal from any immediate relation to the S node. Thus, universally, the agent nominal is the unmarked subject (the logical one). Constraint III, that the subject have a uniform time orientation with respect to the predicate, implies (for all the hypotheses) that the subject of the intransitive predicate would basically precede or follow the predicate in accord with the subject nominal of a transitive predicate.

But notice that the base configuration assigned to VSO systems must, as indicated in (4), be restructured to its preferred shape. Derivative (4a) or (4b) will be necessary to remove the patient nominal from its basic constituency with the predicate. The maneuver, as far as can be determined from the data available for VSO systems, is unmotivated; there is nothing to suggest that the base organization is present in the system. The move that yields (4a) — which requires, in addition, that we allow a switch in structural position as a desirable construct in syntactic theory — or (4b) is motivated solely by a concern to universalize the notion VP, in the sense of a predicate + patient constituent, and impose it on all systems. Most important, hypothesis (1) offers no explanation for the facts in the first section of this chapter.

Hypothesis (2) is a weakening of (1); the universality of base-structuring is given up by limiting the appearance of the VP-construct to SVO and SOV systems:

(6)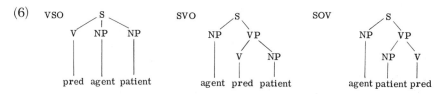

Hypothesis (2), unlike (1), does not (in fact, cannot) require constraint IV. It assumes constraint II, that the subject nominal be given an immediate relation to the S node, but that the subject relation not be defined uniquely in structural terms. As we shall see, all hypotheses other than (1) will have to offset the loss of constraint IV with some substitute construct for the subject relation. In itself, then, the rejection of constraint IV is not a distinctive aspect of hypothesis (2). In fact, this hypothesis has little to recommend it; it has already given up the attractive universality of (1) but offers nothing to replace it. It assumes constraints I, II, and III, and yet offers no explanation for the facts in the first section of this chapter. Indeed, it promises to show how SVO and SOV systems share certain features when, as the facts have indicated, there is more in common between VSO and SOV systems than between SVO and either of the others. Hypothesis (2) does not help, and it may even hinder.

Hypothesis (3) is closest in spirit to (1) in that it claims a universal character for the base organization of all systems — at least in the sense that all and only the same categories appear:

(7)

Whether all linear organizations derive from the same order is another aspect of the universalistic perspective, but one whose discussion will be postponed to the next section of this chapter. Hypothesis (3), like (2), cannot fall back on a structural definition of "subject — which was the chief virtue of hypothesis (1) and constraint IV. True enough "subject" will be — as required by constraint II — a nominal immediately dominated by the S node, but that is not a unique characterization.

Hypothesis (3) is an attractive proposal, not only for its universal domain, but also for its explanation of the facts (B) given above. Recall that true ergative systems, that is, those expressing the transitive relationship as ergative in the unmarked construction, were found only in VSO and SOV systems:

VSO	Pred	AGENT	Patient
	Pred	Agent	PATIENT
SOV	AGENT	Patient	Pred
	Agent	PATIENT	Pred
SVO	AGENT	Pred	Patient
	*Agent	Pred	PATIENT

where capitalization indicates the nominal in subject relation to the predicate. Hypothesis (3) is based on constraints I, II, and III. Constraint III, the requirement that the subject bear a uniform time orientation with respect to the predicate (transitive or intransitive), is apparently the explanation that now emerges. For the first time, we see that what sets VSO and SOV systems apart from SVO systems is that in the former, the subject must have a uniform orientation to the predicate. Constraint I and constraint III are in conflict in an SVO system that is at the same time truly ergative. Constraint III requires the ergative construction to be an unmarked

PATIENT   Pred   Agent

in conformity with the subject orientation of the intransitive predicates. But Constraint I requires that agent precede patient in the unmarked transitive expression in any system. Apparently, given the empirical motivation now available, it must be assumed that constraint I takes precedence over constraint III.

Hypothesis (3), then, seems to take advantage, on the one hand, of the rejection of the VP-constituent entirely, and on the other hand, of its universal leveling of all systems to configurations of S, NP, and V. On the basis of such an equalization, constraint III stands out as a critical factor. It offers an explanation uniquely for the facts (B) above — that SVO systems and true ergative systems are incompatible.

It would seem, therefore, that hypothesis (4) has little to recommend it, for we have said that all the hypotheses under consideration here assume the validity of constraints I, II, and III. Since Hypothesis (3) can dispense with the construct VP, hypothesis (4) appears to be more costly — blatantly so in its neglect of a universal base structure. However, in defense of hypothesis (4), we could say that since it invokes one construct (the VP-constituent) perhaps the other (constraint III) is not necessary. Hypothesis (4) posits the following base types:

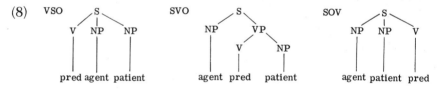

(8)   VSO   SVO   SOV

This hypothesis, as did the others, assumes constraints I and II — the first being the temporal precedence of agent over patient; the second being the immediate domination of the subject nominal by the S node. Can these two principles, plus the VP-construct, explain the facts (B) above? If such a cluster of assumptions can, then the only advantage hypothesis (3) has over hypothesis (4) is its universal aspect; otherwise, (3) requires constraint III for its explanatory value, while (4) requires the system-specific VP-constituent.

It should be fairly clear that hypothesis (4) does offer its own explanation for the incompatibility of SVO and true ergative systems.

The crucial requirement here is constraint II: if the subject nominal must be in immediate association with the S node of its predicate, and if constraint I forces the agent to precede the patient, then the VP-construct rules out an SVO–ergative system. The patient nominal in an SVO system can never be the subject of an unmarked transitive construction.

While hypothesis (4) can dispense with constraint III, it leans crucially on the positing of a language-specific category like VP. Thus, while both hypotheses (3) and (4) explain the facts (B) above, hypothesis (3) would appear, because of its more general character, to be preferable. However, we have yet to consider these alternatives in the light of the facts (A) given above. There, a number of phenomena involving constituency relations built around the predicate suggested certain distinct characteristics associated with VSO and SOV languages, on the one hand, and certain distinct characteristics associated with SVO languages, on the other. Hypothesis (3) assumes the following basic organizations:

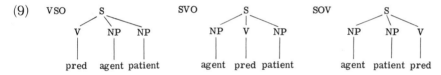

(9) VSO   SVO   SOV

But these subhypotheses of hypothesis (3) can offer nothing to explain the critical facts (A), that while VSO and SOV systems manifest an openness with respect to movement toward the predicate, SVO systems show a resistance to interrupting the predicate–patient sequence. Hypothesis (4) exploits its VP-construct in two ways then—first, in explanation of the nonoccurrence of SVO–ergative systems; second, in explanation of phenomena involving interruptability, placement, and movement with respect to the predicate. It would appear, therefore, that even at the cost of surrendering universality, hypothesis (4) is to be preferred over (3).

IN SEARCH OF AN EXPLANATION

It will be recalled that in giving up hypothesis (1), we recognized a need for finding an alternative to the rejected structural definition of subject. Hypothesis (3), like (4), must cast about for a replacement. Both hypotheses seem to converge on the SVO system as supplying the direction of inquiry, each in its own way requires that agent and subject be identified in an SVO system. For hypothesis (3), constraint

III—the requirement of uniform subject–predicate orientation—
forces the identification; for hypothesis (4), the VP-construct does the
same.

It is interesting that each hypothesis, for its own reason, forces an
identification of agent and subject (in the unmarked transitive expression) in the SVO system. Since this contrasts obviously with the lack
of such a constraint in VSO and SOV systems—recall that true ergative
systems identify the patient and subject in the unmarked transitive
expression—what we are led to ask is whether the SVO system is a
marked or unmarked organization. If marked, does it stand opposed to
two equally unmarked organizations? If unmarked, in what relation
does it stand to the two marked systems?

One argument for the unmarked character of SVO organization is
that as elsewhere in linguistic analysis, when two or more variants of a
construction are in question and the base-derived relationship is not
clear, one criterion that often serves to distinguish the candidates is
that of generality of distribution. For example, if nothing else serves to
indicate the primacy of active over passive in a particular system, we
could ask whether active and passive occur equally naturally in all
clause types (subjunctive, imperative, relative, interrogative), in all
nominalizations, or in all deletion and pronominalization phenomena.
If active turns out to have the wider distribution, we incline to view
that variant as the unmarked member of the set. Such a line of reasoning indicates that accusative systems are unmarked since, among the
VSO–SVO–SOV alternatives, they have the widest distribution. Passive constructions would then be marked, and so would ergative (see
Hale, 1968). Ergative systems, then, would be most marked, since
they have the most restricted distribution; they require a special context within which to develop. A fairly justifiable inference can be extracted from all this—VSO and SOV systems are special contexts that
allow (invite?) ergative systems. Or, perhaps more accurately, the
ergative view of transitivity (being incompatible with SVO organization: VP + constraint I + constraint II) forces a rearrangement of
some unmarked expression toward one (VSO or SOV), which incurs
no violation of these general principles—constraints I and II (and III).

I claim no originality for such a proposal. Intuitive statements from
quite unparochial linguists such as Sapir and Velten go back a good
number of years:

> On general psychological principles, it seems likely enough
> that transitive activities are necessarily more closely con-
> nected in experience with the object [=patient] than with the
> subject [=agent].
>
> (Sapir, 1917)

Though it is always well to be wary of so-called universal
psychological phenomena, one may safely state that it is
natural to refer to the goal or recipient of an action only after
the action itself has been mentioned. This would seem to be
inherent in the analytic system.

                                                    (Velten, 1932)

Velten's last remark is particularly interesting for our purposes; it implies that although uninflected transitive constructions can occur in
all systems (VSO–SVO–SOV), because constraint I requires an announcement of agent followed by patient, the unmarked temporal
sequencing of patient and predicate is naturally predicate followed by
patient.

What sort of evidence would support such speculative proposals?
How else can one argue for the unmarked character of the *predicate-
patient constituent?* There are a number of possibilities, but a good
deal more has to be learned about these areas before anything clearly
confirmatory (or disconfirmatory) will emerge. The possibilities include (a) evolutionary tendencies, (b) natural but nonverbal systems,
(c) language acquisition in children, (d) unmarked interpretations of
predicate–nominal utterances, (e) pidgin developments, and (f) experimental evidence. I will try to say something about each of these
areas, but there is little to report at the moment. Whatever I have
found, however, either does not contradict hypothesis (4) or else supports it.

Little is known about typological development and the accusative–
ergative issue. According to Hohepa (1969), the Polynesian group
offer an attractive laboratory for the investigation of the relationship
between active–passive–ergative constructions, on the one hand, and
VSO–SVO organization on the other. A number of languages show a
relatively fine grading in this respect, suggestive of a process in action
in closely related systems.

There is almost nothing known about natural sign systems like those
of the deaf. It has been observed (A. Cicourel, personal communication) that in schools for deaf children, a private peer-group sign system
is developed that deviates from the conventional system propagated
by the school. Furthermore, when the deaf from different societies
meet, their conventional systems are set aside for a more basic (pidgin)
system that they contrive ad hoc. Since the congenital deaf have no
oral language to prejudice their natural inclinations, the ad hoc systems just mentioned seem to offer clear evidence for or against the
hypotheses discussed here. But, obviously, the facts about such systems are very hard to come by, so that we can expect the evidence for
the next few years to be slow in emerging and fragmentary in character.

Pertinent studies on the development of language in children include those of Gruber (1967) and McNeill (1966), i.e., those focusing
on the relation of subject to predicate. In *topicalization,* what can
serve as the topic? From Gruber's work, it seems that the patient of an
active transitive construction cannot serve as topic. We find expressions like

boy, break toy	('the boy broke the toy')
toy, break	('the toy broke')
toy, broken	('the toy is broken')

but not

*toy, boy break	('the boy broke the toy')
*toy, boy break it	('the boy broke the toy')

This constraint on *topicalization* is clear from discussion of constructions like: (a) *catch me* and (b) *no him no bite.* Construction (a) is only
two ways ambiguous; it is either a transitive predicate (equivalent to
the adult imperative *Catch me!*) or a topicalized agent relation ('as
for me, I catch (something)''); (b) is unambiguously a topicalized version of *he doesn't bite,* it does not mean 'nothing bit him' or 'don't bite
him!' Such findings are interesting but not compelling, given the fact
that they occur in an SVO context. Similar findings emerging in non-
SVO contexts constitute significant support for the unmarked status of
the VP-constituent.

By "unmarked interpretations," I mean that in support of constraint
I, we adduce the fact that in systems or constructions within a system
in which neither the predicate nor the nominals have informative
case-marking, clauses like

$$\begin{bmatrix} \text{Transitive} & \text{Nominal} & \text{Nominal} \\ \text{Predicate} & & \\ {}_{\text{S}} & & \end{bmatrix}$$

$$\begin{bmatrix} \text{Nominal} & \text{Nominal} & \text{Transitive} \\ & & \text{Predicate} \\ {}_{\text{S}} & & \end{bmatrix}$$

whose semantics do not force an interpretation, will be naturally interpreted in an agent–patient order. Similarly, one might argue that an
unmarked nominal in relation to a transitive predicate, if consistently
interpreted in one way rather than another would indicate something
about the natural semantic relations. So, in Squamish, in the basic
active transitive construction, the agent and patient nominals are in

the same case (the absolutive). But the sequence VSO is unambiguous because of Constraint I. The question is, then, what interpretation of the superficially uninformative

$$\begin{bmatrix} \text{Transitive} & \text{Nominal} \\ \text{Predicate} & \\ \text{s} & \end{bmatrix}$$

will be made, if the semantics are left as open as possible? According to Kuipers (1967, p. 172), the only interpretation gives the patient relation, not the agent. This piece of evidence is particularly instructive, in view of the Pred–Nom–Nom interpretation, which gives temporal preference to the agent. The natural semantic primacy of predicate + patient yields to another consideration — the primacy of agent over patient.

Like the natural situation of deaf signers who contrive a system that will make minimal demands (i.e., maximize natural semantic relationships), pidgin systems arise from an attempt to satisfy conflicting systems. The laboratory questions are: If SVO is set in conflict with SOV, what will emerge? If SVO is set in conflict with VSO, what will emerge? Suppose it turns out that SVO prevails with greater than chance frequency; what can be made of that fact? In the case of SVO–VSO conflict, the conclusion is weakened by the fact that every VSO system allows an alternate SVO order. Thus, the fact that Chinook jargon is SVO, while Chinook itself is VSO, is not very persuasive, even though it is surprising that a jargon that leans so heavily for its vocabulary (including pronouns and numerals) on one language would incline another way for its syntax (see Jacobs, 1932; Grant, 1945). More enlightening might be SVO–SOV conflicts involving strict SOV languages, that is, systems that do not allow alternate SVO orders. At the moment, I have no evidence about pidgins that would develop in such conflicts.

Finally, we might discover something about the natural relationships of agent, patient, and predicate from experimental manipulation. In a very limited way, Johnson (1968) showed that phrase structure was instrumental in facilitating learning; but the context was totally English — the experimenter, his subjects, the language of instruction, and the language manipulated were all prejudiced by English-specific structure. What I am suggesting is a similar procedure in various contexts (VSO, SOV, as well as SVO) that can test for the natural constituency relations. A number of variations are possible in the laboratory design, all of which could converge to confirm or disconfirm what is being proposed here.

A MODEST PROPOSAL

What follows is an attempt to reconsider how generalizations like constraint I or the unmarked status of VP-constituency are to be incorporated into linguistic theory. It is clear that a maneuver like

(10)

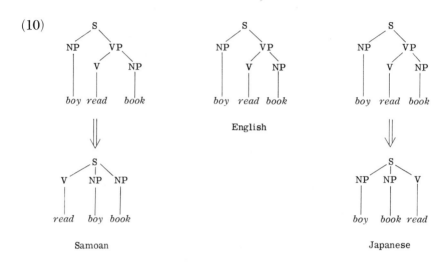

Samoan   Japanese

is of little explanatory value. The maneuver itself is simple and straightforward. We assert a universal base (unmarked configuration), as given in more or less surface English, and then indicate the marked deviation in Samoan and Japanese by attributing a rule to those systems that moves the predicate to first and last position in the proposition, respectively. The move itself is natural, direct, and effective. It produces just the sequencing and constituency in harmony with the facts of the first section of this chapter (both sets A and B), which gave us our point of departure.

But this proposal is to be rejected. As far as the empirical evidence is concerned, it is a gross distortion to claim that Samoan and Japanese have any such transformation characterizing their respective systematic characters. In what way, then, can we satisfy both the universality of principles like constraint I and the unmarked status of VP-constituency, as well as the supposedly marked character of systems like Samoan and Japanese? One rather simple way is to view the universal principles in some hierarchical fashion, seeking optimal actualization. For example, there might be among the constraints, two sets called general and transitive:

General predicative requirements
  a. a predicate to be announced
  b. the time of announcement to be first, last, or neither
  c. time of announcement to be made consistently
  d. if there is a subject, it is to be in a sister relation to the predicate
  e. if there is a subject, it is to be in a uniform time orientation to the predicate
  f. . . .

Transitive requirements
  a. agent to be announced before patient
  b. patient to complement predicate
  c. instrument to be marked as agent
  d. . . .

Obviously, the general predicative requirements are more fundamental than transitive requirements. We will suppose they take precedence over predicate-specific constraints.

Now, suppose we go about trying to satisfy as many of these requirements as possible, always with an eye to obeying the more compelling ones. Then general predicative requirements (a–e) shape a proposition to the extent that they predicate something, that they announce the predicate consistently, that a subject, if manifested, bear the proper relation to the predicate, and so on. A system-specific choice under general predicative requirement (b) gives three possible temporal configurations:

$$(1) \quad [_s V \ldots \ldots]$$
$$(2) \quad [_s \ldots \ldots V]$$
$$(3) \quad [_s \ldots V \ldots]$$

Notice that there is no cost attached to the choice in itself: option (1) is no more to be preferred over (2) than (2) is over (1); and so with (3) in relation to the first two. However, each choice entails certain consequences. For example, in the special case of transitive predicates, options (1) and (2) overrule transitive requirement (b), that the patient complement the predicate. System (1) cannot accommodate this desideratum because of transitive requirement (a) that agent precede patient, which takes precedence over transitive requirement (b). Since agent must precede patient, yet not precede predicate, it is forced to intervene and cancel the natural predicate–patient constituency. System (2) cannot accommodate transitive requirement (b), since the more fundamental option of general predicative requirement (b) in the form of a predicate last bias prevents any complements to the predicate in the strict sense of a temporal completion. Thus, system (3), which can accommodate both transitive requirements (a) and (b), satisfies more general requirements than either of the other systems, and so emerges as the least marked.

Given these assumptions, it is rather mysterious why marked systems such as VSO and SOV should arise at all. I would like to point out general predicative requirement (e), the principle earlier called constraint III — that the subject bear a uniform time orientation with respect to the predicate. Although it was the distinctive component of hypothesis (3), and in my contrived competition between hypotheses (3) and (4), I was obviously favoring (4) and rejecting (3), I nevertheless consider general predicative requirement (e) a valid constraint (or desideratum) in sentence organization. What I wanted to avoid is the suggestion that general predicative requirement (e) is the explanation for true ergative development in VSO and SOV contexts only. In fact, given the precedence of general predicative requirements over particular predicative requirements, hypothesis (3) fails as an explanation for facts (B). The principle critically characterizing hypothesis (3) was general predicative requirement (e), that the subject be uniformly oriented with respect to the predicate in terms of time. But in order to invoke this hypothesis as an explanation of ergative systems and their skewed distribution, we were forced to accept the precedence of transitive requirement (a), that the agent precede the patient, over general predicative requirement (e) (see p. 224). If we are correct in our hierarchy of desiderata, no particular predicative requirement can overrule a general requirement.

At this point in the exposition, having advanced transitive requirement (b) as the essential principle, I would like to implicate general predicative requirement (e) as an accessory. I think the explanation of ergative systems involves an interesting interplay of several constraints. Note that general predicative requirement (b) offers a free choice of time of predicate announcement. General predicative requirement (c) requires that the choice, once made, be made consistently in any one system. If the choice is predicate last or predicate first, then general predicative requirement (e), the uniform subject–predicative orientation, is automatically satisfied. If we give bonuses for clever decisions, then such options at the general predicative requirement level must be highly valued. It seems to be just this value that sustains the option, even at the cost of flouting transitive requirement (b), that the patient complement the predicate. In other words, it is not general predicative requirement (e) that leads to the development of VSO/SOV ergative systems; it is general predicative requirement (b) and its apparent optimization with respect to general predicative requirement (e) that leads to a comparative neglect of transitive requirement (b). This costly dissociation ultimately allows for an ergative view of transitivity.

CONCLUSION AND SUMMARY

It would be easy to misinterpret and overgeneralize this discussion of transitive predication. System (2), the so-called SVO type, seems to be the least marked in this one respect. But there are many other aspects of sentence construction which remain to be considered. Systems (1) and (2), in other respects, may be more highly valued than system (3); or, the three may split up in different ways under different requirements (cf. *WH-fronting* which groups VSO and SVO as the marked types, as opposed to SOV). This chapter is concerned with a very specific syntactic property of natural language, the VP-constituent and its relation to ergative systems. I had assumed a constraint on movement transformations that precluded increase of structure. In VSO and SOV systems, a certain trait—attraction to the predicate—suggested a detached status of the predicate in which the patient nominal was not in a strict complement relation. Given the proposal of syntactic markedness just sketched (end of previous section), we can estimate the cost of this option; that is, it is a bit clearer why in just these systems there is nothing to stop patient nominals from developing into the subjects of unmarked transitive expressions.

As indicated earlier, the adoption of any hypothesis other than (1), that all systems have a VP-constituent, entails the rejection of a unique structural definition of the notion "subject." Hypothesis (4), the account that seems to offer the best explanation of all the facts, is in this sense as costly as (2) and (3) would have been. I am not able, at this point, to say exactly how the "subject-of" relation is to be incorporated into a proposition. There is obviously some flexibility in this respect from language to language. In the case of transitive predication, the so-called double complement verbs (*give, offer, sell*) allow for maximally three possible candidates—some languages restrict it to the agent, others relax it to include the patient (a primary passive), still others extend it to include the beneficiary (a secondary passive: *he was given a choice*). At the moment, I am inclined to view this choice of subject as a lexical redundancy rule rather than a transformation, since the various actualizations of the transitive network seem merely to be a shifting of perspective on the action—which principal in the drama the camera is focusing on, which principals are by default backgrounded as complement structure. Clearly, an important line of inquiry is some clarification of the idea of grammatical subject.

Constraints like general predicative requirements (a–e) and transitive requirements (a–c) represent the set of considerations making for the well formedness of base representations. The constraints are universal, but in their particular interplay from system to system, certain incompatibilities and priorities make for language-specific bias. The constraints have little concern with the semantic content of propositions. What they do is dictate certain shapes (cognitive–perceptual) for successful linguistic performance. The shapes themselves are determined by the mind's eye, not the mind. It will be interesting, as we learn more about these constraints, to discover how much the mind's eye shapes the mind.

REFERENCES

Carroll, V. 1965. An outline of the structure of the language of Nukuoro. Journal of the Polynesian Society 74.192–226, 451–472.

Dixon, R. M. W. 1969. Relative clauses and possessive phrases in two Australian languages. Language 45.35–44.

Fodor, J. and Bever, T. 1965. The psychological reality of linguistic segments. Journal of Verbal Learning and Verbal Behavior 4.414–420.

Grant, R. V. 1945. Chinook jargon. International Journal of American Linguistics 11.225–233.

Greenberg, J. 1966. Some universals of grammar with particular reference to the order of meaningful elements. Universals of Language (J. Greenberg, ed.) MIT Press, Cambridge, Massachusetts.

Gruber, J. 1967. Topicalization in child language. Foundations of Language 3.37–65.

Hale, K. 1968. Review of Hohepa. Journal of the Polynesian Society 77.83–99.

Hohepa, P. 1969. The accusative-to-ergative drift in polynesian languages. Journal of the Polynesian Society 78.295–329.

Jacobs, M. 1932. Notes on the structure of Chinook jargon. Language 8.27–51.

Johnson, N. 1965. The psychological reality of phrase–structure rules. Journal of Verbal Learning and Verbal Behavior, 4.469–475.

Johnson, N. 1968. The influence of grammatical units on learning. Journal of Verbal Learning and Verbal Behavior, 7.236–240.

Kuipers, A. 1967. The Squamish Language. Mouton, The Hague, The Netherlands.

Lewis, G. L. 1967. Turkish Grammar. The Clarendon Press, Oxford, England.

Maclay, H. and Osgood, C. E. 1959. Hesitation phenomena in spontaneous English speech. Word 15.19–44.

McNeill, D. 1966. Some universals of language acquisition. Harvard Center for Cognitive Studies Colloqium, Cambridge, Massachusetts.

Matthews, W. K. 1953. The ergative in modern Indo-Aryan. Lingua 3.391–406.

Naro, A. 1970. Pidginization and natural change. Paper presented to the Linguistic Society of America, December 1970.

Newman, P. 1970. A Grammar of Tera. University of California Press, Berkeley, California.

Pizzini, Q. 1969. Predicate complement constructions in Samoan. Linguistic Notes from La Jolla 2.80–105.

Sapir, E. 1917. Review of C. C. Uhlenbeck. International Journal of American Linguistics 1.82–90.

Schwartz, A. 1972. Constraints on movement transformations. Journal of Linguistics 8.35–85.

Velten, H. V. 1932. The accusative case and its substitute in various types of language. Language 8.255–270.

LAHU NOMINALIZATION, RELATIVIZATION, AND GENITIVIZATION

JAMES A. MATISOFF
University of California, Berkeley

INTRODUCTION

James McCawley is reputed to have said a while ago that if one were to penetrate deeply enough into the workings of English grammar one could come up with the answers to "all questions of interest for linguistic theory" without bothering to look at any other languages. Presumably, McCawley meant that to plumb the depths of any single language—whether English, Yiddish, or Lahu—would provide us with all the answers. Yet even this modified claim is false, as this paper is partly intended to demonstrate. In fact, we would like to lodge a counterclaim: Any language, if studied deeply enough, will supply us with new insights into questions of general theoretical interest; and some of these, at least, will be questions that could not possibly have been raised from the study of other languages.

Lahu is a language of southeast Asia belonging to the Lolo-Burmese family of the Tibeto-Burman branch of Sino-Tibetan. I have been working on Lahu and related languages since 1965, with fieldtrips to Thailand in 1965–1966 and 1970. The most intriguing and exasperating word in Lahu is the particle *ve*, which serves not only as the marker of genitive constructions and relative clauses, but also as a clause nominalizer. These are construction types that may not at first

237

seem to be particularly closely related in languages like English. However, once the connection has been pointed out for a language in which it is obvious and overt, parallel phenomena can be discovered in other languages [see pp. 254–256], and we are challenged to find some theoretical basis for the relationship. We shall observe that in other languages where there is an overt connection between *nominalization* and relative–genitive constructions, there is a strong tendency to treat whole sentences as nounlike objects.

LAHU NOMINALIZATION BY MEANS OTHER THAN VE

Lahu has a rich array of devices for converting clauses into nounlike structures that can then be embedded into larger sentences. These devices are nominalizing particles that are postposed to the clause. All of them except *ve* have clear-cut meanings, and present no particular problems of analysis.

A Lahu clause is defined as a VP plus any (perhaps zero) preceding NPs that are associated with it [LG 2.1].[1] A structure is functioning as a noun if it may be followed by a member of the class of noun-particles $(P_n s)$, crucially the accusative P_n *thà*ꞏ [LG 3.8].

Agentive Nominalizations [LG 6.13][1]: *pā, ma; šē̂-phâ, šē̂-ma*

A clause may be turned into a noun of agent ("the clauser; the one who clauses") by one of several particles, most productively by *pā*. Thus:

(1)   *qhɔ-qhô-lɔ̀-qhô | mâ tâ*ꞏ *e gâ*
        '(They) don't want to climb up into the hills.'[2]

(2)   *{{qhɔ-qhô-lɔ̀-qhô | mâ tâ*ꞏ *e gâ pā} | qò*ꞏ *e phὲ*ꞏ *ve}yò*
        'Those who don't want to climb up into the hills
        may go home.'

Sentence (2) as a whole is nominalized by the *ve* at the end (see p. 246). Despite the relative clause in the English gloss, the embed-

---

[1] Bracketed references are to the author's "Lahu Grammar," to appear in the series University of California Publications in Linguistics.

[2] To obviate somewhat the need for tedious interlinear glosses, the following diagrammatic conventions are used: a solid vertical line (X | Y) separates a NP from a VP; a broken vertical line separates two NPs belonging to the same clause (X ┊ Y); a double vertical line separates two clauses conjoined in the same sentence (X ‖ Y). Nominalized clauses are enclosed in braces, and relative clauses in square brackets. The diacritics over Lahu vowels are tone marks [LG 1.6].

ded clause is clearly functioning as a unitary derived noun: 'the not-wanting-to-climb-up-into-the-hill-ers.' This is obvious when the clause is of simpler structure, so that the English translation tends to be a single noun: *šā | bɔ́ʔ* 'shoot animals'/{*šā | bɔ́ʔ pā*} 'hunter'; *lɔ̀ lɛ́ʔ* 'ask to eat'/{*lɔ̀ lɛ́ʔ pā*} 'beggar', etc.

Locative Nominalizations [LG 6.14]: *kɨ*

The particle *kɨ* has the power to convert a clause into a noun of location ('the place where one clauses'):

(3)   *yɔ̂ ¦ yù tā*
        'He has taken (it).'

(4)   *khâʔ thàʔ ¦ {yɔ̂ | yù tā kɨ}ɔ̄ | qɔ̀ʔ tɛ ò*
        '(He) has already put the crossbow back **where he had taken it from.**'

In (4), the nominalized clause is followed by the locative P$_n$ɔ̄. When the *kɨ* clause is of simple enough structure, a single noun usually serves for an English translation: *mɨ* 'sit'/{*mɨ kɨ*} 'stool, chair'; *te câ* 'cook'/{*te ca kɨ*} 'kitchen'; *cha | hɔ̂* 'sell one's vulva'/{*cha | hɔ̂ kɨ*} 'brothel.'

Purposive Nominalizations [LG 6.15]: *tù*

The verb-particle *tù* indicates that the verbal event is hypothetical, unrealized, or future oriented. Often it is used to mark purpose clauses that are not nominalizations, but rather structures that stand in an adverbial relationship to the higher sentence. We diagram such clauses by enclosing them in inward-pointing arrows.

(5)   {*ŋà | → màʔ-pāw=šī | ca hɔ̂ tù ← là ve*}*yò*
        'I've come **to sell (my) coconuts.**'

Sometimes, however, especially when the main verb is *cɔ̀* 'have, be there,' a *tù* clause functions as a noun of purpose ('that which is for clausing; that which is to be claused'):

(6)   *ɔ̀-vi-ɔ̀-ni thàʔ | qɔ̀ʔ qô ʔ lâ*
        '(I) am speaking once again to my brethren.'

(7)   {{*ɔ̀-vi-ɔ̀-ni thàʔ | qɔ̀ʔ qô ʔ lâ tù*}*thɔ̂ | cɔ̀ šɔ̄ ve*}*yò*
        'There are still **things (for me) to say once again to (my) brethren.**'

When the nominalized clause is simple enough, a single English noun is often the best translation: *câ* 'eat'/{*câ tù*} 'food'; *cì* | *šî* ˀ 'brush teeth'/{*cì* | *šî* ˀ *tù*} 'toothbrush'; *g̈â* ˀ-*mu* | *dɔ̂* ˀ 'hit chicken feathers'/ {*g̈â* ˀ-*mu* | *dɔ̂ tù*} 'badminton racquet.'

Temporal Nominalizations [LG 6.12]: *thâ*

The temporal particle *thâ* 'when' is often used to mark a non-nominalized clause that stands in an adverbial relationship to a higher sentence:

(8)   *yɔ̂* | *šɨ e*
                                     'He died.'

(9)   *yɔ̂* | *šɨ e thâ* ‖ *ŋà* ¦ *yâ-nɛ̀* | *phɛ̀* ˀ *šɔ̄*
             'I was still a young man **when he died.**'

Sometimes, however, when the time in question is focused upon as the main center of interest in the sentence, rather than being an ancillary modifier of the verbal idea, a *thâ* clause may function as a temporal noun ('the time when clause'):

(10)   {*yɔ̂* | *šɨ e thâ thà* ˀ ¦ *ŋà* | *qha-dɛ̀* ˀ *dɔ̂-nɔ̂ šɔ̄*
            'I still clearly remember **the time he died.**'

In (10), the nominalized clause is followed by the accusative P_n *thà* ˀ.

VE AS A SUBORDINATOR

Before going on to consider the role of *ve* as a nominalizer, it is time to examine its occurrences as a subordinator of modifying material to nounheads.

Genitival Subordination

Ve is regularly used to indicate that one nominal nucleus (ν) is modifying another within the same NP in a genitival relationship [LG 3.7]. The possessor nucleus (ν_p) precedes the possessed head (ν_h); thus: *ŋà ve mi-chɔ* 'my shoulder-bag'; *šɨ̂* ˀ-*cɛ̀ ve ó-qō* 'the top of the tree'; *qhâ* ˀ-*šɛ ve ɔ̂-qā* 'the headman's buffalo'; *mà* ˀ-*pāw=šī ve ɔ̂-qú* 'the shell of the coconut.'

Under certain favorable circumstances, particularly when the ν_p is a pronoun, genitive *ve* may be deleted with no change in meaning [LG 3.75]: *ŋà* □ *ɔ̂-mî=ma* 'my wife', *g̈ɨ-ša* □ *ɔ̂-bo* 'the grace of God'; *nɔ̂* □ *phî* 'your dog.' The deleted constituent is symbolized by an empty box.

When the general context is clear, or to avoid repetition of a nucleus mentioned elsewhere in the discourse, the ν_h may be deleted: $\nu_p + ve + \nu_h \rightarrow \nu_p + ve + \square$ [LG 3.76]. These residual structures still behave like nouns and may be followed by P_ns. They have the same semantic relationship to full genitive constructions that English pronominal expressions like *mine, yours,* and *Noam's* bear to their corresponding possessive adjectives plus noun (*my mango, your jackfruit, Noam's durian*). Thus:

(11)   ŋà ve □ ¦ nɔ ve □ a-kɛ́ | yɨ̀ jâ
              'Mine is much longer than yours.'

Into the empty box one may freely stick any appropriate noun (*á-tà* 'stick', *nâˀ* 'rifle', *nī-qhɛ̀ˀ* 'penis').

Relative Subordination

A relative clause (RC) is embedded in a larger sentence in such a way that it modifies the particular noun of the sentence to which it is preposed. The marker of this subordination is *ve* [LG 6.4]:

(12)   [yàˀ-qɔ | jû qay ve] a-pi꞊qu chi ¦ a-šu le
                                N_{rh}
         'Who's this old lady **that's walking along the road**?'

(13) [vàˀ qhe | chu ve] Pîchɔ̂-pā ô tê ğâ ¦ nɔ ve ɔ̀-chɔ̂ lâ
     'Is that Shan man over there **who's fat as a pig** your friend?'

(14)   [vàˀ꞊ó-qō thàˀ | cɔ̂ tā ve] yâ-mî꞊ma lɛ̀ ¦ qhâˀ-šɛ꞊ma yò
         'The woman **who boiled the pig's head** is the headman's wife.'

(15)   [qhâˀ-šɛ꞊ma | cɔ̂ tā ve] vàˀ꞊ó-qō | mɛ̀ jâ
         'The pig's head **the headman's wife boiled** is yummy.'

The noun in the higher sentence that is modified by the RC is the relative head or N_{rh} (*a-pi꞊qu* 'old lady,' *Pîchɔ̂-pā* 'Shan man,' *yâ-mî꞊ma* 'woman,' *vàˀ꞊ó-qō* 'pig's-head'). In general, when the verb of the RC is an intransitive action verb—like *jû qay* 'walk' in (12)—or an adjective—like *chu* 'be fat' in (13)—the N_{rh} is its underlying subject. When the verb of the RC is transitive—like *cɔ̂* 'boil' in (14–15)—the N_{rh} is either its underlying subject (14) or object (15). Sometimes there is ambiguity, when it makes sense to interpret the N_{rh} either as the subject or as the object of the RC: [*šī ve*] *chɔ thàˀ | tâ qôˀ pî* (a) 'Don't tell (it) to the people who know (it)' [N_{rh} is subject]; (b) 'Don't tell (it) to the people (we) know' [N_{rh} is object]. In any case, no RC may contain a noun that is coreferential with the N_{rh}; that is, the underlying subject or object in the RC that is equivalent to the N_{rh} is obligatorily deleted on the surface.

So far, there is nothing very remarkable about the role of *ve* in these constructions. There is an obvious analogy between the possessor nuclei of genitive expressions and relative clauses. Both are structures that are semantically subordinate to a nounhead (ν_h or N_{rh}), and in fact, there are other languages where the same particle is used to mark both relationships. A notable case is the Mandarin *.de*, used both in genitives (*woo .de kuay.tz* 'my chopsticks'; *feiji .de chyan.tour* 'the front of the airplane') and in relative clauses ([*may | shu .de*] *ren*$_{N_{rh}}$ 'the person who sells books'; [*tsorng Meei.gwo | lai .de*] *feiji* 'airplanes that come from America').

NOMINALIZING VE IN NONFINAL CLAUSES

Clauses in Lahu are either final or nonfinal. A final clause (Cl_f) is the last clause of its sentence. Simple sentences comprise a single (therefore final) clause. Nonsimple sentences contain at least one nonfinal clause (Cl_{nf}). A sentence is complex if it contains a Cl_{nf} embedded within the Cl_f, and compound if it has a Cl_{nf} conjoined to the Cl_f [LG 2.1]. The various types of Cl_{nf}s differ from one another and from Cl_fs with respect to the kinds of unrestricted particles that may follow them [LG 4.72, 5.43 et passim]. These details need not concern us here. However, it is convenient to begin our discussion of nominalizing *ve* with those cases where the *ve* clause is nonfinal, since it is here that its nounlike nature is most apparent to our alien eyes.

Embedded ve Clause Followed by a Noun Particle [LG 6.115]

The clearest cases are those where the *ve* clause is followed by a P_n—morphemes that otherwise occur only after natural nouns (or clauses nominalized by one of the particles discussed above, pp. 238–240). The P_ns that may occur after *ve* clauses are *pa-tɔ* "causal" and (more importantly) *thaʔ* 'accusative.' Thus, analogously to (16)–(18), where natural nouns are marked by these P_ns, we have (19)–(21):

(16)   *qhâʔ-še pa-tɔ | hɛ | tú mâ phὲʔ še*
      N P_n
      '**Because of the headman,** (he) can't fire (his) fields yet.'

(17)   *ɔ-šɨ̄ thàʔ | nɔ | mâ ga mɔ lâ*
                 N P_n
                 'Didn't you see **the blood?**'

(18)   *ɔ-mî=ma thà ʔ | nɔ | mâ šī šē lâ*
      N   P_n
     'Don't you know **(his) wife** yet?'

(19)   *{yɔ | hɛ | mâ ga̋ phɔ̀ pɔ̀ šē ve}pa-tɔ | hɛ | tú mâ phɛ̀ ʔ šē*
    '**Due to the fact that he still hasn't finished clearing his fields,** he can't fire them yet.'

(20)   *{ɔ-šɨ̏ | tɔ̂ ʔ la ve}thà ʔ | nɔ | mâ ga̋ mɔ̀ lâ*
    'Didn't you see **that blood was coming out?**'

(21)   *{yɔ̀ ɔ-yâ=pā | ɔ-mî=ma | bà tù ve}thà ʔ | nɔ | mâ šī šē lâ*
    'Don't you know yet **that his son is going to divorce his wife?**'

As the glosses indicate, the meaning of nominalizing *ve* is much more abstract than those of the other nominalizing particles (pp. 238–240 above). *Ve* adds nothing to the meaning of its clause other than the gift of nounhood itself, and is in fact as semantically colorless as the English complementizer *that*. For want of a better term, we may call *ve* an indicative nominalizer, understanding by this nothing more than the semantically unmarked nominalizer.

Ve Clause Not Followed by Any Particle [LG 5.21, 6.11].

Most of the time, the syntactic–semantic relationship of the nonfinal *ve* clause to the rest of its sentence is not signalled overtly by any particle, as in (22)–(27):

(22)   *{{nɔ̀-pa ve ɔ-khɔ̂ | mâ na ve} | dà ʔ ve}lâ*
    'Is it good **not to listen to your father's advice?**'

(23)   *{ŋà-hɨ thà ʔ | Kâlâ-phu=khɔ̂ | mā lâ chê ve} | cɨ́-kɨ̀ | cɔ̀ jâ*
    '**(Your) continuing to teach us English** is very important to us.'

(24)   *{ŋâ nālī | mâ gà ve} | nî chi minì ʔ | cɔ̀ šɔ̄*
    'It's twenty minutes to five' ('**As for not reaching 5:00,** there are still twenty minutes').

(25)   *{nɔ̀ kà ʔ | là ve} | ŋà | ha-lɛ̀ jâ*
    'I'm very happy **that you came too.**'

(26)   *{nɔ̀ | i-kâ ʔ | lɔ̂ pɨ ve} | ŋà | mâ šī*
    'I didn't know **that you could swim.**'

(27)   *{yɔ̀ ve khɨ-šɛ thà ʔ | pɨ | chè ʔ lâ ve} | yɔ̀ | bɔ̀ ʔ jâ cê*
    'He got very angry at **the mosquitoes' biting him on the feet.**'

In all sentences of this type, it is possible to insert a topicalizing un-restricted particle after the *ve* clause. Furthermore, in sentences like (25)–(27), where the *ve* clause may alternatively be considered the object of the higher verb, the P_n *thà*ʔ may be inserted after it.

Where semantically appropriate, as in (23) or (27), the causal P_n *pa-tɔ* may also freely be inserted ('Because of your continuing to teach us English, [you are] very important to us'). The point is, there is still no doubt that these clauses are functioning as nouns, even when a P_n is not overtly present.

Ve Clause Followed by a P_{unf} [LG 6.110]

An unrestricted particle (P_u) is a morpheme of abstract meaning that may occur either after nouns or verbs. P_us are thus more powerful than noun particles, which occur only after nouns, or verb-particles (P_vs), which come only after verbs. A subclass of these are the nonfinal unrestricted particles (P_{unf}s), which occur only in nonfinal position, either after the verb of a nonfinal clause or after a noun that does not come last in its sentence. Sentences whose last structure is a NP (rather than a VP) are minor sentences. See, for example, sentence (14). The presence of a P_{unf} in the middle of a sentence, therefore, is not a criterion for deciding whether a preceding structure is nominal or verbal. Nevertheless, since we find P_{unf}s after natural nouns, naked verbs, and *ve* clauses, and since the meaning of $V + P_{unf}$ is indistinguishable from that of $V + ve + P_{unf}$, it is clear that the only difference between these two is that provided by the nominalizing power of the *ve*. In other words, $V + ve + P_{unf}$ is more like $N + P_{unf}$ than like $V + P_{unf}$. Consider (28)–(30):

(28)　with the conditional P_{unf} *qo*

　　a.　*Lâhū-yâ qo | i-mû | mâ ga cî qay hɛ*
　　　　 N　　 P_{unf}
　　　　'If (he's) a Lahu, he probably won't be able to go on horseback.'

　　b.　*mû-cha | cha qo ‖ i-mû | mâ ga cî qay hɛ*
　　　　　　　　 V　P_{unf}
　　　　'If the sun is hot, (he) probably won't be able to go on horseback.'

　　c.　{*mû-cha | cha ve*}*qo | i-mû | mâ ga cî qay hɛ*
　　　　'If the sun is hot, (he) probably won't be able to go on horseback.' ("If it is a sun-being-hot . . .")

(29)   with the concessive P$_{unf}$ *thɔ̂*
   a.   *yâ-ɛ́ thɔ̂ ¦ ó-qō | dàʔ jâ*
         N   P$_{unf}$
         'Although (he's) a child, he's got a good head' ('the head
         is very good').
   b.   *yɔ̂ | mɔ̂ jâ thɔ̂ ‖ ó-qō | dàʔ jâ*
               V   P$_{unf}$
         'Although he's very old, he's got a good head.'
   c.   *{yɔ̂ | mɔ̂ jâ ve}thɔ̂ ¦ ó-qō | dàʔ jâ*
         'Although he's very old, he's got a good head.' ('Although
         it is a his-being-very-old . . .')

(30)   with the topicalizing P$_u$ sequence *tí qo lɛ̀*
   a.   *ŋà tí qo lɛ̀ | yàʔ-tɔ pɨ̀ à*
         N P$_u$ P$_u$ P$_u$
         'As for me, I'd be awfully embarrassed!'
   b.   *ŋà ¦ á-thâ | mɔ̂ʔ tí qo lɛ̀ ‖ yàʔ-tɔ pɨ̀ à*
               V   P$_u$ P$_u$ P$_u$
         'As for me playing the jewsharp, I'd be awfully
         embarrassed!'
   c.   *{ŋà | á-thâ |mɔ̂ʔ ve}tí qo lɛ̀ | yàʔ-tɔ pɨ̀ à*
         'As for me playing the jewsharp, I'd be awfully
         embarrassed.'

Note that the difference in structure between (30b) and (30c) cannot
be captured in English translation, since English *as for* requires us to
nominalize the following clause anyway. In general, we regard utterances like (28b), (29b), (30b) as ordinary compound sentences, where
the Cl$_{nf}$ is merely conjoined to the Cl$_f$, not embedded within it as in
(28c), (29c), (30c).

Ve Deleted from the Nominalized Clause [LG 5.11]

   Sometimes, especially when the *ve* clause is quite short and the
sentence as a whole is not very complicated in structure, the *ve* itself
may be deleted:

(31)   *{{làʔ | tha (ve)} | šɨ̂ ɛ̀ qay ve}*
             The hand-clapping was boisterous.'

(32)   *{qhâʔ-šɛ | te (ve)} | dàʔ à mē*
             The way the headman does it is really fine!' ('The
             headman's doing it . . .')

(33)   ê ||| {*a-pi* ¦ *qhê* | *tè*ᵖ *(ve)*} | *nù à*
             'Whew! **Grandma's farting** sure stinks!'

It is hopeless to try to formulate precise conditions for the deletability
of this *ve*, just as it would be to try to specify exactly when English
that may be omitted from relative clauses (*the man* [*that*] *I know*).

VE IN FINAL CLAUSES – NONEMBEDDED NOMINALIZATIONS
[LG 4.711, 6.118]

We come now to a phenomenon that is quite alien from the point of
view of standard average European languages but surprisingly widespread elsewhere – the nominalization of entire sentences that are
embedded in nothing larger than themselves.

Ve appears in the final clauses of Lahu sentences with enormous
frequency. [For additional examples, see sentences (2), (5), (7), (22),
and (31) above.]

(34)   {*yɔ̂* ¦ *vên qhɔ* ¦ *mɔ̂* | *ca hɔ̂ qay ve*}
             'He went/goes/will go to town to sell some things.'

As the gloss of (34) shows, *ve* has nothing to do with tense. So what is
it doing in sentences like this? It is tempting to take refuge in such
empty labels as indicative, general, neutral, or actualizable. The situation is actually more straightforward. The verbal event is being objecti-
fied, reified, viewed as an independent fact, endowed with a reality
like that inhering in physical objects – in short, *nominalized*. It is
standing on its own, and is not a constituent of any sentence higher
than the one to which it belongs itself.

In formalizing this interpretation, it is important to avoid setting up
an overly complex underlying structure when a simpler one would do
just as well. Perhaps the most comfortable solution would be to recognize two types of minor sentences – natural and derivative. A natural
minor sentence [e.g., sentences (12), (13), (14)] has a natural noun
phrase as its final constituent. A derivative minor sentence is one that
has been nominalized by a *ve* in its final clause:

(35)   S_minor
                                               deriv

                                        Clause   *ve*

Alternatively, one could recognize sentential noun phrases:

(36)

In any event, it is necessary to guard against being misled by attempts at English translation of these structures. It may help us to understand a sentence like:

(37) {yɔ̂ | là tù ve}
      'He will come.'

by glossing it with painful literality as 'It is the case that he will come' or 'It is a he-will-come case.' But this does not mean that we have to assume that there is some higher verb floating around with the meaning "be the case."

Ve-Clauses Plus P$_{uf}$s

Final *ve*-clauses may be followed by final unrestricted particles (P$_{uf}$s), morphemes of abstract meaning which come at the end of sentences, supplying information about the speaker's propositional attitude toward the sentence as a whole [LG 4.72]. The P$_{uf}$s may be roughly subdivided semantically into several categories—declarative, dubitative, interrogative, persuasive, quotative, and interjectory. They occur equally well after naked verbs and after the final NP in natural minor sentences. However, analogous to the situation described above (p. 244) with respect to P$_{unf}$s, sequences of V + *ve* + P$_{uf}$ are more like N + P$_{uf}$ than like V + P$_{uf}$:

(38) with the declarative P$_{uf}$ yò
      a. yɔ̂ ¦ qhâʔ-šɛ yò
              N   P$_{uf}$
          'He (is) the headman.'
      b. yɔ̂ | qay yò
             V   P$_{uf}$
          'He's going!'
      c. {yɔ̂ | qay ve}yò
          'He's going' ('It is a his-going').[3]

---

[3] As the glosses of (38) indicate, it is more usual (and semantically colorless) to have the *ve* than not. When *ve* is absent, the verb retains an 'untrammeled verbality' which manifests itself as an additional nuance of emphasis. See the discussion of *ve* and negation, p. 249 below.

(39)   with the dubitative P_{uf} *hé*
    a.   *yɔ̂ | qhâ ꞌ-šε hé*
              N P_{uf}
       'He('s) probably the headman.'
    b.   *yɔ̂ | qay gâ hé*
             V P_v P_{uf}
       'He probably wants to go.'
    c.   *{yɔ̂ | qay gâ ve}hé*
       'He probably wants to go.' ('It's probably a his-
       wanting-to-go').

(40)   with the interrogative P_{uf} *lâ*
    a.   *yɔ̂ | qhâ ꞌ-šε lâ*
              N P_{uf}
       '(Is) he the headman?'
    b.   *yɔ̂ | qay lâ*
             V P_{uf}
       'Is he going?'
    c.   *{yɔ̂ | qay ve}lâ*
       'Is he going?' ('Is it that he's going?').

Citation Forms of Verbs

Perhaps the clearest situation where a verb is treated as a nounlike object is when it is cited in isolation—metalinguistically, as it were. Just as we cite verbs with the nominalizer *to*, so the Lahu invariably cite them with *ve*: *qay ve* 'to go'; *chu ve* 'to be fat'; *šɨ ve* 'to twist.' Consider the following:

(41)   *{{qay ve} | Kâlâ-phu꞊khɔ̂ | qhà-qhe qoꞌ ve}le*
       'How do you say "to go" in English?'

(42)   *{≪ {qɔ̂ꞌ dàꞌ ve} ≫ qɔ̂ꞌ qo ‖ ≪ {dê dàꞌ ve} ≫ qɔ̂ꞌ ve}*[4]
      '"To have words with each other" means "to quarrel with each other."'

As a general rule of thumb applicable throughout the Tibeto-Burman family, whenever one discovers the particle used in verb citation, one can be sure of having discovered the most important nominalizer of the language (see pp. 250–251).

---

[4] We diagram embedded clauses governed by verbs of utterance like *qɔ̂ꞌ* 'say' by enclosing them in angular brackets [LG 6.3].

Ve and Negation

After a non-negated verb, *ve* is actually more conspicuous by its absence than by its presence [LG 4.711]. It is as if the Lahu verb were so brimming with potency that it must be gelded by nominalization in order to avoid giving the sentence a special mark of emphasis:

(43) a. {*ŋà-hɨ* ¦ *tê gɛ* | *qay ve*}
          'We go/went/will go together.'
      b. *ŋà-hɨ* ¦ *tê gɛ* ¦ *qay*
          'Let's go together!'; 'We go together!'; or 'We'll
          go together!'.

However, the situation is reversed when the verb is negated by pre-posing the adverb *mâ* 'not' to it:

(44)   a. *yɔ̂* | *mâ hɔ̀*
                                'He's not tired.'
                            b. {*yɔ̂* | *mâ hɔ̀ ve*}
                                'He's not tired!'

Here, the power of the naked verb is sufficiently attenuated by the negative adverb, so that nominalization by *ve* is no longer necessary to avoid special emphasis. It is now the presence of *ve* that is semantically marked. To negate the verbal event and reify it at the same time is to give extra force to the negation.

Natural nouns are negatable in Lahu by preposing them to the VP *mâ hê ʔ* 'is not the case' [LG 6.111]:[5]

(45)   *yɔ̂* ¦ *Lâhū-yâ* | *mâ hê ʔ*
                        'He is not a Lahu.'

Since they are nounlike entities, *ve* clauses may be negated the same way:

(46)   {*yɔ̂* | *hɔ̀ ve*} | *mâ hê ʔ*
                        'He's *not* tired'; 'His being tired is not the case.'

Note that both (46) and (44b) are more emphatic than (44a). In the case of (44b), one is nominalizing a negation; in the case of (46), one is negating a nominalization.

---

[5] *hê ʔ* is a defective verb that always occurs negated (except in disjunctive questions). It is probably related to the noun *ɔ̀-hê ʔ* 'omen; true harbinger,' and is certainly cognate to the functionally parallel Burmese verb *hou ʔ* (< Old Bs. *hut*). In positive identity statements Lahu (like many other languages) requires no verb at all: *yɔ̂* ¦ *Lâhū-yâ yò* 'He is a Lahu.' To say there is an underlying copula here would be to destroy the analogy between *ve* clauses and natural minor sentences.

Citation Forms and Nominalizers Elsewhere in Tibeto-Burman

As hinted above, Lahu is by no means alone in its penchant for nominalizing whole sentences. This is in fact a pervasive tendency throughout the Tibeto-Burman family.

BURMESE

In modern Burmese, verbs are cited with the particle *te*: *hpya ͻ te* 'to cut'; *thwà te* 'to go'; *pein te* 'to be thin.' This same particle appears with great frequency in clause final position, where the standard grammars misinterpret its true function and characterize it by such vacuous labels as nonfuture or general: (e.g., Okell, 1969, p. 119).

(47) {còu | mə-hpyei nain lóu ‖ dà né | hpya ͻ te}
'Because he couldn't undo the rope, he cut it with a knife'
('It is a case of his-cutting-it-with-a-knife-because-he couldn't-undo-the-rope').

The proof that *te* is really a nominalizer is that *te* clauses may be followed by the accusative particle *kou*, which otherwise occurs only after natural nouns:

(48) {hkinbyà | hyí te ‖ mə-hyí te}kou ¦ be hne | thi məlè
'How will I know **whether you're there or not?**'

JINGHPAW [KACHIN]

In Jinghpaw (an important Tibeto-Burman language spoken in northern Burma), verbs are cited with the particle *ͻai*: *lù ͻai* 'to have'; *hkráp ͻai* 'to weep'; *ləgú ͻai* 'to steal.' This particle occurs with tremendous frequency in clause final position:

(49) {Jɨŋhpò ͻ ͻá ͻ məšà ¦ myìt | kəbà ͻai}
'Jinghpaw people are proud at heart.'

Hanson, the pioneer lexicographer of this language, misses the point by calling this *ͻai* a verbal particle, present indicative, third person singular (Hanson, 1906, p. 54). In point of fact, *ͻai* has no special connection with the third person at all, but follows all person markers. Yet strangely enough, on the same page of his dictionary Hanson has a separate entry '*ai*' glossed as a 'noun affix used . . . in the formation of abstract or verbal nouns.' This was in fact close to the truth.

The proof that *ͻai* is a nominalizer is that *ͻai* clauses may be followed by the accusative particle *hpé ͻ*, which otherwise occurs only after natural nouns:

(50)   . . . *Ningawn Wa Măgam* ¦ *dai{sa ai}ni hpe* | *hkap*
        yu yang . . .[6]
        '. . . and when the mighty Ningawn Wa had examined
        those who had come . . .'

Here the *ᵖai* is nominalizing the verb *sa* 'go, come.' This expression, meaning "comer, one who comes" is then modified by the determiner *dai* 'those,' and followed by the noun-pluralizing particle *ni* and the accusative P_n *hpé ᵖ*.

TIBETAN

Classical Tibetan has a morpheme [pa ~ ba] used in the citation-form of verbs: *dogs-pa* 'to fear'; *snyam-pa* 'to imagine'; *snyi-ba* 'to be soft'; *blo-ba* 'to be able.' It occurs frequently in clause final position, where the nineteenth century lexicographer Jäschke (1881) seems almost to have recognized its true function:

> *pa*, an affix . . . which, when attached to the roots of verbs, gives them the signification of nouns, or in other words is the sign of the infinitive and the participle; in the language of common life, however, it is frequently used for the finite tense . . . [p. 321].

PROBLEMS AND INTRICACIES WITH VE NOMINALIZATIONS

Before attempting to relate the nominalizing power of *ve* to its subordinating function, we should mention a few problems that arise in the interpretation of *ve* clauses.

Ve in the Final Clauses of Compound Sentences [LG 6.118]

No matter how long and complicated a sentence is, there is nothing to stop a *ve* from occurring in its final clause. Confining ourselves to relatively uncomplicated compound sentences, we have cases like the following:

(51)   {*chɔ-qhɔ̂* ¦ *qhâ ᵖ-še thà ᵖ* |*mɔ̂ qo* ‖ *phɔ e tù ve*}*yò*
         'If the thief sees the headman, he'll run away.'

(52)   {*yɔ̂* | *mâ hɔ̂ ᵖ gâ thɔ̂* ‖ *ŋà* | *hɔ̂ ᵖ gâ ve*}*yò*
         'Even if he doesn't want to get it, I want to get it.'

(53)   {*và ᵖ-ɡ̈â ᵖ* | *ca hu lɛ* ‖ *hɔ̂ a lɛ* ‖ *vɨ lɛ̀ ᵖ ve*}*tí yò-qo*
         'We just raise pigs and chickens, sell them, and buy them to earn our living.'

---

[6] This example is taken from H. F. Hertz (1935, p. 58), and is left in his orthography.

The question is, does a *ve* appearing in the final clause of a compound sentence nominalize the entire sentence or just the Cl$_f$ alone? Where are we to insert the lefthand brace in the diagram? For example, in (52), if we put it in before *ŋà*, we are analyzing the sentence as meaning 'Even if he doesn't want to get it, it is an I-do-want-to-get-it thing.' If, on the other hand, we regard the nominalizing force of *ve* as extending back to the beginning of the sentence, it would mean, 'It is an even-if-he-doesn't-want-to-get-it-I-do-want-to-get-it thing.' Although it is a hard-to-prove thing, I espouse the wide range of nominalization theory, simply because there is no principled basis for decreeing that the nominalizing force of *ve* is exhausted at some particular point within the sentence.

Similar considerations hold true in fact for any member of the class of final unrestricted particles. In the compound sentence

(54)   *nɔ | qay qo ‖ ŋà | mâ qay qô ʔ-ma*
             'If you go, I'm not going!'

there is no reason to assume that the force of the interjectory P$_{uf}$ *qô ʔ-ma* extends only to the Cl$_f$. One does not first say "if you go," and only then turn on the exclamatory juice, as it were. The whole sentence is an exclamation.

In sentences like (53), containing the conjoining P$_{unf}$ *lɛ*, the situation is particularly clear. It would be absurd to assume that only the last VP is nominalized (*vɨ lɛ ʔ* 'buy to earn a living'), and not the others as well, considering that all three have the same NP (*và ʔ-ġâ ʔ* 'pigs and chickens') as their object.

One argument one could advance in favor of the narrow range theory might be that in the case of permuted compound sentences, where the Cl$_{nf}$ is shifted to the right of the final clause [LG 6a.11], any *ve* in the original Cl$_f$ stays where it was and is not transported to the end of the permuted sentence:

(55)   *ŋà | hâ ʔ gâ ve}yò ʃʃ {yɔ | mâ hâ ʔ gâ thɔ ‖*
                    P$_{uf}$ P$_{unf}$
             'I do want to get it—even if he doesn't.'

But this does not prove anything, since *clause permutation* is a very late rule, applied well after the process of *nominalization* has been carried out.

Appositional Ve Clauses [LG 6.31].

There does exist one situation where a *ve* in a final clause affects only that clause and not what comes before. This happens when two *ve* clauses stand in apposition to one another:

(56)   {yɔ̂ | qôᵖ ve} ¦ {šɔ́-pɔ̄ | qay ve}
            'What he said was, he'd go tomorrow.'

Such sentences are analogous to appositions involving natural NPs:

(57)   khâᵖ-pà-mē-cɨ-câ-kwì ¦ ŋâᵖ tê cɔ̀ yò
            'The racket-tailed drongo (is) a kind of bird.'

Nominalizing Ve versus Relativizing Ve [LG 6.47]

When a *ve* clause is followed directly by a noun, there is often ambiguity according to whether the clause is interpreted as modifying that noun or not. Consider the following sentence:

(58) a.   {tê-qhâᵖ-tê-lɔ̀ | šī ve} ¦ {a-pi꞊qu | šɨ e ve}yò
            'What the whole village knows is, the old lady has died.'
     b.   {[tě-qhâᵖ-tê-lɔ̀ | šī ve] a-pi꞊qu | šɨ e ve}yò
                                  N_rh
            'The old lady whom the whole village knew has died.'

In (58a), the sentence is understood as consisting of two appositional *ve* clauses, such that the noun *a-pi꞊qu* 'old lady' has no connection with the preceding nominalized clause *tê-qhâᵖ-tê-lɔ̀ | šī ve* 'that which the whole village knows'. In (58b), on the other hand, *a-pi꞊qu* is taken as the nounhead of what precedes, so that the *ve* clause is not a nominalization at all, but rather a relative clause. In actual speech, there would be no problem in keeping the interpretations apart; a pause before *a-pi꞊qu* is sufficient to remove the ambiguity of the sentence in favor of the first reading.

Nominalizing Ve versus Ve in Right Relative Clauses [LG 6.497].

Under certain conditions, it is possible to shift a relative clause (*ve* and all) to the right of its N_rh, with little or no change in meaning [LG 6.49]:

(59)   a. {[cɔ̂ tā ve] vàᵖ꞊ó-qō thàᵖ ¦ qhɔ̀ | tɛ tā ve}le
                           N_rh
                'Where have you put the boiled pig's head?'
            b. {vàᵖ꞊ó-qō [cɔ̂ tā ve] thàᵖ ¦ qhɔ̀ | tɛ tā ve}le
                           N_rh
                'Where have you put the boiled pig's head?'

Sometimes it happens to make sense to interpret a given noun either as the head of a right-shifted relative clause or as being included within a nominalized *ve* clause:

(60) a. $\check{s}\hat{\imath}^{\eta}\text{-}c\grave{e}$ [mâ mu ve] kà$^{\eta}$ | thu bà phè$^{\eta}$ ɔ
         N_{rh} RRC P_{unf}
     'You may chop down even the trees that are not high.'
   b. {$\check{s}\hat{\imath}^{\eta}\text{-}c\grave{e}$ | mâ mu ve}kà$^{\eta}$ | thu bà phè$^{\eta}$ ɔ
     'Despite the fact that the trees are not high, you may
        chop them down.'

Under interpretation (60a), the P_{unf} kà$^{\eta}$ 'even' is in constituency with
the natural noun $\check{s}\hat{\imath}^{\eta}\text{-}c\grave{e}$ 'trees,' which is in turn modified by the
switched relative clause. In (60b), kà$^{\eta}$ 'even though, despite' is in
constituency with the entire predicative clause $\check{s}\hat{\imath}^{\eta}\text{-}c\grave{e}$ | mâ mu ve
'(It is the case that) the trees are not high.' See pp. 244–245 for similar
examples of P_{unf}s in constituency with preceding ve clauses.

SUBORDINATION AND *NOMINALIZATION*

The question we now face is whether there is any plausible way we
can relate the nominalizing power of ve to its function as a subordinator (pp. 240–242). It might be claimed at this point that this is a pseudo-
issue. Maybe ve represents the conflation of two separate particles
that now happen to be pronounced the same way through historical
accident? In the first place, there is no evidence for such a claim. But
more importantly, there are many other languages, including some
that do not even belong to the Sino-Tibetan superstock, where the
same morpheme is used for both functions. This cannot be accidental.
At the same time, it is not easy to explain. We are in no position to offer
a definitive solution here, but we will content ourselves with presenting some evidence from other languages.

Particles in Other Languages Having Dual Subordination/
Nominalization Function

JAPANESE

The behavior of the Japanese particle no is strikingly similar to that
of ve. It is, first of all, the marker of genitive subordination: ki no eda
'branch of a tree'; azi no moto 'the wellspring of taste' (monosodium
glutamate); hi no kuruma 'chariot of fire'; zaibatu no zituryoku 'the
real power of the corporations.' Unlike ve, however, no is not used to
connect relative clauses to their heads; the verb of a RC is attached to
its N_{rh} by simple juxtaposition ([kinoo tabeta$_V$] ninzin$_{N_{rh}}$ 'the carrots
(we) ate yesterday').

The other role of *no* in Japanese grammar is that of a nominalizer:

(61) {*issyookenmei ni* | *hataraku no*}*wa* ¦ *karada ni* ¦ *doku* | *desu*
       P_n
      'Working with all one's might is poison for the body.'

(62)   {*haha ga* | *kaette kuru no*}*o* | *matte orimasu*
             P_n
            'I'm waiting for **my mother to come back.**'

In these sentences, the *no* clause is nonfinal. But colloquial Japanese, like Lahu, has a strong tendency to nominalize whole sentences by using *no* in the final clause:

(63)   {*kimi mo* | *iku no*}*ka*
                    P_{uf}
            'Are you going too?' ('Is it a you-going-too thing?')

(64)   {*atasi mo* | *asobitai no*}*yo*
                     P_{uf}
            'I want to play too!' [women's speech]

(65)   {*mada aru no*}
                  'Are there still some left?'

Sentences like (63)–(65) are certainly to be derived from fuller, less colloquial structures where the *no* clause is followed by the copula *da/desu* (the so-called *no desu* construction of standard grammars of Japanese), so that {*iku no*} | *desu ka* 'Are (you) going?' ('Is it a your-going?') is analogous to natural-noun sentences like *mookoo-syuuheki* | *desu ka* 'Is it an epicantheal fold?' Nevertheless, the propensity for copula deletion here does make Japanese look a great deal like Lahu.

MANDARIN

As discussed above (p. 242), the particle *.de* is used as a subordinator both in genitive constructions and in relative clauses. In conjunction with the copula *sh* (the so-called *sh . . . de* construction), it also serves to nominalize clauses:

(66) *ta sh*{*leang dean jong* | *daw .de*}
      'He arrived at two o'clock' ('He is a two-o'clock-arrive thing'),

analogous to natural-noun sentences of the form N_1 *sh* N_2:

(67)   *ta sh yanggoei.tz*
                  'He is a foreign devil.'

According to Benjamin Ts'ou (private communication), it is often possible to omit the copula *sh* from this construction in colloquial speech. It seems likely that the ancestor-particle to *.de* in classical Chinese, *jy*, also had a dual subordinating/nominalizing function.

JINGHPAW

As discussed above, the Jinghpaw particle *ʔai* is used as a nominalizer in verb citations, nonfinal clauses, and final clauses. Exactly as in Lahu, this particle is also used as a subordinator in relative clauses: [*ŋai hpéʔ | kərum ʔai] məšà*$_{Nrh}$ 'the person who helps me'; [*nta shătaw kalaw ai] hpún* 'the wood (we) use for house-posts' [Hertz (1935) p. 51]; [*kəbà ʔai] hpún* 'a tree that is big.'

It seems certain that the Jinghpaw particle used in genitive subordination, *ʔáʔ* (*Jiŋhpòʔ ʔáʔ məšà* 'a person of the Jinghpaw'), is historically connected to *ʔai*, with the final *-ʔ* analogous to the creaky tone acquired by the Burmese particle *te* in attributive position (next section).

Burmese

We have seen above how the Burmese particle *te* is used in verb citations and nominalizations. But it is also used to connect relative clauses to their heads, in which position it assumes the creaky tone (*té*): [*thutóu | mə-yauʔ hpù thei té] əyaʔ*$_{Nrh}$ 'a place they have never been to.'

SUMMARY

The above remarks are admittedly very sketchy. Here are some even sketchier ones. Alan Stevens (personal communication) reminds me that the Indonesian affix *-nja* may have either possessive or nominalizing force. Margaret Langdon (personal communication) has pointed out some fascinating parallels between my findings and phenomena she has discovered in the Yuman languages of southern California and Arizona. The details of the relationship between nominalization and subordination vary from language to language, and a much more thorough study is needed. In any event, this is a topic worthy of the attention of anyone who is truly interested in putting speculations about universal grammar on an empirical basis.

REFERENCES

Hanson, Rev. Ola. 1906. A Dictionary of the Kachin Language. Rangoon. Reprinted in 1954 by Baptist Board of Publications, Rangoon.

Hertz, H. F. 1935. A Practical Handbook of the Kachin or Chingpaw Language (revised ed.) Superintendent, Government Printing and Stationery, Burma. Rangoon, 1935.

Jäschke, H. A. 1881. A Tibetan–English Dictionary with Special Reference to the Prevailing Dialects. Reprinted in 1958 by Routledge and Kegan Paul Ltd., London.

Matisoff, James A. 1967. A Grammar of the Lahu Language. University of California (Berkeley) dissertation. University Microfilms, Ann Arbor, Michigan, 67-11,648.

Matisoff, James A. 1969a. Lahu and Proto Lolo-Burmese. Occasional Papers of the Wolfenden Society on Tibeto-Burman linguistics (No. I), Ann Arbor, Michigan.

Matisoff, James A. 1969b. Verb concatenation in Lahu: The syntax and semantics of 'simple' juxtaposition. Acta Linguistica Hafniensia (Copenhagen) 12.1.

Matisoff, James A. 1969c. Lahu bilingual humor. Acta Linguistica Hafniensia (Copenhagen) 12.2.

Matisoff, James A. 1970. Glottal dissimilation and the Lahu high-rising tone: a tonogenetic case-study. Journal of the American Oriental Society 90.1.

Matisoff, James A. 1971. The tonal split in Loloish checked syllables. Occasional Papers of the Wolfenden Society on Tibeto-Burman Linguistics (No. II), Urbana, Illinois.

Matisoff, James A. 1972. The Grammar of Lahu, University of California Publications in Linguistics, Berkeley, California.

Matisoff, James A. 1973. Lahu–English and English–Lahu Dictionary. University of California Publications in Linguistics, Berkeley, California.

Okell, John. 1969. A Reference Grammar of Colloquial Burmese. Oxford University Press, London.

NAVAHO OBJECT MARKERS AND
THE GREAT CHAIN OF BEING

NANCY FRISHBERG
University of California, San Diego

The problem with Navaho object markers is that there are so many of them. For instance, [yi,] [bi], [ji] and ['a] all mark the third person (nonspeaker, nonlistener) object onto the verb. These forms have been called third person, 3a, third ordinary, 3o, third obliquative, fourth person, 3i, third indefinite, indefinite, and impersonal. However, the various names for the forms do not really give a clue to their meaning.

The purpose of this paper is to define [yi and [bi] and describe their usage in what Hale (1972) has called *subject–object inversion* in Navaho. His forthcoming paper "A note on *subject–object inversion*" Hale (1972) will be the jumping-off point for the discussion here.

Hale observes that in Navaho there are pairs of sentences such as (1) and (2):

(1) a. *łį́į́' dzaanééz yi-ztał*
     horse mule him-kicked
     'The horse kicked the mule.'
    b. *dzaanééz łį́į́' bi-ztał*
      mule horse him-kicked
     'The mule was kicked by the horse.'

(2)   a. *diné 'ashkii yoo'í*
                         man   boy   him-see
                         'The man sees the boy.'
                     b. *'ashkii diné boo'í*
                         boy   man   him-see
                         'The boy is seen by the man.'

Hale indicates that "the third person object prefix is changed from
/yi-/ to /bi-/" [Hale, 1972] and the relative positions of the logical subject and object are reversed. At first this pair of sentences looks related in much the same way as the English translations; that is, active
sentences in (1a) and (2a) and passive in (1b) and (2b). Certainly it
looks here as if sentences with *yi* have the semantic form SOV and
those with *bi* OSV.

The situation is complicated somewhat by such pairs of sentences
as (3) and (4):

(3)   a. *dzaanééz tsé yiztał*
                         mule   stone kicked
                         'The mule kicked the stone.'
                     b. **tsé dzaanééz biztał*
                         stone mule   kicked

(4)   a. **sá   shilíí'   yiyiisxí*
                         old age   my horse killed
                     b. *shilíí' sá   biisxí*
                         my horse old age   killed

                         'My horse was killed by old age.'

In these examples, *subject–object inversion* either cannot take place,
as in the case of (3), or it must take place, as in example (4). Hale finds
that a generalization can be made about those sentences that will invert and those that will not. He postulates a hierarchy of classes of
nouns: (1) human, (2) animate, (3) inanimate. Then he states conditions for *subject–object inversion* as follows:

Subject–object relation	Inversion
Equal in rank	Optional
Subject outranks object	Blocked
Object outranks subject	Obligatory

The conditions permit that sentences (1) and (2) can invert because the
NPs are of equal status. It also explains that (3b) is starred because an
inanimate would appear before an animate in the sentence, and similarly, (4a) has to be inverted to (4b) in order to have the animate noun
precede the inanimate.

There is no question that Hale's conditions work for the sentences he discusses; indeed, I will later make use of his concept of hierarchy in my own statements of the relation between sentences with *yi* and sentences with *bi*. However, this relation between *yi* and *bi* is not as simple as the conditions above, as becomes clear if we take care to construct examples using verbs that semantically could apply either way between the two NPs involved—e.g., *The man kicked the horse* and *The horse kicked the man*. The advantage of working with reversible propositions is simply that potential ambiguities are not obscured or blocked on semantic grounds. A sentence like *The man stung the bee* will be rejected by the informant, not because of any lack of agreement between verb and object or other strictly grammatical reasons, but rather because of the semantic anomaly.

The concept of animacy with which this chapter is concerned is the native Navaho concept. Animate things in Navaho are things that are capable of self-induced motion. This definition includes horses, sheep, cars, wind, rain, and running water. Human beings are, of course, animate but are in a separate category in the great chain of being.

Table I gives examples of some sentences of the form NP NP *yi*-V and NP NP *bi*-V. The first columns gives the order and type of the two NPs in each sentence. For example, numbers 4 and 15 have human and animate NPs followed by a verb, and the examples directly below— 5 and 16 have animate and human as first and second NP. Examples 4, 5, 15, and 16 involve humans and animates. Numbers 6, 7, 17, and 18 include humans and inanimates. The last eight examples have animate and inanimate subjects and objects. Boldface numbers indicate examples that violate the hierarchy.

All the examples with *yi* as the object marker are grammatical and are interpreted as SOV sentences, as shown in column headings. Sentences with *bi* are not quite so straightforward.

Most of these examples—12, 13, 15, 17, 19, and 20—correspond to the sentence type OSV and can be translated by an English passive. Examples 16 and 22 are ambiguous between OSV and SOV readings, and three examples—14, 18, and 21—are ungrammatical. Of these last five examples, all but 14 break the hierarchy conditions (as denoted by the boldface numbers).

Now let us consider sentences with only one NP. Examples in Table II correspond to those on Table I. As Table II shows, Navaho sentences show no overt third person independent pronouns, either as subject or object; there is one NP in each sentence. The first column gives the category of the overt NP. Thus, 23 can be read with a human subject and 'girl' as object, "He burned the girl" or with 'girl' as

TABLE I *Examples of Sentences of the Form NP NP yi = V and NP NP bi = V*

	SOV sentences				OSV sentences			
Hierarchy	Number	NP₁ S	NP₂ O	yi-V	Number	NP₁ O	NP₂ S	bi-V
Human–human	1	*shinaai* my brother	*ana'i* the enemy	*yiztał* kicked	12	*shinaai* my brother	*ana'i* the enemy	*biztał* kicked
Animate–animate	2	*mósi* the cat	*łééchąą'i* the dog	*yizighaas* scratched	13	*mósi* the cat	*łééchąą'i* the dog	*bizighaas* scratched
Inanimate–inanimate	3	*teezh* the sand	*naltsos tsits'aa* carton	*yishjįįzh* crushed	14	**teezh* sand	*naltsos tsits'aa* carton	*bishjįįzh* crushed
Human–animate	4	*shinaai* my brother	*shiłįį́* my horse	*yiztał* kicked	15	*shinaai* my brother	*shiłįį́* my horse	*biztał* kicked
Animate–human	5	*shiłįį́* my horse	*shinaai* my brother	*yiztał* kicked	16	*shiłįį́* my horse (also SOV)	*shinaai* my brother	*biztał* kicked
Human–inanimate	6	*at'ééd* girl	*nímasi* potato	*yidiiłid* burned	17	*at'ééd* girl	*nímasi* potato	*bidiiłid* burned
Inanimate–human	7	*nímasi* potato	*at'ééd* girl	*yidiiłid* burned	18	**nímasi* potato	*at'ééd* girl	*bidiiłid* burned
Animate–inanimate	8	*shiłįį́* my horse	*tsin* branch	*adah ayíítgo'* off pushed	19	*shiłįį́* my horse	*tsin* branch	*adah abiitgo'* off pushed
Animate–inanimate	9	*łįį'* horse	*ei tsin* that branch	*adah ayíítgo'* off pushed	20	*shiłįį́* horse	*ei tsin* that branch	*adah abiitgo'* off pushed
Inanimate–animate	10	*tsin* branch	*shiłįį́* my horse	*adah ayíítgo'* off pushed	21	**tsin* branch	*shiłįį́* my horse	*adah abiitgo'* off pushed
Inanimate–animate	11	*ei tsin* that branch	*łįį'* horse	*adah ayíítgo'* off pushed	22	*ei tsin* that branch (also SOV)	*łįį'* horse	*adah abiitgo'* off pushed

TABLE II *Examples of One-NP Sentences*[a]

Category	Number	NP	yi = V	Number	NP	bi = V
Human	23	at'ééd 'girl' — O {Human, Animate}; S	yidítłid 'burned' — O {Animate, Inanimate}	26	at'ééd 'girl' — S; O {Human, Animate}	bidítłid 'burned' — S {Human, Animate, Inanimate}
Animate	24	shitłį́į́' 'my horse' — O {Human, Animate}; S	yiztał 'kicked' — O {Animate, Inanimate}	27	shitłį́į́' 'my horse' — S; O {Human, Animate}	biztał 'kicked' — S {Animate, Inanimate}
Inanimate	25	tsin 'branch' — O {Human, Animate}; S	adah ayíítgo' 'off pushed' — O {Animate, Inanimate}	28	tsin 'branch' — S; O {Human, Animate}; *O	adah abíítgo' 'off pushed' — S

[a] Deleted NP can be understood as human, animate, or inanimate, according to the alternatives listed.

263

subject and animate or inanimate as object, "The girl burned it." Every one-NP sentence has at least one reading corresponding to a two-NP sentence with subject or object of appropriate rank. There are a few grammatical sentences with two NPs, however, for which the sentence formed by deleting one of the NPs is not grammatical. These are just the cases where a human object occurs with a *yi*-verb. The pronominal human object is not allowed.

How are we to account for the more complex set of data? Father Berard Haile offers a number of interesting comments in his book *Learning Navaho* (Haile, 1941). He says that *yi* is the object marker signaling that the NP directly preceding the V is the object.

> A safe rule to follow is that, whenever the object is mentioned the transitive verb, especially in the thirds [third person], refers to it by the YI-element. . . .
>
> (Haile, 1941, pp. 119–120)

> In reality, then, there is a double object of transitive verbs, the object noun which the speaker announces and the YI-pronoun which refers to the object noun.
>
> (Haile, 1941, p. 110)

Sentences with *yi* in Table I can be characterized in just this way. Sentences in Table II with *yi* have two readings. In one reading, the overt NP acts as object, and the deleted (or pronominalized) subject precedes the object. In the other reading, the overt NP is the subject, and the deletion has occurred between the subject and verb.

Father Haile defines *bi* as the object marker referring to a human object:

> [*bi*] can refer only to human beings. When such pronouns are incorporated into the verb and its subject and object are expressed, the subject must be kept close to the verb, while the object is mentioned first and reference made to it again in the incorporated pronoun. Position of subject and object, therefore are just the reverse of that of the YI-verb.
>
> (Haile, 1941, p. 65)

The data in Table I show that this characterization of *bi* is not correct. A number of examples are grammatical and have nonhuman objects. However by loosening Father Haile's definition slightly it is possible to interpret most of the examples in both tables. Suppose that *bi* implies two things: (a) the object is human or animate and (b) the object is the first NP of two NPs. Sentences 12 and 13 have animate NPs in first position and are therefore grammatical. They fulfill both requirements for *bi*; similarly for examples 15, 16, 17, 19, and 20. These are all grammatical for the same reason. Sentences 14, 18, and 21 have in-

animates in first position and are therefore ungrammatical. Sentence
16 can also be interpreted as SOV. The ambiguity can be explained as
a conflict between the conditions of the definition of *bi* and the hierarchy conditions. Both NPs in sentence 16 are animate and therefore
qualify for the first condition of *bi*. I should mention that the sentences
in Table I that conform to Hale's hierarchy are preferred. In 16, therefore, the hierarchy is violated and the sentence is ambiguous.

Sentence 22, then, is our only remaining problem in Table I. The
sentence is still grammatical and ambiguous if instead of *ei* 'that', we
use *ła'* 'one, a certain,' or *lei* 'this.' The apparent explanation is that by
qualifying an inanimate with a possessive or deictic, sentences like 22
become grammatical and ambiguous. By making it clear that an NP
refers to a specific item, the NP is raised in the hierarchy. The hierarchy therefore seems less like a three-level ranking system and more
like a continuum. Note in Table II that the pronoun object of *bi*-Vs
consistently refers to humans or animates and can be assumed to be
deleted from the first position in the sentence. These pronouns conform to our description of how *bi* works.

Certain facts can now be explained. Hale did not understand why
sentences like

'ii'ni' *łįį'* *yiyiisxį*
lightning horse killed

are optionally inverted to

łįį' *'ii'ni'* *biisxį*
horse lightning killed

That is, he did not understand why this sentence can occur in either
yi or *bi* form. The answer is that by using the native concept of animacy, we will classify 'lightning' with the animates. Then the conditions stated above will apply and switch two equal animates, optionally. We have also seen that the hierarchy is not a strict three-level
system, but more like a continuum, and such concepts as possessed or
unpossessed can enter into decisions about the working of the
hierarchy.

Finally, we have seen that *yi* and *bi* are not synonymous markers
that separate inverted from uninverted sentences as Hale implies.
Rather, they cover different semantic domains. *Yi* applies to all cata-
gories freely in two NP sentences, but does not apply to pronominalized humans. *Bi* strictly applies to animate and human objects. Separ-
ating *yi* and *bi* permits a more thorough description of the data.

ACKNOWLEDGMENTS

This paper is the result of two quarters of the field methods course at the University of California, San Diego taught by Professor Margaret Langdon. I have been helped by many discussions with Suzette Elgin, Alec Bamford, Ed Klima, and Margaret Langdon. The informant for this work was Kathy Begaye, who showed great patience throughout.

REFERENCES

Haile, Fr. Berard. 1941. Learning Navaho. St. Michaels Press, St. Michaels, Arizona.
Hale, Kenneth. 1972. A Note on Subject-Object Inversion in Navajo, in *Papers in Linguistics in Honor of Henry and Renee Kahane*, ed. by Braj B. Kachru *et al.*

THE CROSSOVER CONSTRAINT AND OZARK ENGLISH

SUZETTE HADEN ELGIN
University of California, San Diego

The picture presented by organized transformational grammar today is roughly that presented by organized religion, except that instead of Catholics, Protestants, and Jews, we have lexicalists, generative semanticists, extended standard theorists, and functionalists. The impression given is that of a healthy exchange of ideas, a sort of free enterprise linguistics with lots of competition to clear the air. However, if you go beyond the surface, you discover that this apparent diversity is in many ways only apparent, and that whatever the terminology and methodology of the various sects of transformational grammar, they are all describing the same monolithic dialect. This dialect I shall refer to as Standard American Dialect. Even those who do things like studies of Harlem English or child language acquisition studies seem themselves to have Standard American as their native speech.

This situation constitutes a historical accident, and worse than that, a self-perpetuating historical accident, since all these people who share the same dialect quite naturally find one another's arguments clear. On the other hand, the novice approaching transformational grammar, who finds his own grammatical sentences always turning up as the crucially ungrammatical ones in the literature, is likely to be panicked, give up in despair, and switch to animal husbandry.

It is therefore appropriate to examine another dialect of English,

267

preferably one that differs markedly from Standard American, but that
is not confined to any one specific social or ethnic group, and that
covers a respectably large geographic area. My own dialect, Ozark,
meets these requirements rather adequately.

Ozark differs so radically from Standard American that it would require the space of a dissertation to cover the differences even minimally. I refer not to differences of phonology or specific lexical items,
such as *taters* for *potatoes*, but to syntactic differences of very large
scope. This chapter will take up one syntactic area where Standard
American and Ozark clash markedly and discuss it in some detail,
allowing it to serve as an example for the dialect as a whole.

Now it is striking how the phenomena known as *crossover* permeate
organized transformational grammar. The impression received is that
all of English grammar somehow revolves about the central pivot of
crossover. This is true whether the choice of method for handling it is
in the form of constraints on transformations, surface interpretive
rules, redundancy rules, or whatever other mechanism any one transformational sect prefers. The most complete and intricate formulations of *crossover* are those of Postal (1970) and Grinder (1971), and if
their formulations are to be believed, it is at once obvious that Ozark
simply cannot be described by the rules of Standard American.

This article will make no attempt to present a competing formal
specification for *crossover*, nor will there be any attempt to cover
every English transformation for which *crossover* has been proposed
as a relevant factor. The discussion will instead be confined to an informal description of the situation, with regard to those movement
rules of English that are generally accepted as well described and
motivated.

The first such rule is, of course, the *passive*. The following sentences are all perfectly well-formed for Ozark, with coreference as
marked:

(1)   a. *Hermione$_i$ was shaved by herself$_i$.*
        b. *The professor$_i$ was amused by himself$_i$ throughout
            his entire lecture.*
        c. *Tremaine$_i$ was shot by himself$_i$ in spite of all his
            friends could do to dissuade him$_i$.*

When I first noticed these facts, it seemed puzzling that although all
the sentences of (1) are fine, the sentence *She was bathed by herself*
seems somewhat different. And then I realized that this is because it
has the same surface structure as a sentence with a different deriva-

tion: *She was bathed by herself until she was six and then they decided to bathe her in the same tub as her big sister*, where *by herself* is in effect the same as *alone*. Prepositional phrases, particularly if S-final, have some very interesting syntactic repercussions in Ozark, and this is one of them. This topic will be taken up in more detail below.

It should be pointed out that for Ozark, just as for Standard American, sentence (2) is clearly ungrammatical.

(2)   *Himself was shaved by John.*

This, however, is not due to a constraint on the crossing of coreferential NPs, but rather to the fact that the ordering of rules must be *passive* and then *reflexive*. This ordering is necessary in any case to derive sentences like (1a).

The second movement rule involving coreferential NPs and crossing is *Wh-Q movement;* since it operates exactly as does *Wh-rel movement*, these two rules will be discussed together. The two sentences of (3) are fully grammatical Ozark sentences:

(3)   a.   *Who$_i$ did perjuring himself$_i$ bother?*
         b.   *I knew a man$_i$ who$_i$ perjuring himself$_i$ bothered.*

These data lead us to an interesting problem. Ozark English has a rule that does not appear to be a part of the grammar of Standard American, and which will be referred to as *clausemate pronominal antecedent* deletion. It is an optional rule, and it operates to remove the pronominal antecedent of any clausemate pronoun, unless that antecedent is itself the subject of the relevant verb.

Where it is subject of the highest verb, as in *He shaved himself*, the transformation is blocked by the independent constraint that requires all English sentences to have an overt subject. In the case of a pronominal antecedent serving as subject of an embedded verb, as in *Mary said he shaved himself*, it appears that deletion is blocked because it would bring about the automatic formation of an infinitive, thus yielding a sentence identical with the output of an entirely different derivation. This is consistent, since the derivation of *Mary said to shave himself* from *Mary said for him$_i$ to shave himself$_i$* is perfectly good Ozark.

All the sentences of (4) are fully grammatical for Ozark and are transformationally derived from those of (5).

(4)   a.   *Shaving himself was enormous fun.*

 b. *Hermione said that it would be difficult to control*
   himself when the riot started.

 c. *Voy's claim that shaving himself before applying for*
   work was equivalent to prostituting himself
   irritated John.

 d. *Bill said it would be difficult to behave himself.*

(5) a. *His$_i$ shaving himself$_i$ was enormous fun.*

 b. *Hermione said that it would be difficult for him$_i$ to*
   control himself$_i$ when the riot started.

 c. *Voy's claim that his$_i$ shaving himself$_i$ before applying*
   for work was equivalent to his$_i$ prostituting him-
   self$_i$ irritated John.

 d. *Bill said it would be difficult for him$_i$ to behave*
   himself$_i$.

Although some of the above data might be accounted for by postulating that the constraints on *super-equi deletion* are different for Ozark than for Standard American, there is no way that *super-equi* could account for sentences like (4a). Therefore, we must assume that Ozark has both *super-equi NP deletion* — with differing constraints — and the antecedent deletion rule described above.

As would be expected, the sentences of (4) and (5) are synonymous in Ozark. Sentences like (4d) are ambiguous, however, since there is no way to tell whether it is *Bill* or a deleted *for him* that has served to reflexivize the final NP.

At this point it should be mentioned that the proposal that free deletion transformations be restricted to deletion of category representatives could apply to *clausemate pronominal antecedent deletion* if we could assume that a structure like *Shaving himself was fun* could result from a deep structure like the following:

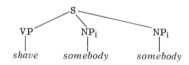

Further, John Grinder's (1971) proposal that what we have heretofore called "free deletion" be looked upon instead as optional lexicalization could also apply, if coreference is stipulated for nodes rather than for lexical items, and if the problem of stipulating gender and number for reflexive pronouns could be dealt with satisfactorily. For the moment, however, it will suffice simply to mention these possibilities. A full discussion of the concepts involved can be found in Grinder (1971) and Fauconnier (1971).

In view of this situation, it is interesting that the sentences of (6) below are not synonymous with those of (7) in this writer's dialect, although they can be for some speakers of Ozark English.

(6)   a.   *Who$_i$ did perjuring himself$_i$ bother?*
        b.   *I knew a man who$_i$ perjuring himself$_i$ bothered.*

(7)   a.   *Who did his perjuring himself bother?*
        b.   *I knew a man who his perjuring himself bothered.*

For my dialect, in the sentences of (6), *who* and *himself* must be coreferential, while for (7), *who* must never be coreferential with *his* and *himself*. For other Ozark speakers, the sentences of (7) are ambiguous as to coreference.

It seems clear, then, that for this dialect the rule of *equi-NP deletion* precedes *clausemate pronominal antecedent deletion* and removes the antecedent of the pronoun before the latter can apply. Further, *clausemate pronomial antecedent deletion* is blocked from application in the sentences of (7) by a transderivational constraint, which blocks that application when the output thereof would be identical to the surface output resulting from prior application of *equi-NP deletion*. It will be seen below that this is an entirely consistent strategy for Ozark English.

The next rule to be mentioned is that of *about movement*. For Ozark, the following derivation holds:

(8)   *I talked to Robert$_i$ about Robert$_i$* $\xrightarrow{\text{reflexive}}$
    I talked to Robert about himself $\xrightarrow{\text{about movement (optional)}}$
    I talked about himself to Robert.

The identical situation holds for *indirect object movement*, as shown by (9):

(9)   a.   *Fred showed Hermione$_i$ a picture of herself$_i$.*
        b.   *Fred showed a picture of herself$_i$ to Hermione$_i$.*

In his recent book on *crossover*, Postal discusses three rules that move NPs about and that seem to offer parallel phenomena, with frustrating differences that cannot be satisfactorily correlated. These are the rules of *passive* (already discussed above), *tough movement*, and *it-replacement*. He finds it annoying that the obvious close relation of these three rules cannot be made more complete, more elegant, and less subject to idiosyncratic differences. He will perhaps be pleased to learn that for Ozark these three behave in absolute parallel, so that all the following derivations hold:

(10)   a.   *It was difficult for John to shave Joseph* $\xrightarrow{\text{tough movement}}$
       Joseph was difficult for John to shave.

       b.   *It was difficult for me to shave me.* →

       I was difficult for $\begin{Bmatrix} me \\ myself \end{Bmatrix}$ *to shave.*

       c.   *It seemed to me for John to be sick.* $\xrightarrow{\text{it replacement}}$
       John seemed to me to be sick.

       d.   *It seemed to me for me to be sick.* →

       I seemed to $\begin{Bmatrix} me \\ myself \end{Bmatrix}$ *to be sick.*

       e.   *John shaved Bill.* $\xrightarrow{\text{passive}}$
       Bill was shaved by John.

       f.   *I shaved I.* →
       I was shaved by myself.

This seems a tidy way to handle the situation, in terms of the data. What it accomplishes in view of the differing reasons Postal has proposed for the ungrammaticality in Standard American of the coreferential sentences, I have no idea.

Where *psych movement* is concerned, it appears to be beyond the scope of this brief paper. It should simply be pointed out that with the exception of those sentences that are out because of selectional restrictions (like *The corn on the cob tasted me*), every sentence judged ungrammatical by Postal is perfectly correct for Ozark. A few examples are the following, all with coreference of pronouns:

(11)   a.   *I am pleasing to myself.*
                        b.   *I was irritating to myself.*
                        c.   *I was annoyed at myself.*

It will be noted that all the sentences so far have involved reflexive phenomena, and it seems safe to state that there is no restriction on the crossing of coreferential NPs in Ozark when one of those NPs is a reflexive pronoun or some other clausemate pronominal form such as *his own*. The question to be considered, then, is whether this freedom applies also to sentences involving other kinds of NPs.

Since it is the *Wh-Q* and *Wh-rel* sentences that are most severely restricted for *crossover* in Standard American, we will use examples of the application of these two rules to investigate the *crossover* question. First, consider sentence (12) below:

(12)   *The man who she$_i$ married left her$_i$* $\xrightarrow{\text{Wh-Q movement}}$
       Who$_i$ did the man she$_i$ married leave?

This sentence is not only perfectly grammatical in Ozark as written, but in fact the only possible interpretation is the one indicated by the referential indices. If *who* and *she* are not intended as coreferential, *she* has to be pronounced with emphatic stress, and even then it is an awkward sentence.

Sentences (13) and (14) also show that it is quite all right to cross coreferential NPs in Wh-Q and Wh-rel movement rules in Ozark, even without the reflexive factor:

(13)   *The book$_i$ which$_i$ the man who ordered it$_i$ said would be dull turned out to be interesting after all.*

(14) $\begin{Bmatrix} Whom_i \\ By\ whom_i \end{Bmatrix}$ *were the rumors which slandered her$_i$* $\begin{Bmatrix} denied\ by? \\ denied? \end{Bmatrix}$

Ideally, it would now be possible to state that Ozark simply does not have the *crossover constraint* in any form. Unfortunately, this is not true. For Ozark, as for Standard American, the following sentence is ungrammatical:

(15)   **Who$_i$ did she$_i$ claim Melanie hated?*

It would be satisfying if this particular configuration could somehow be explained away as due to some factor other than *crossover*. And Postal (1970) has some remarks that seem pertinent:

> Given a sentence with multiple occurrences of nominals designating the same entity, the question marker must go on the leftmost, where leftmost is defined not on surface structures but on the structures at the point where WH-Q MOVEMENT applies [p. 74].

Ozark does have this constraint, except that it applies not to all questions, but only to those having the configuration of (15) above. If this is true, then *crossover* disappears from Ozark entirely.

A few Ozark sentences seem to argue against this conclusion. One of them is the sentence referred to previously in the discussion of the *passive, She was bathed by herself.* Another is (16), which illustrates application of the rule of *conjunct movement:*

(16)   *Elizabeth shaved me with* $\begin{Bmatrix} myself. \\ me. \end{Bmatrix}$

These sentences would be a problem, except that they reflect a single relevant factor about Ozark, one that can perhaps be most easily demonstrated by sentence (17):

(17)   *John was told to stand by Mary.*

Sentence (17) is fully grammatical for Ozark, of course, but it cannot be a passive derived from *Mary told John to stand.* It can only be an alternative realization of sentence (18):

(18)   *John was told to stand beside Mary.*

In other words, for Ozark, the passive interpretation is not possible if a derivation exists in which the *by* phrase would be a locative. The only way to produce a passive derived from the sentence *Mary told John to stand* is to say *John was told by Mary to stand.* Sentence (16) above is ruled out by precisely the same situation; that is, it presents a surface pattern identical to sentence (19):

(19)   *Elizabeth shaved me with a razor.*

Thus, the agentive interpretation is not possible when an alternative derivation exists where the prepositional phrase would be an instrumental.

There seems to be a conspiracy in Ozark that works to maintain case distinctions on NPs and blocks sentences that would tend to obscure such distinctions. This is consistent with the fact that for many speakers of Ozark the *who/whom* distinction is still fully operative, which is not so for Standard American. It is not surprising that a dialect that has such freedom of movement for NP constituents would seek to compensate for that freedom by maintaining distinctions of case. Further, it appears that Ozark is extremely sensitive to the constraint on identical surface structures resulting from different derivations. These two factors work hand in hand, and in fact interact, in Ozark to prevent a degree of ambiguity that would not be tolerable.

Having reached the end of the discussion of *crossover* phenomena for Ozark, it should be pointed out that similar papers could be written with regard to the *complex-NP constraint*, the *coordinate structure constraint*, the *Pied Piping constraint*, the choice and placement of complementizers, and the formation of nominalizations, as well as for many other areas of the grammar.

REFERENCES

Postal, Paul. 1970. Crossover Phenomena. Holt, New York.

Grinder, John. 1971. On Deletion Phenomena in English. Unpublished Ph.D. thesis. University of California, San Diego, California.

Fauconnier, Giles. 1971. Theoretical Implications of Some Global Phenomena in Syntax. Unpublished Ph.D. thesis. University of California, San Diego, California.

AUTHOR INDEX

Number in italics refer to the pages on which the complete references are listed.

SUBJECT INDEX

A

About movement, in Ozark English, 271
Again, as factor in the great causative
    verbs debate, 154–155
Almost, scope of, 117, 118, 120–122, 141,
    152
Ambiguity in causative verbs, 117, 120,
    121, 122, 126, 133–135
A/M verbs, *see* Aspectual/modal verbs
Anaphoric complement deletion as
    evidence for output conditions, 167,
    168
Antonymy, *see* Negative pairing
Aristotle, 6, 14
Aspectual modal verbs, 30, 31, 37–47
    diachronic developments of, 39–42
    with nominalizations, 37–39
    polysemy of, 42–47
    subclassification of, 30

B

Backward gapping is really conjunction
    reduction, 202ff
Being deletion as evidence for output
    conditions 168–169

C

Causative verbs, 117–156, *see also*
    specific items
    action-result analysis, 120–123, 140,
    142, 153
    in Japanese, 127–137, 143–149
    prelexical hypothesis, 117–156
    arguments against prelexical
    hypothesis, 125–137, 151–156

McCawley's revised prelexical
    hypothesis, 129, 130, 140
    rationale for prelexical hypothesis, 123
*Clausemate pronominal antecedent
    deletion,* 269, 270, 271
Conjunction reduction, 199ff, 206–210
Coordinate structure constraint as ev-
    idence against backward gapping,
    203ff
Crossover, 94, 268
Cycle, 64ff, 81–111
    primary motivation for, 82–84
    secondary motivation for, 82–84
Cyclic grammars, formal properties of,
    70–77

D

Deep structure
    of believe, 22
    of conditionals, 22
Do-so transformation, 130, 131
Doubling constraint
    effects on linguistic theory, 178–186
    as evidence for global rule, 172ff
    minimal criteria for formalization of,
    172–178
Doubling violations, characterization of,
    160–171

E

Embedding deletion in nonrestrictive
    relative clause formation, 195ff
Epistemic logic, 8–11
Equi-NP deletion as evidence for global
    rule, 174–175